Effective Intervention
with the
Language Impaired Child

Second Edition

Martha L. Cole, M.Ed.
Valley View Elementary School
Las Cruces, New Mexico

Jack T. Cole, Ph.D.
New Mexico State University
Las Cruces, New Mexico

AN ASPEN PUBLICATION®
Aspen Publishers, Inc.
Rockville, Maryland
Royal Tunbridge Wells
1989

Library of Congress Cataloging-in-Publication Data

Cole, Martha L.
Effective intervention with the language
impaired child/Martha L. Cole, Jack T. Cole.--2nd ed.
p. cm.
"An Aspen publication."
Bibliography: p.
Includes index.
ISBN: 0-87189-798-9
1. Children--United States--Language. 2. Language disorders in children--United States.
3. Language arts--United States--Remedial teaching. I. Cole, Jack T. II. Title.
LB1139.L3C575   1988   371.91′4--dc19   88-19003
CIP

Editorial Services: Marsha Davies

Library of Congress Catalog Card Number: 88-19003
ISBN: 0-87189-798-9

Printed in the United States of America

1 2 3 4 5

Table of Contents

Preface

The success of the first edition of this book has necessitated the writing of a second edition. In the eight years since the initial publication of *Effective Intervention with the Language Impaired Child* there have been significant advancements in the approaches to the treatment and teaching of language delayed children. Included among these advancements are

- pragmatic techniques
- microcomputer application in the field of language disorders
- new testing materials
- improved instructional materials

It has been our objective to incorporate the new while retaining what we consider to be the tried and true methods for working with children experiencing language problems.

Martha L. Cole
Jack T. Cole

Acknowledgments

We would like to express a very special debt of gratitude to Dr. Ann Beth S. Deily for her very thorough critique and most helpful suggestions in the development of this second edition.

We would also like to thank Dr. Stephen Farmer, Department of Special Education/Communication Disorders, New Mexico State University, for his input during the early stages of this project. Finally, a special thanks to Judith Zimmerman, speech/language pathologist from the Las Cruces Public Schools, who gave assistance in obtaining current language training materials.

Chapter 1

Normal Acquisition of Language: An Introduction

Language is the vocal communication of thoughts and ideas, a process by which meaning is conveyed or expressed from one person to another. Language assumes two specific functions for the individual. First, it serves as a cognitive tool by which individuals use the linguistic code to represent their thoughts. As a cognitive tool, language helps people organize and categorize the information their senses convey to them. It aids them in formulating their perceptions and ideas into speech. Language is the overt manifestation of cognitive functioning. It enables people to demonstrate their thought processes to others.

Second, as a social tool, language provides for interactions between people, setting the stage for interpersonal communications and for the mutual expression of feelings. Language enables the individual to give and receive information, thoughts, and ideas.

Children without language are limited in engaging in the most human of all skills—communicating with others. Therefore, they cannot indicate when they are ill, hungry, or thirsty, except by primitive gestures or sounds. They are not able to verbally share ideas or to express personal experiences, events, or even feelings. But perhaps most devastating of all, they are not able to use language to decode other bodies of knowledge.

Because many areas of learning are language related, the child without language may have great difficulty in one or more cognitive areas. For example, children with limited receptive language cannot approach the skill of reading without comprehending the abstract concepts prevalent in this subject area. No matter whether they are taught to decode words phonetically and can "call" words, what use is this skill if they have no understanding of what they have read? Engelmann (1969) related a problem often encountered by teachers. He stressed that even if children are able to read a sentence such as "The bug ran under the log," they may not understand the underlying concepts of bug, ran, under, or log. This, Engelmann emphasized, is not a reading problem per se, but a language problem. If children do not comprehend a reading passage, perhaps it is because the language practitioner has not dealt sufficiently with the language concepts found therein.

Furthermore, children with language deficits will most likely have difficulty in the expressive phase of the language system—in speaking, writing, and spelling. Many of our schools and classrooms are organized in a question-response instructional format. Children who participate in class discussions and verbally respond correctly to the teacher's questions tend to be viewed more favorably than those who do not participate.

In addition, verbal and written expression gives the teacher a view of children's cognitive processes. Through spoken and written language, the teacher is able to determine what children are thinking, the content of their ideas, and their mode of expressing concepts. The verbal and written expression of the child is a primary means by which the teacher is able to evaluate whether the child has mastered the concept taught or the body of knowledge covered in the instructional process. If a child is nonverbal and has no skills in writing language, the teacher, parent, or other involved adult is denied this means of evaluating the intellectual abilities and achievement of the child.

Language also facilitates the learning of mathematical concepts. Indeed, the area of mathematics may be considered a language in itself. Understanding relationships of size, quantity, space, and position in mathematical symbols is often difficult for the child with little or no language.

Understanding cause and effect relationships, deriving meaning from human interaction, and interpreting and using what they see and hear are complex cognitive and social skills for young children. Without language, children are inhibited in the use of the skills necessary to make sense of the world around them.

Surprisingly, there are many children who exhibit language delays. They may be found in special education programs of all descriptions or in regular elementary classrooms. Language delayed children may be identified during their preschool years, when a parent, doctor, or other concerned individual recognizes that the toddler is not developing speech as rapidly as other children the same age. Or they may be identified in their early school years, when they stand out as being significantly "different" in comparison to their peers. If these children have not been identified before entering school, it becomes the responsibility of the educator to make an effort to identify them and to provide intensive language intervention to remediate any problems found.

If language training is initiated early, more serious language deficits may be ameliorated or even prevented.

THE DEVELOPMENT OF LANGUAGE

Some linguists and educators take a nativistic view that language is an innate capacity, based on a code that the individual is equipped with at birth. The most orthodox of the nativistic school take this view even further, believing that the child will acquire the code naturally and that no amount of language intervention will help the child develop language. This is based on the assumption that the child will outgrow the language problem. The manifestation of this theory in the instruction of the child is exemplified by an "experiential" approach, which provides the child with perceptual and linguistic input, but no formal skills of expression or production. The child is supposed to acquire language vicariously through experience.

Though the authors do not deny the existence of linguistic competence, or that there may be some internalized set of rules guiding the child in expression, they do believe that language can be learned and that specific intensified language training can help develop this internal code. It is the intent of this book to demonstrate that language can be developed as a combination of this innate capacity and experience. Furthermore, this book will demonstrate how providing the child with a sequenced language acquisition program coupled with structured environmental events will assist the child in acquiring constructions that may not have been acquired if left to chance or natural development.

Providing early language training may be the only hope language delayed children have to unlock the code that will enable them to view their world in a logical order.

THE COMPONENTS OF LANGUAGE

A discussion of language would not be complete without describing the components of language and how they develop in the young child. Understanding these components is crucial to appropriately identifying the underlying basis of a language deficit. These components include phonology, syntax, morphology, semantics, and pragmatics.

Phonology

Phonology, usually the first component to develop in the child, is the system of speech sounds. An infant's early attempts at using personal vocal mechanisms include crying, vocalizing, babbling, and producing distinct consonant and vowel sounds, all part of the initial process of developing communication.

Initial studies in phonological development dealt primarily with the acquisition of individual sounds (segments); later research focused on the acquisition of sounds by distinctive features, the acquisition of prosodic features, and methods by which a child internalizes phonological rules and processes.

In a classic review of the literature, McCarthy (1954) summarized the findings of studies on the phonological development of children. Some of the most important points for the purposes of this discussion are the following. (1) Vowel sounds appear before consonant sounds and outnumber them in frequency throughout the first year of a child's life. At about two years of age, vowel frequency increases rapidly. (2) By age 29 to 30 months, most children have in their repertoire 27 of the 35 phonemes common to adult speech. (3) When consonants are considered, initial consonants exceed final and medial sounds. (4) Final consonants are virtually nonexistent in the first six months, but accelerate soon thereafter, though never exceeding initial or medial consonants.

Somewhat later the child begins to blend these sounds to show evidence of using intonation and stress. Children gradually become aware of likenesses and differences in sounds. At about 12 months of age most children begin to use one-word utterances (Morehead & Morehead, 1976; McNeill, 1954).

Also during this period, children begin to interact meaningfully with significant adults in their lives, receiving reinforcement from parents and family for initiating new sounds and words. During the period between 12 and 18 months, the child develops a vocabulary of approximately 50 words, and between the ages of 18 and 24 months, the child begins to develop two-word utterances.

During the period from 24 to 36 months, children are also rapidly increasing receptive awareness. They are beginning to develop comprehension of requests and commands from adults and to develop an understanding and use of many nouns, especially functional words in their environment— "ball," "mama," "dada," "doggie," etc. In addition, they learn to combine sounds and words to name family members, pets, and household items.

By the age of 36 months, most children have developed a large number of phonemes, or speech sounds, though their speech may be characterized by substitutions and omissions of medial and final consonants (Berry, 1969).

Phonemic development continues at a steady rate until age seven or eight years, when most consonants, consonant blends, and digraphs are acquired, and proficiency is well underway.

In addition to the ways that children acquire individual sounds or segments, other research focused on how sounds are developed through the child's perception and production of distinctive features. Menyuk (1968, 1972); Chomsky and Halle (1968); Cairns and Williams (1972); and others have developed systems of categorizing phonemes based on contrasts, and they subsequently sought to describe phonemic acquisition of normally developing children.

Another aspect of phonemic acquisition focused on how and when children acquire adultlike intonation. Crystal (1979) developed a description of five stages of prosodic development in children.

- *Stage I (birth to two or three months).* The infant uses vocalizations and exhibits differentiation in the types of crying and other vocalizations.
- *Stage II (three to six months).* The child exhibits an awareness of changes in adult intonation and other prosodic contrasts.

- *Stage III (six months).* The infant's vocalizations begin to include changes in loudness and pitch and resemble adult prosodic patterns.
- *Stage IV (six months to one year).* The child begins to use rhythm, pitch, pause, and tone. At this stage, adults are often interpreting these utterances as having specific functions or purposeful intent.
- *Stage V (about one and one-half years).* The child begins to blend and integrate tones into two-element sentences.

Studies have also sought to describe a child's phonological development in terms of how phonological rules and processes are internalized. Shriberg (1980) described the way a child uses rules that govern the distribution and sequence of phonemes in a word. He also discussed phonetic rule changes in which each phoneme sounds and is pronounced slightly differently because of different combinations of sounds. Ingram (1974) described six phonological rules that account for the progression to an adult phonemic system.

1. *Reduplication.* An initial syllable is repeated, e.g., "baba" for bottle.
2. *Diminutive.* A vowel (often i) is added at the end of a word, sometimes with repetition of the first syllable, e.g., "wawi" for water.
3. *Weak syllable deletion.* A child deletes an unstressed syllable, e.g., "bout" for about.
4. *Cluster reduction.* A child reduces a consonant cluster to a single consonant, e.g., "poon" for spoon.
5. *Voicing.* A child voices an initial consonant but does not voice a final consonant, as in the substitution of "do" for shoes.
6. *Assimilation.* The child incorporates a neighboring sound with another syllable, e.g., "kiki" for kitty or "hamburber" for hamburger.

Syntax

Syntax and morphology together make up the component referred to as grammar. Syntax refers to word order and the way that words and sequences of words are combined into phrases, clauses, and sentences.

As syntax develops, normal children learn quite early—at about 18 months—that there is an order to words. They learn to use sentences with the order of subject, verb, and object, often omitting articles. An example of this stage in a child's development is the expression of eating an apple as "Me eat apple." This reduction of utterances, utilizing the most functional words of the sentence, has been termed "telegraphic speech" by Brown and Bellugi (1964).

By age 30 months, most children have begun to use articles such as "a," "an," and "the," allowing them to connect nouns and verbs into more meaningful phrases. By age three and one-half years, they have increased their use of auxiliary verbs. Phrases are expanded into simple kernel sentences, with some use of questions. At age four and one-half children are extending and expanding expressions into compound and complex sentences. By seven or eight years of age the children are able to use all forms of sentence structure.

Lee (1966) described four levels of syntactic development in normal children.

Level I–Two-Word Combinations

This phase is characterized by the use of pivot words such as "that," "thatsa," and "there." A child's first combination at this level might resemble

> there dog   thatsa ball
> that house   there cat

Level II–Noun Phrase

In this phase, the pivot words increase in variety to include articles such as "the" and "a," pronouns such as "my," possessives, numbers, and adjectives. Typical expressions in this phase are

> my big doll   the big chair
> the red car   no more cookie

Level III–Constructions

In the construction phase, two-word responses may be expanded into designative constructions by adding articles, possessives, quantifiers, and adjectives, forming such phrases as

> that my ball   here a car
> that a chair   that big dog

Verbs may also enter at this level, forming predicative constructions such as

> the chair broken   my chair broken

Level IV–Sentences

During this phase, the child begins to form sentences such as the following.

> That is a big dog.
> There goes a horse.

Declarative kernel sentences such as "The cat is there" may also be formed. Finally, at this stage the child may enter into the phase of making transformations, including interrogatives and negatives. Crystal, Fletcher, and Garman (1976) found similar acquisition patterns, stressing that, for the most part, normal children develop syntax in the same relative order. Yet they also explain that the rate at which children develop these syntactic constructions is the variable factor. They set out to describe syntactic development in children, and they provided a syntactic profile chart that could be utilized as an assessment tool and remedial procedure, the Language Assessment, Remediation and Screening Procedure (LARSP).

Crystal et al. (1976) found that children develop constructions in a particular manner, though they cautioned that stages were not finite entities and that children make subtle transitions from one stage to another. Briefly outlined here are seven stages of syntactic development.

Stage I (9 to 18 months). One-Element Sentences

Children use purposeful single utterances in a social context, such as in greetings, names, or stereotypic utterances, e.g., "peekaboo." The authors explained that, though some researchers speculate on intent of the child's utterances and have multiple categories for classifying them, what the child says is more than frequently ambiguous with respect to any categorization scheme. With regard to coding syntax at this stage, a child's utterances may be classified as either questions or commands.

Stage II (18 to 24 months). Two-Element Sentences

Some subject-verb and verb-object structures have begun to emerge at this stage. Children's sentence structure patterns at this stage may be classified as *commands*, such as "kick ball," *questions*, such as "where ball" and *statements* such as

subject-verb	boy run
subject-object-complement	kitty milk; ball big; man mad
verb-object-complement	read book; be cold
adverbial-X(subject, object, verb, complement)	here ball
negative-X	no milk; not run

Children's phrase structures at this stage may include such patterns as

noun-noun	boy boat
adjective-noun	big car

determiner-noun	my shoe
verb-verb	go eat
verb-particle	come out
preposition-noun	on chair
Interrogative-X	down there
Others, such as adjective-adjective	big blue

Stage III (two to two and one-half years). Three-Element Sentences

At this stage, children begin to blend clause and phrase structure and expand their repertoire of clauses. For example, the subject-complement from Stage II "ball big" might be expanded to "red ball big." Expansions can also occur in the complement-object phrase, the adverbial phrase, and the verb pattern position.

Among the new structures to be added at Stage III are

New Clauses

subject-verb complement-object	boy eat apple
subject-verb-adverb	boy go school
verb complement-object-adverb	take boy car (Take the boy in the car)
verb-direct object-indirect object	give bone doggie (Give the bone to doggie.)
negative X-Y (X and Y are any elements)	no candy box (No candy in the box)

New Clauses—Questions

Q-X-Y	what mommy doing (What is mommy doing?)

New Clauses—Commands

Verb-X-Y	take boy house (Take the boy to the house.)

New Phrases

noun-adjective-noun	boy blue car (boy's blue car)
adjective-adjective-noun	big black cat
determiner-adjective-noun	this blue car
preposition-determiner-noun	on the table
copula	boy is mean

auxiliary	boy could swim
pronouns	her go store, him do it

Between Stages II and III morphological markers begin to emerge. These inflections include

-ing (present progressive)	jumping
-s (plural)	boys
-ed (past tense)	jumped
-en (past participle)	eaten
-s (3rd person singular, or noun verb agreement)	he eats apple
's (possessive)	doggie's bone
-n't (contracted negative)	can't
-'s (contracted copula)	she's mad
-'s (contracted auxiliary)	she's going
-est (superlative)	meanest
-er (comparative)	funnier
-ly (adverbial suffix)	happily

Stage IV (two and one-half to three years). Sentences of Four Elements or More

During this phase, as in Stage III, children begin to expand three-word phrases into four and more words. For example, the three-word sentence structure "boy eat apple" becomes the subject-verb-object structure "The boy ate the apple."

In addition, the children increase clause acquisition to include the following.

New Clauses—Statements

subject-verb complement-object-adverb	Boy's eating the apple now.
subject-verb-direct object-indirect object	She gave the book to me.
adverb-adverb-X-Y	We go to the library in the morning.

New Clauses—Questions

Question-X-Y-Z	Where are you going?

New Clauses—Commands

subject (the subject is expressed as a command)	You come with me.

New Phrase Structures Added at Stage IV

noun-preposition-noun	boy in the car
2 auxiliary verbs	She has been running
preposition-determiner- adjective-noun	on the blue chair
negative X	not my doll
X-conjunction-X	bread and butter; hot and tired
conjunction-X	and mommy

The authors stated that by the end of this stage—three years old—children have acquired all elements of structure and the main elements of phrase structure.

Stage V (three to three and one-half years). Recursion

At this stage the children begin to expand by sequencing several clauses together, connecting them with such words as *and* and *so*, *because* and *now*. The result is more mature sentences that coordinate and subordinate clauses.

Stage VI (three and one-half to four and one-half years). System Completion

The authors stressed that this is a stage of "error analysis," noting that although all of the elements of structure are present, children are in the process of using immature word forms, such as verb tense, irregular noun inflections, and pronoun errors. In this phase children begin to use initiators, coordination patterns, and more complex verb forms.

Stage VII (four and one-half years and beyond). Discourse Structure, Syntactic Comprehension, and Style

In the discourse structure, fewer and fewer errors are noted at this stage, but learning is not complete. Children learn refinements of language by including sentence-connecting devices such as however and although. Children learn to vary word order to control emphasis, as in the sentence "Boy, did I." Intonation becomes refined to emphasize certain aspects in need of emphasis.

With regard to syntactic comprehension, children begin to understand the intricacies of adult speech and to discriminate between the different meanings inferred from two identical structures.

Ask me to do it.
Tell me to do it.

In refining a style, children begin to individualize elements of style in communicating with others. These may be influenced by familial language traits, the school environment, and personal choice.

In addition to the development of constructions in the seven stages identified by Crystal et al., Garman (1979) sheds further light on the grammatical development of children at these stages by including research done on mean length of utterance, word classes, and vocabulary size. The main summary of the findings is reported in Table 1-1.

When is the acquisition of syntax complete? Morehead and Morehead (1976) indicated that acquisition of syntax is greatest during the period between 18 months and 4 years. Chomsky (1969), however, stated that active syntactic acquisition continues beyond the age of 9. She stressed that even though children vary in their rate of acquiring syntactic constructions, sequence of construction acquired remains relatively constant.

Morphology

Morphology is the division of grammar that deals with the forms and internal structure of words. It is the study of morphemes, the smallest meaningful unit of speech. Morphology is concerned with word endings and inflections, prefixes, suffixes, and compound words. It is concerned with how words are transformed in response to changes in tense, number, and case. As children mature they begin to learn, by hearing others and by gradually internalizing for themselves, the rules that govern morphological change. Singular nouns develop into plurals. Present tense verbs evolve into appropriate usage of past and future tense verbs. The child begins to change verb endings to agree with the plurality of the noun used. Use of

Table 1-1 Grammatical Development of Children

Stage	Age	Mean Length of Utterance	Word Classes	Vocabulary Size (Approximate)
I	18 months	1.2	Mostly nouns (61%) 11% action words 10% modifiers, personal-social	50 words
II	2 years	1.7	Verbs develop latter half of stage	300 words
III	2.5 years	2.7	Child develops more adjectives	470 words
IV	3 years	3.4	Little change in relative proportions of word classes	920 words
V	3.5 years			
VI	4 years	4.8		1900 words

possessive pronouns and comparative forms of adjectives emerges. The normal child increasingly becomes aware of how words change in relation to each other and begins to generalize the rules to form novel sentences with correct morphological markers.

Berko (1958) studied the morphological development of children between the ages of four and seven and found evidence that children use morphological rules to generalize plurality, progressive and past tense, comparative and superlative adjectives, third person singular, and compound words. In this study, Berko gave 56 children nonsense situations in which they were to complete sentences using a nonsense word with the proper allomorph (word ending). For example, to determine whether children generalized rules governing plurals, they were presented with a statement such as this.

This is a wug. Now there is another one.
There are two of them. There are two _____.

The child was required to complete the sentence. If the answer was ''wugs,'' it was assumed that the child had generalized the plural allomorph/z/to a novel situation.

The evidence from Berko's study indicates that children in this age range do indeed operate with morphological rules that allow them to generalize inflectional endings to new unfamiliar words. What are some of these morphological rules that change words, and how do children acquire them?

Brown (1973) studied the beginning language of three children and identified their acquisition of 14 morphemes. From these data, and drawing from the work of Cazden (1968), Brown established a mean order of acquisition for these 14 morphemes with three children. Table 1-2 represents an adaptation of Brown's work in studying the development of these morphemes, along with examples of their use in children's language.

With minor variations from Brown's rank order of occurrence in these 14 morphemes, deVilliers and deVilliers (1973) presented data that correlated highly with Brown's findings. In addition, the deVilliers predicted an order of acquisition based on grammatical complexity.

Using the predictions from the deVilliers study, along with information from Lee's Developmental Sentence Scoring chart (1974), we have developed a table to compare the relative appearance of morphological constructions. Table 1-3 illustrates the order of acquisition.

It can be seen from Table 1-3 that singular nouns appear before plural nouns, regular plurals appear before irregular plurals, and regular adjectives appear before comparative adjectives. Similarly, present progressive verbs occur before past tense verbs. Within the class of past tense verbs, irregular verbs tend to occur before the child develops regular verbs. Past tense verbs also occur before future

Table 1-2 Morphemes in Order of Acquisition

Morphemes in Order of Acquisition	Examples
1. Present progressive form of verb	is eating
2.-3. Prepositions in, on	in chair, on table
4. Plural (regular)	cats, dogs, witches
5. Past irregular tense verbs	went, came, fell
6. Possessives	boy coat, Daddy hat
7. Uncontractible copula	Here I *am.*
	There it *is.*
	Here we *are.*
	I *be* good.
8. Articles	a ball, the doggie
9. Past regular tense verbs	jumped, poured, waded
10. Third person regular verbs	Daddy *drives.*
11. Third person irregular verbs	Debbie *does.*
	Mommy *has.*
12. Uncontractible auxiliary verb	I *am* working.
	Boy *is* running.
	Girls *are* jumping.
	They *be* working.
13. Contractible copula verb	He's boy.
(contraction form of a copular verb)	We're happy.
	She's a mommy.
	I'm good boy.
14. Contractible auxiliary	I'm working.
(contraction form of an auxiliary verb)	He's running.
	She's sewing.
	We're playing.

tenses. And finally, first and second person pronouns appear in development before third person pronouns.

Derwing and Baker (1979) replicated the findings of such researchers and confirmed Brown's mean order of acquisition by establishing a hierarchy of difficulty from the most frequently correct morpheme to the least.

1. progressive morpheme, e.g., He is walking.
2. plural morpheme, e.g., cats, dogs
3. past tense morpheme, e.g., walked
4. possessive morpheme, e.g., girl's coat
5. present (third person singular) morpheme, e.g., He eats.

In addition, they concluded that children master these inflections as a whole class of stem types rather than on a word by word basis. They also pointed to factors of rule strength and to rules governing the use of derivational endings,

Table 1-3 The Relative Acquisition of Morphological Constructions

Initial Constructions	Subsequent Constructions
Singular nouns (cat) ⟶	Plural nouns (cats)
Regular plurals (dogs, cats) ⟶	Irregular plurals (children, men)
Regular adjectives (big) ⟶	Comparative adjectives (bigger)
Present progressive verbs (eating, ⟶ playing)	Past tense verbs (ate, played)
Past tense irregular verbs (saw, ate, ⟶ went, ran)	Past tense regular verbs (jumped, worked)
Past tense verbs (ate, went, jumped) ⟶	Future tense verbs (will go, is going to go)
First and second person pronouns ⟶ (I, me) (mine, you)	Third person pronouns (he, she, her, him)

emphasizing the need for further research in explaining the relationship between frequency and acquisition order.

Semantics

Semantics refers to the component of language most concerned with the meaning or understanding of language. Children begin to build their receptive vocabularies far faster than their expressive vocabularies. They also develop an understanding of abstract language concepts as well as cause and effect relationships. They begin to understand consecutive directions or commands given to them by an adult. They learn to categorize and classify objects and, through these processes, glean new meaning from words, phrases, and sentences.

How does the child begin to attach meaning to words? Bowerman (1976) described a process by which children acquire a conceptual framework before they begin to speak.

> During the period before he speaks, the child is busy building up a repertoire of basic cognitive concepts—ways of organizing and understanding his experiences. His task is to discover the linguistic devices by means of which such concepts can be expressed. In other words, acquiring language consists in large part of learning how to map or translate from one representational system (the child's prelinguistic notions) into another system. (p. 101)

Clark (1973) hypothesized that when children first begin to use understandable words, they may not fully comprehend their meanings as an adult would. Rather, they may associate a word with a relatively small number of features. As they mature, they begin to add more identifying features to the meaning of the word. For example, when they begin to use the word "kitty," they may be attending to only one or two characteristics, such as the number of legs or that it is a furry object. When children see other similar furry four-legged animals such as a horse, dog, goat, or cow, they may mistakenly call them "kitty" also. Clark termed this generalized use of one word to other objects "overextension." Gradually, as children mature, they begin to attend to more features of an object or concept.

Clark explained the semantic feature hypothesis further.

> . . . when the child first begins to use identifiable words, he does not know their full (adult) meaning: he has only partial entries for them in his lexicon. So the child identifies the meaning of a word with only one or two features. So the acquisition of semantic knowledge consists of adding more features of meaning to that word. (p. 136)

Bloom (1971) emphasized the semantic content of children's first utterances, stressing that a child's development of syntactic constructions is affected by the context in which the construction appears. In another study, Bloom (1973) indicated that children beginning to acquire language often express their perceptions of actions using constructions relating actions and people, as well as relationships between objects and people. In describing semantic categories of children's two-word phrases, she noted four grammatical relations that account for a great number of children's two-word utterances. They are

1. agent-action, action-object, agent-object
2. possessive
3. attributive
4. locative

She described agent-action relations that show how children express actions in terms of who performed the action. An example of the agent-action category would be "Mommy read" or "Daddy sit." Children were also observed describing what received the action. An example of this action-object category might be "read book." An agent-object relationship might be expressed as "Mommy sock," indicating that the child's mother was helping the child put on a sock.

Bloom further indicated that children use possessives, such as "Daddy car;" attributives, a category commonly including adjectives, such as "big truck;" and locatives, a category indicating the location of objects, such as "ball table."

Bloom also delineated three grammatical functions into which children's utterances fall: (1) existence, (2) nonexistence, and (3) recurrence.

The first, existence, was used by children to indicate that they recognized objects. This category includes phrases such as "this ball" or "that dog." The second category of function is nonexistence, which the child typically uses to indicate when something is gone. For example, a child might indicate "all gone juice" or "no more milk." Finally, the child at the two-word stage might typically indicate a recurrence of an action. For example, "jump again" may indicate the child's wishes for the action to occur again, and "more milk" may indicate when the child desires more of the object.

Weiss and Lillywhite (1976) emphasized the development of vocabulary and indicated an order of word acquisition by grammatical category. They stated that normal development of word acquisition follows this sequence.

- nouns
- verbs
- adjectives
- pronouns
- adverbs
- prepositions
- articles
- conjunctions
- interjections

They also pointed out that there are variances in this sequence from child to child and stressed that variations exist in order and time of acquisition.

How do children acquire this core vocabulary? What factors influence the order of acquisition? Clark (1979) postulated that there are three factors affecting the development of vocabulary. They are parental influence in the selection of words used with the child; semantic complexity; and the child's knowledge, the context, and the strategy.

Parental Selection of Words

Clark emphasized that the research shows that parents select words for their children to learn in the course of conversing with them and by supplying labels that are progressively more specific as the child matures.

Semantic Complexity

Stated simply, a child learns terms that represent concepts to comprehend first. Some of the factors contributing to this complexity include

- Dimensional terms.   The concept of size is first learned as the most simple dimension, such as the term *big*. Later, more difficult variations of the size dimension, such as *long*, *tall*, and *wide* may be comprehended.

- Kinship terms. Easier terms of the familial structure, such as *mother* and *father*, are learned before terms requiring more abstract understanding.
- Possession verbs. The actions of *give* and *take* are learned quite early, whereas more complex verbs such as *buy* and *sell* are comprehended much later.
- Spatial terms. Prepositional placement of *in* and *on* are learned before such terms as *between* and *below*.
- Diectic terms. Children learn *I* and *you* differentiations early, but other relational terms as *here* and *there* and *come* and *go* evolve later in the child's usage.

Knowledge, Context, and Strategy

The child's current knowledge about the environment coupled with the context of the situation affects the acquisition of vocabulary and gives the child strategies to understand and use new words.

Berry (1969) provided a table that summarizes oral language development in the young child between three and eight years of age. Table 1-4 represents these developmental milestones.

PRAGMATICS

The functions and uses of language provide an even more thorough investigation into the development of a child's competence in language. The child uses language as a social tool, defined and shaped by the context of the situation and the intent of the speaker. Viewing these elements together offers another perspective on the way that children acquire the skills necessary to communicate.

Emphasis on the pragmatics of language has enabled researchers to examine language in its social/communicative role, and through sophisticated categorization systems, to code infant-adult, child-adult, and adult-adult interactions. Thus, a child's development in the functions and uses of language can be described.

Pragmatics has offered a way of looking at the production of language in a new light. Lucas (1980) emphasized that the interaction of phonology, syntax, and morphology with semantics forms a pragmatic system that enables the child to communicate.

The environmental context of the communication becomes an important part of the interaction. Craig (1983) stated that "Pragmatics is the additional set of skills that the child acquires for using language structure in different conversational contexts" (p. 105). Simon (1985) stated it even more concisely. "Pragmatics is a

Table 1-4 Development of Some Aspects of Oral Language, 3-8 Years

Age: Years, Months	Phonological Development	Syntactic Development	Semantic Development
3.0	*Fairly intelligible speech.* Substitution, omission, and distortion of many phonemes inconsistent, varying with position in word and context. Final consonants appear more regularly than at 30 months. *Speech melody* develops rapidly although easy repetitions are present. Voice usually well controlled.	Generative grammar develops (development by his own rules). Experiments with *many syntactic forms.* *Two-word phrases* most frequent form: *That boy (is) naughty; Mommy car stop (Mommy's car stopped; wouldn't run).* *Designative constructions* coming into use: Phrases expanded into subject-predicate sentence. *(What that thing go round?)* *Mean length of response:* 3.4 words.	Egocentric speech prevails. Dramatizes, combining words and actions for his own pleasure. Asks questions about persons, things, processes. Names two colors. Tells sex; full name. Verbalizes toilet needs. *Vocabulary.* Mean number of words: 896.
3.6	*Phonemic gains.* All English vowels and following consonants are used: /m-/, /-m-/, /-mi; /n-/, /-n-/, /-n/; /ŋ-/, /-ŋ/; /t-/; /t-/; /k-/; /p-/, /-p-/; /b-/, /-b-/; /f-/, /-f-/; /h-; /w-/, /-w-/. Articulation still characterized by omission of many medial consonantal phonemes and syllables; does not remember unstressed bits. *Speech melody.* Blocking on initial syllables frequently interrupts rhythm. Rate of speech increased. Many responses in loud voice or yell.	*Grammatical categories.* Speech is made up of: nouns 17% conjunctions 2.2% verbs 22.8% prepositions 6.7% adjectives 6.5% interjections 1.7% adverbs 10.1% articles 6.9% pronouns 19.8% unclassified 6.3% Uses new adjectives: *strong, new, different.* Uses new adverbs: *maybe, too.* Uses auxiliaries: *might, could.* Gains skill in *permutations:* Makes questions from declarative statements. *Mean length of response:* 4.3 words.	*Closed-cycle linguistic development.* Egocentric speech, perception, and inner language reciprocally augmented. *Communicative speech* developing. Directive speech: Commands, requests, threats. Question asking, "why" stage. Relates experiences with fair understanding of sequence and closure. Says nursery rhymes. Names primary colors. Repetitive use of one in counting; *one light and one light,* etc. *Vocabulary.* Mean number of words: 1222. Misuses many words, imperfect understanding.

4.0 *Phonemic development.* 98% of speech intelligible. Articulatory omissions and substitutions sharply reduced. *Speech melody (prosody).* Vocal pitch controlled. Uses some adult patterns of rhythm. Repetition reduced, thus improving rhythm. Some blocking and associated overt mannerisms may continue.

Skill increasing in *transformations* (modification in sentence which transforms kernel). *Sentence structure* advances rapidly. Beginning to use complex and compound sentences, 6-8 words in length. Mean sentence length: 4.2 words. *Grammatical categories.* Speech is made up of:

nouns	16.3%
verbs	23.1%
adjectives	6.7%
adverbs	10.4%
pronouns	20.3%
conjunctions	2.8%
prepositions	7.5%
interjections	1.3%
articles	7.5%
unclassified	4.1%

Verbal syncretism still dominates understanding, but he is beginning to show interest in isolated word meanings. In general still deals with whole sentences without analysis of words. Uses many *how* and *why* questions in response to speech of others. *Perception still is realistic, first person.* Ideation, however, becoming less concrete: alludes to objects, persons, events not in immediate environment. Engages in collective monologues with other children but there is little cooperative thinking. Tells tales; talks much; threatens playmates. Counts 3 objects. *Vocabulary.* Mean number of words: 1540. Uses slang.

4.6 *Phonemic gains.* Appearance or stabilization of phonemes: /s-/, /-s-/; /ʃ-/, /-ʃ-/, /-ʃ/; /tr-/; /kr-/; /-tʃ-/, /-tʃ/. Phonemes /l/, /r/, /s/, /θ/ not stabilized in any position. Reverses order of sounds within word occasionally; reflects lack of memory for bits.

Use of complex and compound sentences increasing. Reverses syllabic and word order occasionally in sentence. Elaborates sentence by use of conjunction; makes spontaneous corrections in grammar. Mean length of response: 4.7 words.

Egocentric speech declining; uses more adaptive language (social communication). *Verbal syncretism* still dominates understanding. Employs extension of meaning in interpreting speech of others. *Discrimination.* Perceives differences in concrete events. *Recall.* Links past and present events.

Table 1-4 continued

Age: Years, Months	Phonological Development	Syntactic Development	Semantic Development
	Speech melody. Frequently disturbs basic melody by beginning sentence with (Am) or (A). Voice well modulated and usually takes on intonational and rhythmic patterns of mother.		*Vocabulary.* Mean number of words: 1870. Vocabulary now reflects his linguistic culture; uses many colloquial expressions. Defines simple words. Tries to use new words, not always correctly.
5.0	*Phonemic gains.* Articulation generally intelligible but phonemes /f/, /v/, /l/, and /s/ are not stabilized in all positions or in all contexts.	*Grammar.* Reasonably accurate. Makes many spontaneous corrections. Sentence structure expanding rapidly in accuracy and complexity. *Embedding* more common. Develops relative clause. Mean length of response: 4.8 words.	Engages in *responsive discourse.* Gives and receives information; change from egocentric speech to rational reciprocity. *Develops percepts* of numbers, speed, time and space. *Shows inner logic* in recounting plots of children's plays (television and theatre). *Names and describes objects* in composite pictures. Names penny, nickel, dime. Employs some *imaginative thinking,* but is mainly realistic. *Abstraction* still is meager. *Categorizes* concrete events on basis of likeness and difference. *Vocabulary.* Mean number of words: 2072. Percentage increase in *vocabulary of use* slight; *comprehension of vocabulary* increasing markedly. Defines simple words.

5.6   Intelligibility of speech: 89%-100%.

Permutations.
Great gains in sentence making of all types.
Uses all basic structures.
Mean length of response: 4.9 words.
Grammar. Makes some errors but corrects them spontaneously.

Language is becoming symbolic.
Significant gains in relating present and past events.
Conversation is socialized in sense that listener is associated with speaker; little true collaboration of thought. Child still speaks chiefly of own actions, and thoughts.
Primitive argument develops: clash of un-motivated assertions.
Advances in *categorization and synthesis* of percepts.
Vocabulary. Mean number of words: 2289.

6.0-7.0 *Phonemic proficiency* established in /l-/, /ʃ/, (-t-); /-t-/; (θ-/; /-r/, /-r-/; /j-/.
Sentence melody imitative of adults in environment.
Child experiments with rhythmic patterns.
Facial expression accompanying speech changes with rhythm; more varied patterns of expression.

Grammatical categories. Speech is made up of:

nouns	17.1%
verbs	25%
adjectives	7.6%
adverbs	10%
pronouns	19.2%
conjunctions	2.6%
prepositions	7.6%
interjections	1%
articles	8.3%
unclassified	1.6%

Sentence length and complexity develop sharply; has command of every form of sentence structure.
Mean sentence length: 6.5 words.

Comprehension of morphemic sequences develops sharply. Anticipates closure in speech of others.
Perception and inner language make great gains; asks for explanations, motives of action, etc.
Understands roughly differences between time intervals.
Understands seasons of year.
Generally distinguishes left from right in himself.
Attempts to verbalize causal relationship.
Counts three objects without error.
Vocabulary. Comprehends meaning of 4000 words; uses (mean number of words): 2562 (7 years).

Table 1-4 continued

Age: Years, Months	Phonological Development	Syntactic Development	Semantic Development
7.0–8.0	*Phonemic proficiency* established in /-z-/; /ð-/; /-ɚ/; /-st/; /-lz/; /-lθ/; /-tr/; /-kt/. *Speech melody.* Subtle rhythms and intonational contours present. Facial and hand gestures underscore speech rhythms.	*Grammar.* Chief errors now are common to his cultural environment. Mean length of response: 7.2 words.	*Egocentric speech* has gone underground, and inner language shows marked development. *True communication* develops. Ideas shared; speech reflects understanding of causal or logical relations. *Vocabulary.* Comprehension of words races far ahead of vocabulary of use. Understands 6000-8000 words. Vocabulary of use: 2562 to 2818 words (7-8 years).

Source: Mildred Freburg Berry, *Language Disorders of Children*, © 1969, pp. 225–229. Reprinted by permission of Prentice-Hall, Inc., Englewood Cliffs, New Jersey.

study of the interaction of four variables: the speaker, the listener, the content, and the context'' (p. 21).

There have been many categorizations of pragmatic structures. Austin (1962) described the relationship between utterances and their meanings in three phases: locutions, illocutions, and perlocutions. Locutions consist of the actual utterance and the content of the message. The illocutionary part of a speech act is the speaker's intent, whereas the perlocutionary phase includes the effect the utterance has on the listener.

Searle (1969) provided a distinction between the proposition, or content of the utterance, and the illocutionary force, or how the utterances are to be received.

Dore (1974) identified nine primitive speech acts (PSAs) that serve as a child's intent in communicating. Dore observed and analyzed these PSAs.

1. labeling	4. requesting (action)	7. greeting
2. repeating	5. requesting (answer)	8. protesting
3. answering	6. calling	9. practicing

In his research, Dore discovered that children showed differences in linguistic forms, but even greater differences in linguistic functions. In other words, some children's utterances directly influenced the adult more.

Halliday (1975) described three phases in language learning.

Phase I

The child, from the period of about 10 to 18 months, begins to develop a functional linguistic system. The child uses vocalizations and sounds to express these functions.

- Instrumental function. Children use language to obtain objects and items for their needs.
- Regulatory function. In an attempt to persuade someone to do something, children use vocalizations that are intended to mean ''Do as I say.''
- Interactional function. This includes ways for children to interact and includes greetings and names.
- Personal function. This is characterized by expression of feelings, such as disgust and pleasure.
- Heuristic function. This enables children to learn more about the environment. This includes requests of why, and in its earliest form, requests for the names of objects.

- Imaginative function. Here, children use language to create a ''let's pretend'' environment.
- Informative function. Children use language to inform others that there is information to be communicated.

Phase II

From approximately 18 to 36 months, the child uses two primary functions: the *pragmatic* or language as doing and *mathetic* or language as learning.

Phase III

The beginning of the third year marks the beginning of the adult system. The child utilizes the *ideational* function, a transition from the mathetic, which enables the child to talk about events. The *interpersonal* function arises from the pragmatic and primarily serves as a tool for social interaction. A third function, the *textual* that Halliday noted, is the system of spoken words and sentences that mediates the ideational and interpersonal functions.

Bates, Camaioni, and Volterra (1975) and Bates (1976) sought to substantiate the acquisition of specific pragmatic functions at the different Piagetian stages of development. Research concluded that pragmatic functions serve as the link between linguistic, cognitive, and social development.

SUMMARY

Developmental data as presented in this chapter serve the following functions. First, they serve as a comparison of language acquisition in the normal and language delayed child. This comparison can provide a guideline for decision making, e.g., should the child who shows a lag in language development be further evaluated for obtaining more detailed information on the specific language deficits? These data can also serve as a base from which to communicate with the parents of the child suspected of having a language delay. Parents desire and need to know how their child compares with other children in language development. Consequently, developmental norms may serve as their guide in determining subsequent action.

Second, developmental data serve as a normative standard to be used in the assessment of language disorders. Most commercially developed assessment instruments have incorporated research findings and developmental language data in an effort to evaluate and quantify language functioning.

Finally, developmental data provide a basis for language programming. Through observation of how normal children acquire language, some guidance is offered for making decisions on the sequence and content of the language intervention program.

REFERENCES

Austin, J.L. (1962). *How to do things with words*. London: Oxford University Press.

Bates, E. (1976). *Language and context*. New York: Academic Press.

Bates, E, Camaioni, L., & Volterra, V. (1975). The acquisition of performatives prior to speech. *Merrill-Palmer Quarterly, 21* (3), 205–226.

Berko, J. (1958). The child's learning of English morphology. *Word, 14,* 150–177.

Berry, M. (1969). *Language disorders of children* (p. 225). Englewood Cliffs, NJ: Prentice-Hall.

Bloom, L. (1971). Why not pivot grammar. *Journal of Speech and Hearing Disorders, 36,* 40–50.

Bloom, L. (1973). *One word at a time*. The Hague, Netherlands: Mouton Press.

Bowerman, M. (1976). Semantic factors in the acquisition of rules for word use and sentence construction. In D. Morehead & A. Morehead (Eds.), *Normal and deficient child language* (p. 101). Baltimore, MD: University Park Press.

Brown, R. (1973). *A first language: The early stages* (p. 274). Cambridge, MA: Harvard University Press.

Brown, R., & Bellugi, U. (1964). Three processes in the child's acquisition of syntax. In E. Lennenberg (Ed.), *New directions in the study of language* (p. 140). Cambridge, MA: MIT Press.

Cairns, H.S., & Williams, F. (1972). An analysis of the substitution errors of a group of standard English speaking children. *Journal of Speech and Hearing Research, 15,* 811–820.

Cazden, C. (1968). Acquisition of noun and verb inflections. *Child Development, 2,* 433–448.

Chapman, R., & Miller, J. (1975). Word order in early two and three word utterances: Does production precede comprehension? *Journal of Speech and Hearing Research, 18,* 355–371.

Chomsky, C. (1969). *The acquisition of syntax in children from 5 to 10*. Cambridge, MA: MIT Press.

Chomsky, N., & Halle, M. (1968). *The sound pattern of English*. New York: Harper & Rowe.

Clark, E. (1973). *What's in a word*? In T.E. Moore (Ed.), *Cognitive development and the acquisition of language*. New York: Academic Press.

Clark, E. (1979). Building a vocabulary. In P. Fletcher & M. Garman (Eds.), *Language acquisition* (pp. 149–160). Cambridge, UK: Cambridge University Press.

Craig, H.K. (1983). Applications of pragmatic language models for intervention. In T.M. Gallagher & C.A. Prutting (Eds.), *Pragmatic assessment and intervention issues in language*. San Diego, CA: College Hill Press.

Crystal, D. (1979). Prosodic development. In P. Fletcher & M. Garman (Eds.), *Language acquisition: Studies in first language development* (pp. 33–48). Cambridge, UK: Cambridge University Press.

Crystal, D., Fletcher, P., & Garman, M. (1976). *The grammatical analysis of language disability*. New York: Elsevier.

Derwing, B.L., & Baker, W.J. (1979). Recent research on the acquisition of English morphology. In P. Fletcher & M. Garman (Eds.), *Language acquisition* (pp. 209–223). Cambridge, UK: Cambridge University Press.

DeVilliers, J., & deVilliers, P. (1973). A cross sectional study of the acquisition of grammatical morphemes in child speech. *Journal of Psycholinguistic Research, 2,* 267–278.

Dore, J. (1974). A pragmatic description of early language development. *Journal of Psycholinguistic Research, 3*, 43–350.

Engelmann, S. (1969). *Preventing failure in the primary grades* (p. 83). Chicago, IL: Science Research Associates.

Garman, M. (1979). Early grammatical development. In P. Fletcher & M. Garman (Eds.), *Language acquisition* (pp. 177–208). Cambridge, UK: Cambridge University Press.

Halliday, M.A.K. (1975). *Learning how to mean*. New York: Elsevier.

Ingram, D. (1974). Phonological rules in young children. *Journal of Child Language, 1*, 49–64.

Lee, L. (1966). Developmental sentence types: A method for comparing normal and deviant syntactic development. *Journal of Speech and Hearing Disorders, 31*, 311–330.

Lee, L. (1974). *Developmental sentence analysis* (pp. 134–135). Evanston, IL: Northwestern University Press.

Lucas, E.V. (1980). *Semantic and pragmatic language disorders*. Rockville, MD: Aspen.

McCarthy, D. (1954). Language development in children. In L. Carmichael (Ed.), *Carmichael's manual of child psychology* (p. 509). New York: John Wiley and Sons.

McNeill, D. (1954). The development of language. In L. Carmichael (Ed.), *Carmichael's manual of child psychology* (p. 1062). New York: John Wiley and Sons.

Menyuk, P. (1968). The role of distinctive features in children's acquisition of phonology. *Journal of Speech and Hearing Research, 11*, 138–146.

Menyuk, P. (1972). *The development of speech*. New York: Bobbs-Merrill Studies in Communicative Disorders.

Morehead, D., & Morehead, A. (1976) (Eds.), *Normal and deficient child language* (p. 11). Baltimore, MD: University Park Press.

Searle, J.R. (1969). *Speech acts: An essay in the philosophy of language*. Cambridge, UK: Cambridge University Press.

Shriberg, L.D. (1980). Developmental phonological disorders. In T. Hixon, L.D. Shriberg, & J. Saxman (Eds.), *Introduction to communication disorders*. Englewood Cliffs, NJ: Prentice Hall.

Simon, C. (1985) (Ed.), *Communication skills and classroom success*. San Diego, CA: College Hill Press.

Weiss, C., & Lillywhite, H. (1976). *Communicative disorders* (p. 59). St. Louis, MO: C.V. Mosby.

Chapter 2

Characteristics and Problems of Language Delayed Children

For services to be provided to the language delayed child, criteria must be established that enable the language practitioner to properly identify children with language deficits. The authors have defined several terms that serve to establish these criteria.

The term "language delayed" refers to a deficit in one or more of the following language components: phonology, morphology, semantics, syntax, or pragmatics, to the extent that the child is impaired in the ability to understand or use spoken language and to the extent that the present level of receptive and/or expressive language differs significantly from that expected at the child's chronological age.

DeVilliers and deVilliers (1978) identified three types of language delay.

1. late onset of intelligible speech
2. lagging rate of acquisition once the child has begun speaking
3. a final level of language significantly less than that of normal adult language

Furthermore, deVilliers and deVilliers distinguished between the terms "delayed" and "deviant." Delays fall into the three categories listed above and refer to the time of language acquisition. Deviant language, on the other hand, refers to an abnormality in *what* children acquire or *how* they acquire constructions. More specifically, a deviancy may occur in the sequence of development or as a divergence from normal syntactical development.

This book is intended as a guide for language practitioners dealing with both slow development (delay) and language deviance.

A nonverbal child is one who exhibits less than one-word utterances and who relies heavily on gestures and sounds to communicate. In terms of our previous comments, one may view this as a lag in the onset of speech.

Children with significant language problems can be further identified by characteristics and problems that they possess and that differentiate them from normal children. Following is a discussion of these characteristics, signs for suspecting language problems, and a description of the more common language problems encountered by language delayed children.

CHARACTERISTICS OF LANGUAGE DELAYED CHILDREN

Children with language problems exhibit certain characteristics that will alert the adult to a problem. Often these traits can be directly observed by the individual responsible for the welfare or education of the child. Yet other times the signs of language delay are more subtle and thus more difficult to recognize. The teacher or parent who suspects a language delay should begin by observing the child in the immediate environment to determine whether further screening or assessment is warranted.

Children with language delays may exhibit problems in both receptive and expressive language. Likewise they may manifest social, emotional, and physical characteristics differentiating them from their peers. The language practitioner must be aware of these characteristics so that early identification can be made.

Receptive Language Problems

Receptive language refers to the ability to comprehend the spoken word. Children with receptive language problems are often noticed when they fail to follow directions given by an adult. Often these children appear to be inattentive or may seem as though they do not hear or listen to directions. When asked to "Get the red book and put it on the table," the child may complete only the first part of the instruction, stopping before the second phase.

The child who has problems receiving language may appear to understand speech better if it is accompanied by gestures rather than oral speech alone.

Children with receptive language problems may have great difficulty understanding words or vocabulary that represents abstract concepts. They may be disoriented when responding to concepts of space such as left, right, up, and down. They may not comprehend concepts of prepositional placement such as on, in, under, between, or beside. In addition, they may confuse concepts of time such as yesterday, tomorrow, before, or after.

Another characteristic of children with receptive language problems involves inappropriate responses to questions. The example of Sally, a child of six, illustrates this characteristic. When greeted by an adult with the query, "Hi, what's your name?" Sally responded with, "Fine," indicating that she did not understand the adult's question and therefore responded stereotypically to what she thought was the question.

Children with receptive language difficulties may not comprehend the meanings in stories read orally by another and often cannot answer even the simplest literal questions pertaining to the story. Nor can they respond correctly in relating the sequence of events in a story.

These signs of poor receptive language functioning represent difficulties in the comprehension of spoken language and may indicate the presence of a language delay.

Expressive Language Problems

Expressive language refers to the verbal or oral utterances of communication. Children with expressive language difficulties exhibit distinct characteristics. They may be reluctant to participate in large group activities, especially if this requires verbal interchange. These children may exhibit a limited vocabulary, relying on the same core of words no matter what the situation. This obviously results in a great deal of inappropriate language.

Children with expressive problems may have difficulty in activities that require them to remember sequences of words in rhymes or songs.

The child may appear to use immature speech, utilizing such utterances as "Me want cookie" well beyond the age of acceptable baby talk.

Finally, these children may have difficulty in relating personal experiences such as what they did the previous night. They may exhibit confusion relating sequential events, such as recounting the main occurrences in a story.

Adults who work with children should become aware of these characteristics and be observant of children's behavior so that suspected language problems can be identified. Early identification of children who seem to exhibit a language deficit can lead to further assessment to pinpoint the specific problem.

Social and Emotional Characteristics of the Language Delayed Child

Because language delayed children are hampered in their ability to communicate, they often appear to have low cognitive skills. This misconception often leads peers to assume that the child is "dumb" or "retarded." Often, normal peers will avoid interaction with the child, forcing the child to play and associate only with children who have similar problems.

If the language problem is more overt and the disability more evident, the child will often be the subject of jokes, laughter, and ridicule, a devastating experience for any child.

Often, teachers are openly asked by "normal" children from the regular classroom, "What's the matter with him?" or "Why can't she talk right?" in an honest attempt to understand the apparent deviancy. Unless these questions are handled with discretion and sensitivity, they will only serve to increase the emotional suffering of the language delayed child.

Another problem that language delayed children exhibit is that, because of the language delay, they express themselves at a much lower developmental level. Their speech and understanding of language is at a significantly less mature level than their age peers. Consequently, language delayed children are frequently forced to play with children younger than themselves to communicate and interact in a social situation.

Because children with language problems have difficulty communicating and interacting with others, they may show signs of frustration. One example in the authors' own experience is a child who had such multiple misarticulations that it was difficult to understand him when he tried to communicate his thoughts. One time in particular, the child tried to tell his teacher what he wanted for Christmas. The child repeated the word several times to his teacher, who could usually decipher the majority of his misarticulations. This time, however, the teacher could not discern what the approximated word was. Finally, in frustration, the child stamped his foot in great exasperation and walked away. After a few minutes, he returned with the word "train" spelled incorrectly on a piece of scratch paper. Fortunately for this child, his reading and writing skills were sufficient at this time to communicate his wish. Think how frustrating it is for the child who has no alternative means of expression other than the verbal mode.

All of the above problems may manifest themselves in low self-esteem. It is easy to see how a child who has significant language problems can perceive himself as an inadequate human being.

Physical Characteristics of the Language Delayed Child

Language delayed children may have problems that are not attributable to physical causes. In these cases, the appearance of the children may not deviate significantly from their peers. One example is a particularly handsome child who from all outward appearances seems normal. After interacting with him on the playground, teachers frequently remark "But he looks so normal."

In other cases, language delayed children may show signs of physical problems that may or may not be the cause of the language problem. These physical characteristics may include, but are not restricted to, cleft palate, deviant orthodontal structure, or problems with the vocal mechanism.

Children with language problems may have oral muscular coordination problems so that forming sounds used in speech is slower than normal. They may also experience excessive salivation and feeding problems as a result of the lack of oral coordination. Children with language problems may also suffer from continuous allergy problems, respiratory difficulties, or frequent colds.

Another characteristic of language delayed children may be hearing loss, either temporary or permanent. Chronic ear infections can cause definite losses affecting the acquisition of language and subsequently may cause a lag in language development. Though problems of deafness can indeed have a significant negative impact on language development, this book does not deal specifically with problems of deaf or hearing impaired children. However, the contents will deal with common language problems and language programming that certainly have some applicability to the education of deaf children.

Specific Signs of Language Delay

It is most important to recognize early if a child exhibits a language delay. But how does one determine whether a language delay is suspected? The answer lies in guidelines that compare a child's language functioning with "normal" developmental standards. These developmental standards provide information on the sequence of acquisition of language constructions.

Beyond this, however, specific behavioral events must be observed in the child who is suspected of being language delayed. Weiss and Lillywhite (1976) offer the practitioner a list of signs that may signal the presence of language problems. Possible signs of expressive language problems include the following.

- By 18 months the child is not saying at least six words with appropriate meaning.
- By 24 months the child is not combining words into phrases such as "go bye-bye," "want cookie."
- By 30 months the child is not using short sentences such as "Mommy see dolly," "Daddy go bye-bye."
- By 36 months the child has not begun asking simple questions.
- By 48 months the child's sentences are telegraphic, reversed, or confused, such as "Me car go," "Baby loud crying," "Candy me want."
- By 48 months, the child is not using auxiliary verbs, such as "is," "have," and "can."
- By 60 months, the child is not using the personal pronoun "I," such as "me (instead of I) want a cookie," or uses name instead of pronoun, such as "Bobby (instead of I) want a drink."
- By 60 months the child consistently uses incorrectly past tenses, plurals, and pronouns, such as "Them throwed a ball."
- By 60 months the child's expressive vocabulary is limited and shallow, fewer than 200 to 300 simple words.

- The child's language has not improved in sentence length, complexity, and accuracy within any six-month period after age two.
- The child has difficulty in self-expression, according to the age level, or is concerned or teased about the language used.

In addition to these specific milestones that stress the forms of syntax and morphology used in expression, there are pragmatic considerations that must be addressed. Is the child communicating the ideas intended, or are there so many restrictions in conversation that the listener is left puzzled about what the child said? More specifically, the practitioner or parent may evaluate the child's overall performance as a communicator with these questions as guidelines.

- Does the child frequently exhibit an unsystematic combination of ideas when speaking?
- Does the child use the same sentence patterns repeatedly?
- Does the child exhibit incoherent sequencing of details when discussing an event?
- Does the child have difficulty finding the right words or labels for objects?
- Does the child often repeat phrases at the start or middle of sentences?
- Does the child's volume or speech rate detract from the content of what is being related?
- Does the child have difficulty staying on a topic when conversing with another?
- Does the child usually restate the same information, using the same words or restricted vocabulary, when asked to repeat a statement or question?
- Does the child frequently revert to egocentric or tactless comments within a conversation?

If these problems frequently occur in a child's conversation, it is possible that the child is not saying what was intended and that as a communicator the child is ineffective.

If the language practitioner or parent uses these guidelines and finds that persistent language problems occur over a period of time, a language delay or problem may be suspected. Further information on more specific techniques of assessing language problems will be elucidated in Chapter 3.

COMMON LANGUAGE PROBLEMS

Children who are language delayed exhibit a wide range of language problems. Fundamental to any discussion of common syntactical, morphological, semantic, or pragmatic errors associated with the language delayed child is the fact that the errors, in and of themselves, do not constitute deviance. It is only when they occur far past the chronological age at which most normal children have begun to use the more appropriate form of the construction that they are considered deviant or inappropriate.

For example, if a two year old child uses the phrases "more juice" or "want juice," it would not seem inappropriate. However, if the same phrases are used by a five year old child rather than a more mature statement such as "I want some more juice, please" or "May I have some more?" then this would be cause for concern. Errors commonly made by language delayed children are considered deviant when they are still occurring late in the child's development. The reader may wish to refer to the developmental milestones in Chapter 1 to place these problems in perspective.

Several attempts have been made to classify or describe typical language problems. Coughran and Liles (1976); Morehead and Ingram (1978); Leonard, Bolders, and Miller (1976); Simon (1979); and Damico (1985) have all contributed to descriptions of the expressive and pragmatic language problems of language delayed children. Explanations of the most common problems are described in the remainder of this chapter.

Nonverbal Children

Perhaps the most severe language problem is that of nonverbal behavior, or the absence of any meaningful oral language. Nonverbal children have as their primary mode of communication gesturing and using noises to call attention to their basic needs. Or a child may be syntactically at the level of single-word responses, where immature speech vocalizations such as "baba" and "choo choo" substitute for the more mature forms of the words "bottle" and "train." At the one-word response level the child may have a vocabulary of several functional nouns and verbs, but may not be able to combine them into phrases with meaning such as "boy run" or "hit ball."

Echolalia

Another serious language problem is echolalia, defined as the partial or complete imitation and repetition of phrases or words that children hear modeled. When a seven year old girl, Sarah, was asked, "Hi, Sarah. How are you?" Sarah replied with a smile, "Hi, Sarah. How are you?" The extent of the problem is evident. Echolalic children either do not understand the question and merely repeat what they hear, or they do not process the message they hear, which prevents them from responding meaningfully. Echolalia warrants special attention and procedures for remediation.

In discussing specific language problems, we will use a framework to add structure to descriptions. The format, developed by Simon (1979), effectively combined emphasis on the child's use of language structures, with a focus on pragmatic use of language. Simon separated language problems, or language incompetence, into three areas: form, function, and style. Form refers to the expressive production of language structures used by the child. It includes errors in syntax and morphology; and problems in vocabulary development. Function refers to the manner the child uses language for different social purposes and contexts, and how effective the child is at communicating intent. Style refers to the individual's characteristics of speaking that hinder the rhythm, flow, and continuity of the message.

Simon's format has been adapted with examples of incompetent language obtained from language samples of language delayed children. (See Exhibit 2-1.)

As mentioned earlier, there are several language problems common to language delayed children. It should be noted, however, that the possession of one or more characteristics does not automatically mean that the child has a language delay. Nor does incorrect usage of constructions alone confirm a language delay. However, when these problems occur far beyond the age when most normal children have acquired the more mature constructions, there may be cause for concern.

The following language samples are included to illustrate the quality of expression of language delayed children. The samples included represent spontaneous language from three language delayed children. The children sampled were asked to retell familiar fairy tales using a storybook as a visual stimulus. Their narrations were tape recorded and later transcribed. Note the age of the children.

Language Sample: ''Snow White and the Seven Dwarfs''

Student: Charles, age ten years and two months

The wicked witch say, ''Mirror, who the fairy in the world?'' And Snow White cleaning the step. Snow White run and the king he not kill her. And Snow White saw somebody play the animals. And Snow White see inside the house. And Snow White cleaning the floor. And Snow White see the bed. And then seven dwarfs come back and Snow White wake up and say the names of. And Snow White dancing and Wicked Witch say the king fool her. And the Wicked Witch give the poison apple to Snow White and the Wicked Witch say, ''Take this for eating.'' Then the seven dwarfs run the house. And Snow White dead. And then seven dwarfs so sad. And the Prince come to kiss her. And Snow White come alive.

Though this sample of language will not be analyzed in detail here, it can be readily seen that the student exhibits a number of difficulties. Among these are

- use of present tense verbs and few past tense verbs
- omission of auxiliary verbs
- lack of alternatives for the conjunction "and" in making compound and complex sentences
- incoherent sequencing of details
- unsystematic combination of ideas

The significance of these difficulties is magnified when the child's age is revealed. By the age of ten, most normal children are using these constructions correctly and are much more advanced in the use of morphological endings, syntactical development of sentences, and use of effective illocutionary speech acts.

Language Sample: "The Three Little Pigs"

Student: Becky, age seven years and four months

One little pig was making the straw of the house. Was happy because it was fixed up and he was so happy. Then he went to 'nother house. The first pig went to 'nother house. Two pigs and two pigs were running, singing, dancing. The fox was hungry and the third little pig was so busy. O-O-O-O-O, he was so busy. The little pigs—they talking to him. And say, "Want to play with us?" He was so busy. They went running, dancing, singing. The pig said, "not my chinny chin." And the fox say, "I'll blow your house." And he puff, puff, and he blow it. He went running he could. And the first little pig went the second little pig. And they peek outside and look out the door and they sing and dance in the stick house.

The fox is . . . fox is lamb. "Not my chinny chin." He hide under the lamb. And he is a fox. And he blow and blow and puff and puff and it broke. He puff, puff, puff, and it so strong. They went to the third pig and he puff and puff and puff, and was too strong. And he went down and he got the soup—inside the soup and he say, "OW! That hurts!" And they was so happy and dancing.

The student responded in this language sample with several well formed sentences. However, she still omitted some very vital function words. In the utterance "Was happy because it was fixed up," she omitted the subject of the sentence, until she added it in as an afterthought at the end, "And he was so happy.'' And in the utterance, ''And say, want to play with us?'' the subject is again omitted. The student also has difficulty with using past tense verb markers, both regular and irregular. Other sentences illustrate complete omission of phrases. In the sentence ''He went running he could,'' she omitted the simile phrase ''as fast as,'' assuming that was the intent of her expression. Again, these difficulties become relevant in comparison to other seven year olds, where the differentiation in language development between ''normal'' and ''language delayed'' becomes evident.

Pragmatically, the language of this child illustrates the difficulty she had in systematically combining ideas with the use of transitional or connecting words. Mazes and false starts detract from the continuity of details, and limited vocabulary makes subordinating ideas within sentences infrequent. The total result is an incoherent account or sequence of events. A high frequency of restricted sentences greatly affects the meaning of this story.

Language Sample: ''Hansel and Gretel''

Student: John, age ten years and two months

The boy got away. They're look. The boy is taking the rocks. The boy kissing. The boy taking a walk and the boy eating the house. The woman looking to the boy. The woman put the boy sleeping. The woman got warm and the girl mopping. And the boy in the cage and the girl putting water in there.

The girl's gonna push that in the fire. And the girl and boy are dancing, and the girl and boy is feed the bird and that's the end.

This child exhibited incorrect verb usage and omission of auxiliary verbs. In addition, however, sentences are restricted in a semantic sense because they show limited vocabulary and indefinite referents. The child had no ability to relate cause and effect and no way of connecting the events of the story. Rather, his narrative sounds like simplified statements of unrelated events. Pragmatically, this child cannot express a sequence of events.

These language samples were included to illustrate two points. First, they offer the reader actual descriptive language representative of typical language delayed children. Second, they illustrate the problems of form, function, and style commonly seen in the language of children with language delays.

To delineate specific problems for remediation, however, a more thorough analysis of language is necessary. Chapter 3 offers the reader techniques in the evaluation and assessment of language.

Exhibit 2-1 Characteristics of Incompetent Language

Incompetent Language Form

Problem	Example
Limited vocabulary	You hit it with a, a, _____. (hammer)
Syntactic and morphological errors	Me, momma cake, happy birthday everybody yum, yum. Where kids? Boy go. On Monday me long time sleepy.
Syntactic patterns re-used	The boy is eating. The girl is swimming. The dog is running.
Difficulty with	
verbs	Yesterday I see parade. Tomorrow I go town. She like to play. I see three dog.
plurals	
Lacks consistency in tense and number reference	She eats chips. She eats hamburgers. She ate a cookie. The boy swim.
Uses ambiguous pronouns	The girl's gonna push that in the fire.
Misuse of pronouns	Me know. Her going home. I see shes ball.
Unsystematic combination of ideas	The man look. The man eating chicken. The man going to get the boy and the boy sing.

Exhibit 2-1 continued

Problem	Incompetent Language Function
	Example
Wanders from conversational topic	**Language Practitioner:** Tell me about your house.
	Child: Well, in my house we have an upstairs. And I sleep downstairs. You know what? My grandmother is coming to visit.
Ineffective illocutionary speech acts	Child lacks the ability to use specific phrases for specific purposes.
	Instrumental. Child cannot describe what is needed or wanted.
	Regulatory. Child cannot give directions for a task or use appropriate polite commands. "You put the thing in the thing and it goes around and around."
	Interactional. Child does not use appropriate ways of interacting socially, e.g., taking turns in conversation, responding to greetings, or providing relevant answers to questions.
	Personal. Child may not be able to supply basic information about himself/herself.
	Language Practitioner: How many brothers do you have?
	Child: Uh, I have one, uh, and I gotta think.
	Language Practitioner: Tell me their names.
	Child: One is Daniel and then Matt, and Steven and David.
	Language Practitioner: That's a lot of brothers. One, two, three, four.
	Child: Did I put Daniel?
	Language Practitioner: Yes. Daniel, David, Mat, and Steven. Is that all?
	Child: And also my dad.
	Child may not be able to express an opinion or attitude.
	Language Practitioner: What do you like to do for fun?
	Child: I don't know.
	Heuristic. Child is not able to ask appropriate questions to find out about events and may lack curiosity about objects.

Imaginative. Child does not typically engage in role playing. The child is not able to sequence details to relate a story.

Informative. Child may have difficulty relating a sequence of events, even when provided with picture cues. Take, for example, a 6 year old girl describing the process of communication with her father, who was absent from the home.

Child: I have—I saw—I have a tape recorder—and I just talk to my daddy in here. But he can never hear me. He can't come here. He's in Germany. He can't come. He's a long time, and he can't—he can't—he just can't hear us. Because we're gonna mail this (points to a tape) to Germany. Because when we mail it he's gonna ask us—he can hear us.

Likewise, the child may not be able to explain the functions of common objects with clarity. One child, shown an eggbeater, was asked to tell how it could be used. Instead of a verbal description, the child merely gestured with his hands how to beat a mixture.

Opinions stated as fact

Child: My uncle's dog? Nobody feeds him. He only gets water.

Relies on a restricted code

Child uses idioms and cliches. Pronouns are frequently used instead of more descriptive words (nonspecific referents)

Child: Then—then he said 'Get the dog on the side.' And they, then they came and he caught the dog. So they went home and when he went home the frog followed his footprints.

Informal, social uses of language

Here, the child may use inappropriate vocabulary in more formal settings. The child may not be able to switch codes with varying contexts of school, home, and/or play.

Afraid to ask questions

Child may lack curiosity or be apprehensive about asking an adult for further information. This is frequently seen in the school setting, where the child prefers to struggle alone rather than ask for more specific directions.

Limited language flexibility

Child is not able to adapt language to different social contexts of age of conversant, status, affiliation of the listener, setting or environment, formality of the situation, or familiarity with surroundings and people involved.

Tactless statements

Why do we have to do that again? I'm tired of doing that.

Exhibit 2-1 continued

Problem	Example
Restates the same information	**Child:** What will happen if you keep on doing it without touching the thing? **Language Practitioner:** I'm sorry. I didn't understand your question. **Child:** How come you have to do it without touching the thing?

Incompetent Language Style

Problem	Example
Egocentric comments	**Language Practitioner:** Tell me what you do to help around the house. **Child:** Make my bed. Dry the dishes. I'm tired. Is it time to go yet?
Incoherent sequencing of details	One child's description of the story of *Jack and the Beanstalk*: He's eating apple. She making coat. She's saw the green bean. The boy take care of the cow. The man pulling the cow. The boy looking out. The boy climbing up. The boy going to eat it. The woman laying the food. Oh, oh! The man run in the house and eat the boy. The boy taking money. The boy climb again. The woman drop the boy in there—in the box. The man look. The man eating chicken. The man going to get the boy and the boy sing.
Word finding difficulty	**Child:** An he said he was going to take the cow to um, um—⎯⎯⎯ **Language Practitioner:** Market? **Child:** Yeah.
False starts and mazes	I got a . . . I got a boy. I . . . I don't got a boy scout suit, but I got a . . . I am a boy scout.
Speech slurred in a series of giant words. Frequently, giant words are unintelligible	Henawan (He doesn't want) Eena chip (Eating a) chip.
Rapid jerky speech rate	Unusual rate causes the child to sound unintelligible
Speech volume not adapted to context	The child may speak loudly in a setting requiring softer tones.

Source: From *Communicative Competence: A Functional-Pragmatic Approach to Language Therapy* (pp. 1–47) by C.S. Simon, 1979, Tucson, Ariz.: Communication Skill Builders, Inc. Copyright 1979 by Communication Skill Builders, Inc. Adapted by permission.

SUMMARY

Language delayed children may possess a wide range of characteristics setting them apart from their normal peers. Physical, social, and emotional characteristics and specific traits representative of receptive and expressive language problems serve to differentiate and further isolate language delayed children. The language practitioner must be aware of these characteristics, for they signal possible language delay.

Similarly, recognizing and identifying some of the most common language problems should help the language practitioner in the observation of children, pinpointing possible areas of deficit and laying the groundwork for further assessment of specific problems.

REFERENCES

Brown, R. (1973). *A first language* (p. 74). Cambridge, MA: Harvard University Press.

Coughran, L., & Liles, B. (1976). *Developmental syntax program* (p. 6). Austin, TX: Learning Concepts.

Damico, J. (1985). Clinical discourse analysis: A functional approach to language assessment. In C.S. Simon (Ed.), *Communication skills and classroom success: Assessment of language-learning disabled students* (pp. 165–207). San Diego, CA: College Hill Press.

DeVilliers, J., & deVilliers, P. (1978). Language acquisition (p. 230). Cambridge, MA: Harvard University Press.

Leonard, L., Bolders, J., & Miller, J. (1976). An examination of the semantic relations reflected in the language usage of normal and language delayed children. *Journal of Speech and Hearing Research, 19,* 371–392.

Morehead, D., & Ingram, D. (1978). The development of base syntax in normal and linguistically deviant children. In M. Lahey (Ed.), *Readings in childhood language disorders* (p. 55). New York: John Wiley and Sons.

Simon, C.S. (1979). *Communicative competence: A functional-pragmatic approach to language therapy* (pp. 1–47). Tucson, AZ: Communication Skill Builders.

Weiss, C., & Lillywhite, H. (1976). *Communicative disorders* (p. 177). St. Louis, MO: C.V. Mosby.

Chapter 3

Assessment of Language Problems

LANGUAGE ASSESSMENT: TRADITIONAL OR DESCRIPTIVE

Traditionally, assessment of children's language has utilized formalized standardized measures of the production of language structures by children. These typically concentrated on the sentence as the unit of study. Sentences were exposed to scrutiny by coding and scoring syntactical, morphological, and semantic characteristics.

With the shift toward pragmatics, however, the emphasis was placed on the interaction of two communicators within a given context. Thus, larger units of conversation were studied. The assessment of language skills, then, focused on how well the child communicated intent. Questions such as these were the prime concern.

- Can the child relay an accurate message?
- Is the child's vocabulary flexible and sufficient enough for the child to speak specifically?
- Can the child adhere to a topic without abrupt transitions to new topics?
- Does the child respond to questions and statements appropriately?

Emphasis on the functions of language became primary research concerns, ones that traditional standardized language tests could not assess. More descriptive measures such as Clinical Discourse Analysis (Damico, 1985) and Let's Talk Inventory for Children (Wiig and Bray, 1983) have been developed to address the issue.

Muma (1981, 1983) perhaps best summarized the case for descriptive assessment of language by offering five criteria for consideration.

1. *Relativity*. Verbal behaviors are relative to one another, so language must not be observed in absolute terms, which are measured in many formalized tests.

42

2. *Conditionality*. This is important when viewing verbal production. The content of what is said should not be viewed as one characteristic of the child's language. Rather, the context in which it is produced has a direct bearing on the utterance.
3. *Complexity*. Verbal expression is a complex behavior; therefore, attempts to simplify and isolate different language constructions, and yield specific data, do not produce total evidence of the multifaceted characteristics of a child's language competence or incompetence.
4. *Dynamism*. The fact that language is in a constant state of flux or change means that a one-time assessment of language is not sufficient. Rather, language is dynamic and ever changing, making frequent continuous assessment a mandate for the language practitioner.
5. *Ecology*. This refers to the notion that assessment and intervention should be based on speech behaviors in a naturally occurring environment. Therefore, the language practitioner should assess interaction and dialogue to obtain descriptions of a child's language rather than rely on discreet measures provided by formalized test scores.

Should formalized measures of the analysis of language be disregarded? The authors believe that the language practitioner can effectively utilize both formalized measures and descriptive measures. Standardized testing and systematic language sample analysis can yield important information on the child's receptive language skills and expressive use of syntactic and morphological rules, or the forms of language competence. This is important information. Likewise, pragmatic considerations or the functions language has for the child are also of importance when assessing the child's ability to effectively interact with others. Use of both molecular and molar assessment of language will contribute to a holistic view of language competence.

The authors in describing techniques and specific assessment tools have tried to include both standardized and descriptive techniques. Measures of discreet analysis, such as the mean length of utterance, developmental sentence scoring, and the properant will be described so that the language practitioner may utilize and quantify syntactic and morphological characteristics of the child's language. In addition, descriptive techniques of language sampling will be offered to aid the language practitioner in assessing the child's pragmatic use of language in interactions with others. Finally, this chapter will offer specific information on commercially produced assessment instruments for consideration in a total assessment plan.

Fundamental to any good language training program is the assessment plan. Assessment must take place at the beginning and end of the training program, and additionally, provision should be made for continuous assessment within the program itself.

Assessment at the beginning of the program, or formative assessment, is used to determine the child's strengths and deficits. Formative assessment determines whether a child is eligible for a particular training program and provides the information for developing instructional objectives.

During the language training program, it is necessary for some type of continuous monitoring to determine whether the child is making satisfactory progress toward the stated objectives or if there is a need to make modifications in the training program.

Finally, assessment must take place at the end of the training program. This is known as summative assessment. Summative assessment determines whether the child has achieved the terminal objectives and serves to provide information on the effectiveness of the training program itself.

THREE APPROACHES TO ASSESSMENT

There are basically three approaches to assessment. These include the etiological approach, the diagnostic-remedial approach, and the task analysis approach (Bateman, 1967). Although there are fundamental differences between these approaches, they are not necessarily mutually exclusive in terms of use. In fact, most language practitioners use a combination of all three assessment approaches. However, they do differ in the type of information that they provide.

Etiological

The etiological approach is concerned with causation. It is an assessment approach based on the medical model and focuses on identifying the cause of the language delay. Its goals are prevention and treatment. For example, a child's language delay may be diagnosed as resulting from brain injury at birth.

It certainly cannot be denied that it is important to identify the cause of the problem in hopes of eventually preventing its recurrence and even determining a medical cure. However, this assessment approach provides little useful information to the practitioner whose job is to teach language to the child. Although it is mildly interesting to know what caused the problem, etiological assessment does not tell the language practitioner how or what to teach the child. Therefore, it is of limited value to the practitioner who must work with the child on a daily basis.

Diagnostic-Remedial

The next approach to assessment is the diagnostic-remedial approach. This approach deals with identifying the cognitive process that does not function correctly and that results in language problems. Then the objective is to remediate the area of cognitive dysfunction. The diagnostic-remedial approach concentrates on the receptive, integrative, and expressive functions of the mind.

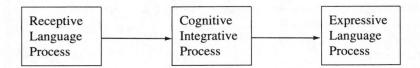

Advocates of the diagnostic-remedial approach state that there is a correlation between the dysfunction in one or more of the three process areas and the particular language problem. The language problem, then, would be corrected by the language practitioner's efforts to remediate the particular process dysfunction. Let us say that the child was diagnosed as functioning poorly in the area of auditory sequential memory. Instruction would involve remediating the problem by giving the child intensive exercises in activities involving auditory sequential memory. The object is to strengthen this process area in hopes that by doing so the child will experience improved language abilities.

A great deal of attention has been given to the diagnostic-remedial approach over the past decade, and many assessment instruments based on this approach have been developed. Likewise, the reader is probably familiar with some of the many perceptual-motor training programs that have been developed as a result of this approach. Unfortunately, research has not been overly supportive of the efficacy of the diagnostic-remedial approach (Rosenberg, 1970; Carroll, 1972; Hammill, 1975; Newcomer & Hammill, 1976). Research has found that though having the child practice in the area of the process deficit may improve performance on those activities, it does not necessarily improve the child's performance in other areas such as language. The carry-over of training does not seem to occur frequently or strongly enough to justify the great expenditures of instructional time. As Thomas Lovitt stated in a very excellent book entitled *In Spite of My Resistance . . . I've Learned from Children*, "If you want to teach kids to crawl, do it; if you want to teach them to read, do that. Just don't expect that when you teach kids to crawl, they'll learn to read." (Lovitt, 1977, p. 137).

The same advice should be applied to language training.

The overall problem with advocating the diagnostic-remedial approach, and its reliance on correlations, lies in the interpretation of correlation data. When two variables correlate positively, such as auditory-sequential memory and language development problems, it means that a relationship between the two may exist. But further experimental research is necessary to determine whether there actually is a cause and effect relationship.

Unfortunately, early claims based on correlation data have only attempted to suggest cause and effect relationships that have not held up under later experimental studies. This is much like the study in one community that found a high positive correlation between the increase in the number of churches over time and the increase in alcoholics over the same period. This example illustrates the fallacy in attempting to draw cause and effect conclusions from correlation data.

Task Analysis

Task analysis is the third and final approach to assessment. The task analysis approach is not concerned with either causation, as in the etiological approach, or cognitive theories, as in the diagnostic-remedial approach. Advocates of task analysis believe that knowledge of the cause of the problem is of limited value to the person who must teach the child language. Nor are they particularly impressed with the indirect approach to instruction provided through the diagnostic-remedial approach.

The task analysis approach to assessment is based on the principles of behavioral psychology. This behavioral approach to assessment focuses on the resulting behavior of the child when presented with a specific stimulus. For example, when presented with a visual stimulus such as a ball and asked to verbally name the object, the child's behaviors are carefully observed and recorded. If the child's verbal response is incorrect, then systematic procedures are used to shape and modify the response until the child can recognize the ball and say its name correctly. The focus of the assessment, then, is to precisely identify the language skills that the child exhibits and those that the child needs to learn, rather than to identify the cause of the problem or the cognitive process deficit.

Task analysis assessment arranges the identified language skills to be taught in a carefully sequenced hierarchy. This provides the language practitioner with a series of instructional steps that are directly related to the child's language problem and sequenced in a manner to ensure success. This approach to assessment has proven to be the most useful to language practitioners who must set, and attempt to achieve, clearly defined instructional objectives.

NORM REFERENCED TESTS VERSUS CRITERION
   REFERENCED TESTS

Language tests can be placed in one of two major categories or a combination of both. These major categories identify language tests as being norm referenced or criterion referenced. It should be noted, however, that some tests have characteristics from both categories.

The norm referenced test is designed to compare an individual's test performance with the test performance of other individuals. More specifically, the individual's score on the test is compared with a normative group. The normative group is the sample of persons that the test makers used in the construction of the test items to determine average levels of performance. The norm referenced test is used when the examiner plans to obtain a measure of variability in performance among those who take the test. Norm referenced tests are used to screen children who might be eligible for a specific language training program because they give scores that compare the child's performance to a normal population of the same age. The scores on norm referenced tests are frequently stated in terms of age equivalents, grade equivalents, percentile rankings, language quotients, etc.

Criterion referenced tests, on the other hand, are used to determine an individual's language performance with respect to a predetermined level of performance. In other words, the examiner is not concerned with how the individual's test performance compares with the performance of others. What the examiner is interested in is whether the individual can meet the predetermined level of performance. For example, does the child's expressive language exhibit correct sequencing or word order in sentences? Or can the child use correct morphological endings in speech? Scores on criterion referenced tests are usually based on simple pass/fail criteria or in terms of percent correct.

Criterion referenced tests provide many advantages for the language practitioner. The criterion referenced test enables the language practitioner to develop and teach toward specific instructional objectives. Furthermore, it permits direct interpretation of pupil progress in terms of these objectives. This type of test enables the language practitioner to monitor pupil progress at regular intervals and provides a comprehensive record of the child's mastery of language skills. Finally, the criterion referenced test allows the language practitioner to evaluate the effectiveness of different instructional methods and materials.

CULTURAL IMPLICATIONS OF LANGUAGE ASSESSMENT

More than ever before, tests are being criticized because of their cultural bias. Intelligence tests have especially received a great deal of criticism, both in and out of the courts. There are some serious doubts as to whether the traditional intelligence test will survive in its present form. The basic complaint is that intelligence tests are discriminatory against most ethnic minorities.

Litigation efforts have been initiated in some states to ban the use of intelligence tests in public schools. A historic court case in California may set legal precedent for the rest of the country. The suit, *Larry P. vs. Riles* (1979), was filed on behalf of six San Francisco black children who had been improperly placed in special education classes on the basis of low intelligence test scores. The suit charged the

California State Public School Superintendent, the California State Board of Education, and the San Francisco Unified School District with violating the Fourteenth Amendment and other federal laws dealing with discrimination. Federal Judge Robert Peckham ruled in favor of the six black children. In effect, this ruling stated that, for some ethnic minorities, the use of IQ tests could be considered a violation of civil rights. The concern about testing bias is beginning to be felt in other areas of standardized assessment as well, including the assessment of language problems.

Cultural differences, then, can be the major reason for poor performance by many individuals on standardized norm referenced tests. In the past, test publishers have rarely established separate normative data according to ethnic or cultural minorities. An observation by Jane Mercer, a researcher in the field of nonbiased assessment, best summarizes past conditions regarding the assessment procedures used to determine the abilities of children from minority groups. (Mercer, 1975)

> A disproportionately large number of minority children are assigned to education programs that limit upward mobility, such as classes for the mentally retarded, the slow learner, and the "basic" student. (p. 130)

In 1977, a task force of professionals assembled by the Southwest Regional Resource Center in Salt Lake City, Utah, developed general guidelines that the professional can use in determining the degree to which a test is nonbiased. (Saunders, Blake, & Decker, 1977)

- Is the normative population of students used directly parallel in all important factors to the characteristics of the students to be tested?
- Are there references to content areas where the student has no documented history of information exposure and of success on assessment measures for the data used on the test administered?
- Does the language of the test conform to the language dominance of the student as identified by the diagnostic instruments for language dominance specified for each student being examined?
- Are categories of materials included that allow and provide norms for nonverbal and nonwritten evaluations that are appropriate to the students being tested, e.g., body language, taped responses from young children, signing for deaf children, etc.?
- Are the language pattern and complexity of sentence structure set parallel to the sentence patterns found on the instruments designated for use, i.e., use of humor, private or phatic language, analogies and metaphors, idiomatic expressions, etc.?

- Is there a detailed specification of analogical and metaphorical language use on the test, e.g., idiomatic and literary allusions? Each cultural history exemplified by the students tested will be reviewed for usage of these language variables, and a test will be provided.
- Is a student penalized for using a particular cultural habit pattern for learning or for having adopted a given style/level of problem solving? By limiting the criteria for success on test materials to traditionally formalized test norming and evaluation criteria, many students are unfairly evaluated. (p. 22)

Although the cultural biasing nature of language assessment instruments is much less controversial than intelligence tests, the problem exists, nevertheless. The student diagnosed as language delayed may actually be a minority child who would be better served in a bilingual education program or in an English-as-a-Second-Language (ESL) program.

This does not imply that children of ethnic minorities do not exhibit language problems. However, it becomes the responsibility of the language practitioner to determine the difference and assist other professional personnel in determining the most appropriate placement for the child.

The remainder of this chapter will be devoted to examining measures of assessing language. More specifically, formal and informal measures for determining language development and language deficits will be discussed. The practitioner will be provided with a variety of assessment instruments that will facilitate the identification of specific language problems and hopefully suggest a starting point for initiating language instruction.

THE CHECKLIST OF EXPRESSIVE LANGUAGE

At the beginning of the school year or at the time of the first clinical contact, when the language practitioner initiates the assessment process, obtaining an accurate evaluation of language is difficult. This is largely because children entering a new environment for the first time are likely to be apprehensive and quiet. Furthermore, if the language practitioner does not know the child, it may take time to establish a personal relationship and to gain the rapport necessary to begin formal testing. Failure to establish a working relationship between the language practitioner and child may result in an unproductive testing situation, where the child remains partially or totally unresponsive to questions or test activities.

Two examples illustrate this phenomenon. One situation occurred when a decision was made to assess a student's language on the first or second day of school, before the child had a chance to become familiar with the school, her classmates, the teacher, and her classroom surroundings. The child being evaluated was a seven year old Hispanic female who sat down at the table as requested, but folded her arms over her chest, gritted her teeth, and refused to even look at the test materials.

On another occasion, an educational diagnostician came to the classroom unannounced and attempted to get an eight year old boy to go to her office for testing. The child immediately scrambled under a table, refusing to come out.

These instances indicate that much more time and thought must go into the effort to formally assess children's language and that informal evaluation procedures are likely to yield more accurate information at this initial stage in assessment. The language practitioner has several alternative measures available for assessing language at the beginning of the school year.

The Checklist of Expressive Language is an excellent tool for gaining information about the language skills of children (see Exhibit 3-1). And because it is administered in a less structured environment while the child is engaging in free play, it yields information about the spontaneous language skills rather than elicited language.

The intent of the Checklist of Expressive Language is to provide the language practitioner with a starting point for assessing language skills. Results from the checklist will provide the language practitioner with sufficient information to determine which formal tests are most appropriate for the language level of the child. One would be wasting time and, in fact, it would be impossible to administer one of the more complex analyses of a child's sentences if the child is spontaneously producing only two-word strings. The checklist will yield enough information to determine basal entry skills in language and will enable the language practitioner to select the most appropriate measure for further assessment.

The checklist is administered as the language practitioner observes the children at free play. By establishing an environment conducive to children's interaction, the language practitioner may observe the nature of spontaneous communication. Therefore, the language practitioner should structure this play environment by selecting and placing on tables toys that lend themselves to cooperative play rather than solitary or parallel play. Building blocks, table games requiring more than one child's participation, and/or self-directed large muscle activities are likely to increase opportunities for expression and to yield valuable data about the language capabilities of each child.

The language practitioner or adult should remain a passive observer rather than an active partner in the play situation. The language practitioner should begin the observation process equipped with the observation checklist, already partially completed with the children's names, the date, and the starting time of the observation period. The language practitioner should remain seated in a corner of the play area, close enough to hear and see the interactions, yet maintain enough distance so that the children do not rely on the language practitioner for support or interaction.

Exhibit 3-1 The Checklist of Expressive Language

Date(s) _____

Time _____

+Construction Present
−Construction Absent

Test(s) to be administered

Child's Name	Gestures	Uses a few recognizable words	Uses two- and three-word phrases	Uses simple sentences	Correct word order	Uses more than present tense (past and present)	Uses auxiliary verbs (is, are)	Uses plurals	Uses pronouns	Uses subject-verb agreement	Uses articles	Uses prepositions	Uses transformations (wh-questions, negations, con-joining)

The period of time needed to gain the information necessary will vary, depending on the number of children to be observed. The language practitioner may need to take two or three 20-minute observations to obtain the data needed. A longer observation period may be advisable, giving the children a chance to become acquainted with each other. It is suggested that the language practitioner observe one child at a time to determine the nature of the constructions used rather than try to observe all children to see whether they establish a specific construction. This way the language practitioner follows one child at a time until most or all of the checklist categories are completed. Then the language practitioner may proceed to the next child, recording that child's interactions, until all the children have been observed.

A simple means of scoring is used in the observation checklist for a quick criterion referenced check of what constructions the child actually exhibits. A plus (+) score is given if the child exhibits the construction listed or an affirmative answer can be given to the item. A minus (−) is given if the construction is not present in spontaneous language or a negative response can be given to the item.

After the language practitioner completes the checklist, the information may be used to determine areas in need of further assessment. In addition, the language practitioner may use this information, coupled with descriptions of commonly used language tests found in this chapter, to determine which formal measures to use for pinpointing the language problem.

TAKING A LANGUAGE SAMPLE

More specific information can be obtained by taking a larger sample of the child's expressive language and submitting it to various analyses. Measures such as Developmental Sentence Scoring (DSS), mean length of utterance (MLU), and the properant will be discussed. Further consideration will be given to the pragmatic analysis of a child's language samples. First, however, there are several issues to be considered in language sampling.

ISSUES IN LANGUAGE SAMPLING: ELIMINATING BIAS

Taking and using a language sample involves three steps.

1. eliciting the child's language and audiotape or videotape recording the child's spontaneous utterances
2. transcribing the child's verbal responses into a written record
3. analyzing the child's language sample for complexity and maturity

Eliciting the language sample, although yielding valuable information, can be very time consuming and susceptible to error. Unless the practitioner is aware of common problems and areas where bias can enter, the time spent may be wasted. Inaccurate results may give the language practitioner a false picture of the child's language as it actually exists.

Lee (1971) and Emerick and Hatten (1979) suggest considerations that may serve to maximize the accuracy of results in taking a language sample. Following is a summary of their most salient points.

- In eliciting language from a child, the language practitioner needs to generate the child's interest in initiating verbal behavior. The use of interesting stimulus materials such as toys and pictures has proven to be successful. These materials should reflect the interest level of the child. In this respect, it is important for the language practitioner to know the child and the child's interests well enough to choose stimulus materials that will maximize verbal output.

- The aim of taking a language sample is to obtain the most mature language possible from the child and to elicit complete sentences. Therefore, the language practitioner should refrain from asking questions that can be answered with a yes/no one-word response. A stimulus such as "Tell me what is happening in this picture" is much more appropriate.

- To determine whether the child has a higher level grammatical form, such as future tense, past tense, plurals, etc., the language practitioner should use these forms in questions. If the child has the linguistic form in his/her verbal repertoire, it will usually be used in response to questions from the language practitioner. For example, the language practitioner may use the question, "What will the boy do next?" to see if the child responds with a similar use of the future tense, "The boy will. . . ." If the same construction is not used, it is possible that the child's expressive repertoire does not contain the more mature form.

- When recording, it is most useful for the language practitioner to repeat what the child has said so that a clear model is available in case the child articulates poorly. In addition, static from the tape recorder, extraneous noise, or interruptions may result in a poor quality tape recording. Repeating the child's responses gives another model for transcription. It eliminates guesswork, thereby decreasing the error in transcription.

- The person who has collected the language sample on tape should also transcribe it. The rationale for this is that the person who was present remembers the context of the conversation, what the child said even if it was misarticulated, and what stimulus materials were used. This procedure decreases error from misinterpretation.

If the language practitioner is aware of these potential areas of bias, steps may be taken to minimize errors and to provide greater accuracy in language sampling.

LANGUAGE SAMPLING IN NATURALISTIC CONTEXTS

Recent emphasis on pragmatics has focused on assessment using language samples taken in a more naturalistic setting. The main premise is that in an environment familiar to the child, one more like the home surroundings, a language sample will be more representative of the child's behavior in that context. It is believed that in a physical setting with interesting toys, games, and activities, the child will exhibit curiosity, begin to explore, and eventually communicate intents and offer utterances more freely.

The language practitioner should be aware, however, that assessment time may be increased in a naturalistic context, because there may be a lower incidence of structures of utterances to base the analysis. Also, there should be an awareness that the presence of the language practitioner may act as an intrusion on spontaneity of expression.

The authors support the idea that this type of context for language sampling frequently yields more representative language from the child, yet realize that elicitation of responses is the prime goal. The use of creative techniques at eliciting language in many different contexts or settings may provide optimum conditions for obtaining a representative sample of language.

STORY NARRATIVES OR CONVERSATIONAL
PARTICIPATION

There are several types of analysis of children's language that may utilize a language sample. The language practitioner needs to be aware of this before organizing the sampling session. One type of language sampling involves the story narrative. To obtain a story narrative, a child is typically asked to look at pictures, a book, or stimulus cards and to retell a story. In the story narrative, there is very little interaction with the examiner. With emphasis on pragmatics, however, there is more utilization of interactional approaches in obtaining language samples. Researchers such as Damico (1985) stress that because language is a product of context and of exchange between two or more persons, the imposition of a set story plot or pictures with limited solutions may stilt the utterances of the child and produce a monologue description of a finite set of events.

Conversational participation or dialogue, on the other hand, enables the examiner to take into account the context of the situation, what was said just before an utterance, and how that affects the content and intent of the child's next utterance.

Both the story narrative and conversational participation can yield important information for the language practitioner. The story narrative will yield more information on the child's ability to use vocabulary, to connect events in a sequence, and to combine ideas systematically; and it will help determine whether the child can maintain a topic. The use of interactional discourse will yield information on whether the child appropriately uses language for instrumental purposes and whether the child can use appropriate ways of interacting socially, e.g., conversational turn taking, use of greetings, and answering questions appropriately. Moreover, it will indicate to the language practitioner whether nonverbal signs of intent occur with speech acts. Gestures, eye gaze, body posture, and motor movements all lend clues to the child's manner of communication.

Story narratives and conversational participation as assessment tools, therefore, are not mutually exclusive. The use of both will yield a more holistic view of the child's total communication skills.

MICROCOMPUTER APPLICATION IN ASSESSMENT OF LANGUAGE SAMPLING

Computer technology has added a new dimension to providing speech and language services for children and adults. The application of microcomputers has affected several areas in the field of communication disorders. Its impact can be seen in the training of speech/language pathologists and audiologists (Rushakoff, 1984), in report writing (Cassidy, Koller, & Schwartz, 1984), in developing individualized education plans (Schwartz, Koller, & Cassidy, 1984) and in preservice and inservice education of speech/language pathologists (Payne, 1984). Similarly, microcomputers have been used in the area of language assessment (Schwartz, 1984, 1985). It is the area of microcomputer assessment that we now address.

Programs such as the Computerized Language Sample Analysis (CLSA) by Weiner (1984), the Lingquest 1: Language Sample Analysis by Mordecai, Palin, and Palmer (1982), and the Systematic Analysis of Language Transcripts (SALT) by Miller and Chapman (1983) aid the language practitioner in analyzing a language sample. The process is initiated by obtaining a language sample. Depending on which of the programs are utilized, the language practitioner codes and/or inputs the utterances of the child into the computer. Although each of the above mentioned programs is unique, the computer then analyzes the utterances for things such as

- frequency and accuracy of grammatical categories
- diversity of vocabulary
- substitutions and omissions of categories
- mean length of utterances

- complex sentence structures
- frequencies of words by structure or function
- verb tense analysis

From these programs, a comprehensive analysis of the child's utterances may be generated in the form of reports, tables, graphs, transcriptions, and error profiles.

To determine the potential of microcomputers in assessing language samples specifically and, in a broader sense, the place of microcomputers in the total language assessment plan, the language practitioner must be aware of the advantages and disadvantages of their use.

Advantages

Time

Microcomputer software designed to aid in assessing language skills can process large amounts of data rapidly, affecting a time savings for the language practitioner. The time for inputting and/or coding assessment information is the same whether the language practitioner does it manually or inputs it into the computer, yet the output time is considerably reduced by computer.

Written Reports

The language practitioner, after inputting data from standardized tests or language samples, can obtain output in the form of written reports. This is possible when adapting word processing software to standard report formats with the use of templates, or if this characteristic is built into the language assessment software itself.

Generation of Individualized Education Plans

The language practitioner may utilize test information output to generate the child's Individualized Education Plan (IEP) in speech or language.

Costs

Cost of the language practitioner's time in hand scoring tests, in comparison to the computer's time, is greater.

Potential for Applied Research

Language practitioners, though concerned mainly with instruction of the child, may find it possible, with the use of microcomputers, to use assessment information in applied research and study.

Disadvantages

Monetary Cost

With programs costing up to $700, the purchase of microcomputer software may not be possible for the language practitioner on a tight budget. Though individual use may be prohibitive, a school district may be able to purchase one program for use by several language practitioners in a centralized location.

Time

Regardless of how easy the software program is supposed to be, it will take time for the language practitioner to study the program manual and to progress through simulated case studies to the point of proficiency and comfort with the software program. This is compounded by the fact that different assessment software programs use different commands and functions.

Fear, Intimidation, Frustration

The average language practitioner may have an aversion to using a "packaged" assessment program for the first time. This is based on fear of the unknown, or in some cases, previous negative experiences using software that jams or has glitches.

Processing Ambiguities

The language practitioner, having past experience with a child being tested, may be able to infer meanings from the child's utterances, intonation, and non-verbal messages. The computer cannot process intents. It can only process coded information. Therefore, analysis of the child's pragmatic use of language is only as good as the code format of the software, the accuracy of the person entering the data, and the appropriate use of the program.

Though the discussion of the pros and cons may have shed some light on the issue of microcomputer use in assessment of language problems, the language practitioner will be the deciding factor on whether the programs will be of use in the total assessment plan.

Specific programs such as the CLSA, the Lingquest 1, and the SALT will be previewed in more detail with language assessment instruments at the end of this chapter.

ANALYZING THE LANGUAGE SAMPLE

The following corpus of sentences was collected in a tape-recorded language sample gathered during an informal exchange between a language practitioner and a child. The language practitioner and child were both seated on the floor in a carpeted room. Several popular fairy tales were used as stimulus materials to elicit language. The child was first asked to select a story that was familiar. As the language practitioner and child looked at each page, the child was asked to describe the events pictured. Sentences such as "Tell me about this picture" and "Tell me what is happening in this picture" were used to elicit the child's responses. The responses have been separated into complete sentences, a procedure used for later analysis.

Language Sample: "The Three Bears"

Student: Becky, age six

- Baby bear, Momma bear went shopping.
- That's Momma chair, Daddy chair, Baby's bed, Momma's bed, Daddy's bed.
- Momma's cooking soup.
- Little girl open that house and see who there.
- That little girl sit down baby chair.
- It's too soft.
- Momma sit down her chair and somebody sat on it.
- Somebody sit down my chair and broke it.
- Somebody eat my soup.
- Now theys coming up.
- Somebody's sleeping my bed.
- And the girl went away.

Once a language sample has been gathered, it can be analyzed for several useful forms of information. Several of these measures will be discussed here. (1) MLU, (2) DSS, (3) the properant, and (4) pragmatic use of language.

Mean Length of Utterance

Mean length of utterance is one measure of the student's language maturity. It is based on the average length of a child's utterances stated in numerical form. The higher the MLU, the more lengthy and, thus, it is assumed the more complex the child's responses. The process of calculating MLU involves counting the number of morphemes in each utterance and getting an average count over several sentences. A morpheme is the smallest unit in the English language that carries meaning. A word can contain more than one morpheme. For example, the word "opening," when divided into its separate parts, contains two morphemes.

Exhibit 3-2 Guidelines for Calculating MLU

Number of Morphemes	Utterance
5	1 1 1 1 1 Momma's cooking soup.
9	1 1 1 1 1 Little girl open that house 1 1 1 1 and see who there.
7	1 1 1 1 1 1 1 That little girl sit down baby chair.
4	1 1 1 1 It's too soft.
10	1 1 1 1 1 1 Momma sit down her chair and 1 1 1 1 somebody sat on it.
Total 35	

$$\text{MLU} = \frac{\text{Total Morphemes}}{\text{Number of Sentences}} = \frac{35}{5} = 7.00$$

"Open" is the basic action verb and "ing" indicates that the action is ongoing. Both are separate morphemes. However, the word "opening" could not be further broken down without changing the meaning.

Brown (1973) gave rules for counting morphemes and calculating the MLU. He indicated that all inflections, e.g., plurals, third person singular, regular past, and progressive endings, should be counted as separate morphemes. Auxiliary verbs such as "is," "are," and "will" count as separate morphemes. Other single words that cannot be divided into more than one meaningful unit are counted as one morpheme. Irregular past tense verbs such as "ran," "saw," and "went" count as only one morpheme, because it is assumed that the child is only relating to these words as present forms. Diminutives such as "kitty" and "Mommy" count as only one morpheme, as do compound words. Cantenatives such as "gonna," "hafta," and "wanna" also count as only one morpheme.

The following five sentences in Exhibit 3-2 were obtained from the language sample illustrated above for the purpose of illustrating how to calculate MLU. In reality, one would take a much larger sample for a more valid picture of the child's level of language functioning. Brown suggested obtaining a corpus of 100 utterances, stressing that the language practitioner should disregard the first few sentences for a better representative sample.

To calculate MLU, the language practitioner must count the morphemes in each utterance, using the guidelines proposed by Brown. The total number of morphemes for all utterances must then be totaled. The final step, dividing by the number of utterances sampled, will result in an MLU.

Taking an MLU gives two important measures of information. First, it gives a normative measure of language development in relation to chronological age. Mean length of utterance usually increases proportionately to the child's chronological age. For example, a child one year of age has a mean sentence length of 1; a child of two has an MLU of approximately 2; a child of three may exhibit an MLU of approximately 3; a child of four, an MLU of approximately 4; a child of five, an MLU of approximately 5; and a child of six, an MLU of approximately 6. Thus, if we present this information in the form of a simple graph, we can plot normal language development in terms of MLU and compare it with a specific child's MLU.

If a child of five had an MLU of 2.5, that could be plotted and compared to the normal linear curve plotted in Figure 3-1. It can be shown graphically that this child is below average compared with age peers.

Figure 3-1 Growth of MLU with Chronological Age

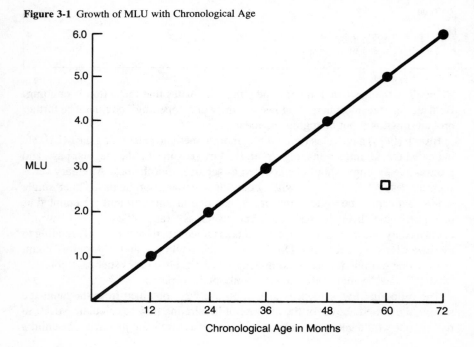

Second, the MLU can provide the language practitioner with an informative pre-postmeasure of learning. The language practitioner can analyze MLU scores before and after language training to determine the effectiveness of the program or method of instruction and to further ascertain the extent of increase in language functioning.

Developmental Sentence Scoring

Developmental Sentence Scoring (DSS) is a normative analysis of children's sentences developed by Laura Lee (1974). Using this method, the language practitioner collects a sample of 50 complete intelligible sentences. To be considered complete, each sentence must contain a subject-verb relationship. The sentences must be different, containing no repetitions and being nonecholalic, and may include no imitation of the examiner's utterances. They must be consecutive utterances, following each other in sequence, except when eliminated from the corpus for failing to meet the complete sentence requirement.

Once the core of sentences has been transcribed onto a DSS chart, the sentences are analyzed to determine whether they contain the following eight grammatical categories.

1. indefinite pronouns
2. personal pronouns
3. primary verbs
4. secondary verbs

5. negatives
6. conjunctions
7. wh questions
8. interrogative reversals

Words in these eight categories are given weighted point values according to developmental complexity. Table 3-1 illustrates the eight categories along with specific examples of the construction of each level within the categories. The column on the left margin of the chart represents the point values for the construction found at that level.

A sentence point is also awarded if the utterance meets all the requirements of adult grammar. Once the points are computed for each sentence and totaled for all 50 sentences, dividing by 50 gives the numerical score or the DSS. The formula is calculated much like the MLU.

$$DSS = \frac{\text{Total points for all sentences}}{50}$$

Table 3-2 illustrates how 30 sentences are scored by DSS.

The specific DSS score can also be compared graphically to developmental norms for DSS scores by chronological age to obtain a relative measure of the child's language level. Similar to the MLU, the DSS can also give an indication of

Table 3-1 The Developmental Sentence Scoring Reweighted Scores

Score	Indefinite Pronouns or Noun Modifiers	Personal Pronouns	Main Verbs	Secondary Verbs
1	it, this, that	1st and 2nd person: I, me, my, mine, you, your(s)	A. Uninflected verb: I *see* you. B. Copula, is or 's: *It's* red. C. is +verb + ing: He *is coming.*	
2		3rd person: he, him, his, she, her, hers	A. -s and -ed: *plays, played* B. Irregular past: *ate, saw* C. Copula: *am, are, was, were* D. Auxiliary *am, are, was, were*	Five early-developing infinitives: I wan*na see* (want *to see*) I'm gon*na see* (going to *see*) I gotta *see* (got *to see*) Lemme [to] see (let me [to] *see)* Let's [to] play (let [us *to*] *play)*
3	A. no, some, more, all, lot(s), one(s), two (etc.), other(s), another B. something, some- body, someone	A. Plurals: we, us, our(s), they, them, their B. these, those		Non-complementing infinitives: I stopped *to play.* I'm afraid *to look.* It's hard *to do* that.
4	nothing, nobody, none, no one		A. can, will, may + verb: *may go* B. Obligatory do + verb: *don't go* C. Emphatic do + verb: I *do see.*	Participle, present or past: I see a boy *running.* I found the toy *broken.*
5		Reflexives: myself, your- self, himself, herself, itself, themselves		A. Early infinitival comple- ments with differing subjects in kernels: I want you *to come.* Let him [*to*] *see.* B. Later infinitival complements: I had *to go.* I told him *to go.* I tried *to go.* He ought *to go.* C. Obligatory deletions: Make it [*to*] *go.* I'd better [*to*] *go.* D. Infinitive with wh-word: I know what *to get.* I know how *to do* it.
6		A. Wh-pronouns: who, which, whose, whom, what, that, how many, how much I know *who* came. That's *what* I said. B. Wh-word + infinitive: I know *what* to do. I know *who(m)* to take.	A. could, would, should, might + verb: *might come, could be* B. Obligatory does, did + verb C. Emphatic does, did + verb	

Negatives	Conjunctions	Interrogative Reversals	Wh-Questions
it, this, that + copula or auxiliary is, 's, + not: It's *not* mine. This is *not* a dog. That is *not* moving.		Reversal of copula: *Isn't* it red? *Were they* there?	
			A. who, what, what + noun: *Who* am I? *What* is he eating? *What book* are you reading? B. where, how many, how much, what . . . do, what . . . for *Where* did it go? *How much* do you want? *What* is he *doing*? *What* is a hammer *for*?
	and		
can't, don't		Reversal of auxiliary be: *Is he* coming? *Isn't he* coming? *Was he* going? *Wasn't he* going?	
isn't, won't	A. but B. so, and so, so that C. or, if		when, how, how + adjective *When* shall I come? *How* do you do it? *How big* is it?
	because	A. Obligatory do, does, did: *Do they* run? *Does it* bite? *Didn't it* hurt? B. Reversal of modal: *Can you* play? *Won't it* hurt? *Shall I* sit down? C. Tag question: It's fun, *isn't it*? It isn't fun, *is it*?	

continues

Table 3-1 continued

Score	Indefinite Pronouns or Noun Modifiers	Personal Pronouns	Main Verbs	Secondary Verbs

7	A. any, anything, anybody, anyone
	B. every, everything, everybody, everyone
	C. both, few, many, each, several, most, least, much, next, first, last, second (etc.)
		(his) own, one, oneself, whichever, whoever, whatever
		  Take *whatever* you like.
			A. Passive with *get,* any tense
			  Passive with *be,* any tense
			B. must, shall + verb:
			  must come
			C. have + verb + en:
			  I've eaten
			D. have got: *I've got* it.
				Passive infinitival complement:
				With *get:*
				  I have *to get dressed.*
				  I don't want *to get hurt.*
				With *be:*
				  I want *to be pulled.*
				  It's going *to be locked.*

8			A. have been + verb + ing
			  had been + verb + ing
			B. modal + have + verb + en: *may have eaten*
			C. modal + be + verb + ing:
			  could be playing
			D. Other auxiliary combinations:
			  should have been sleeping
				Gerund:
				  Swinging is fun.
				  I like *fishing.*
				  He started *laughing.*

Source: From *Developmental Sentence Analysis* (pp. 134–135) by Laura L. Lee, 1974, Evanston, Ill.: Northwestern University Press. Copyright 1974 by Northwestern University Press. Reprinted by permission.

the child's growth in language. Furthermore, it can be used as a tool for prescribing a language program for the individual child. By noting the level of functioning in each of the eight grammatical categories, the language practitioner can prescribe a language training program to facilitate the acquisition of new constructions on the next highest and more complex level.

The Properant

The properant is a more general tool for assessing the presence of a particular form or construction. It was originally intended to assess correct usage of

Negatives	Conjunctions	Interrogative Reversals	Wh-Questions
All other negatives: A. Uncontracted negatives: I can *not* go. He has *not* gone. B. Pronoun-auxiliary or pronoun-copula contraction: I'm *not* coming. He's *not* here. C. Auxiliary-negative or copula-negative contraction: He *wasn't* going. He *hasn't* been seen. It *couldn't* be mine. They *aren't* big.			why, what if, how come how about + gerund *Why* are you crying? *What if* I won't do it? *How come* he is crying? *How about* coming with me?
	A. where, when, how, while, whether (or not), till, until, unless, since, before, after, for, as, as + adjective + as, as if, like, that, than I know *where* you are. Don't come *till* I call. B. Obligatory deletions: I run faster *than* you [run]. I'm *as big as* a man [is big]. It looks *like* a dog [looks]. C. Elliptical deletions (score 0): That's *why* [I took it]. I know *how* [I can do it]. D. Wh-words + infinitive: I know *how* to do it. I know *where* to go.	A. Reversal of auxiliary have: *Has he* seen you? B. Reversal with two or three auxiliaries: *Has he been* eating? *Couldn't he have* waited? *Could he have been* crying? *Wouldn't he have been* going?	whose, which, which + noun *Whose* car is that? *Which book* do you want?

phonemes in articulation therapy (Garrett, 1973). However, its use is more universal. In obtaining a properant score, the language practitioner tape records a sample of the child's language, giving the child an opportunity to make a minimum number of target constructions. If, for example, the language practitioner intends to evaluate whether the child is using plural nouns appropriately, the child would be given opportunities to use plural nouns in conversation. The language practitioner may utilize pictures that illustrate plural objects or persons to elicit this target construction. The properant score would be the ratio of the number of times the child used the construction or form correctly to the number of times it was actually possible to use the form.

Table 3-2 Hypothetical Corpus of Thirty Sentences Illustrating Developmental Sentence Scoring

Name:

Recording date:

Birth date:

CA:

DSS: 13.63

	Indef. Pro.	Pers. Pro.	Main Verb	Sec. Verb	Neg.	Conj.	Inter. Rev.	Wh-Q	Sent. Point	Total
1. Boy eat.			—						0	0
2. Boy eat cookie.			—						0	0
3. The boy is eating a cookie.			1						1	2
4. The boys are eating cookies.			2						1	3
5. They ate them.		3,3	2						1	9
6. They didn't eat them.		3,3	6		7				1	20
7. Didn't they eat them?		3,3	6		7		6		1	26
8. Why didn't they eat them?		3,3	6		7		6	7	1	33
9. Why didn't they?		3	6		7		6	7	1	24
10. All the cookies were eaten.	3		7						1	11
11. I want to eat some cookies.	3	1	1	2					1	8
12. I want him to eat some cookies.	3	1,2	1	5					1	13
13. I tried to find some cookies.	3	1	2	5					1	12
14. Could you find them?		1,3	6				6		1	17
15. You couldn't find them, could you?		1,3	6		7		6		1	24
16. Nobody knows where to find them.	4	3	2	5		8			1	23
17. Who knows where she keeps them?		2,3	2,2	5		8		2	1	20
18. I looked but I couldn't find them.		1,1,3	2,6		7	5			1	26
19. I like eating cookies.		1	1	8					1	11
20. Nobody told me that I shouldn't eat them.	4	1,1,3	2,6		7	8			1	33
21. I only ate a few.	7	1	2						1	11
22. Somebody else must have eaten all the rest.	3,3		8						1	15
23. Let's eat some more.	3,3		1	2					1	10
24. Mommy said, "Don't eat those cookies."		3	2,4		4				1	14
25. That isn't what she said.	1	6,2	1,2		5				1	18

26. Him can't have some.	—		—	4	0	8
27. What you eating?		1	—		0	3
28. Her don't gots any.	7	1	—	—	0	7
29. Mommy find out.		1	—		0	0
30. You want to get spanked?		7	—	2	0	8

TOTAL   409

409/30 = 13.63 DSS

Source: From *Developmental Sentence Analysis* (p. 164) by Laura L. Lee, 1974, Evanston, Ill.: Northwestern University Press. Copyright 1974 by Northwestern University Press. Reprinted by permission.

$$\text{Properant Score} = \frac{\text{Number Correct}}{\text{Number Possible}}$$

In this illustration, if the child were given the opportunity to use ten plurals and correctly responded nine times, the properant score would be expressed in this manner.

$$\text{Properant Score} = \frac{\text{Number Correct}}{\text{Number Possible}} = \frac{9}{10} = .9$$

This may also be viewed as the percentage of the target construction correctly used. The closer the properant score is to 1.00, the more accurately the child used the construction. The closer the properant score is to .00, the less capable the student is of producing the form correctly.

The applicability of the properant score to almost any construction the language practitioner plans to evaluate is perhaps its greatest asset as an assessment device. Once it has been determined what construction or form the child needs to develop, whether past tense verbs, plurals, or any other specified construction, the properant score can be an efficient criterion referenced measure of the student's ability to produce it.

Pragmatic Use of Language

With the abundance of inventories available for pragmatic assessment of language, the language practitioner should carefully study each for its potential use. Many instruments have been developed for coding pragmatic language interactions in research settings and may not lend themselves for use by the language practitioner who collects assessment information for the purpose of planning intervention. Furthermore, many contain such complex coding systems that they require specific training, often making their use by the language practitioner impractical.

The authors suggest an eclectic approach to finding the appropriate instrument to assess pragmatic use of language by the child. Several formats will be offered so that the language practitioner can use specific items to adapt an instrument best suited for use in the practitioner's individual context and/or setting.

The first example, Exhibit 3-3, shows a recording form that analyzes a language sample for MLU and characteristics such as mazes, reversals, substituted forms, and words run together or omitted. In addition, the language practitioner must judge whether the sentence is restricted and whether the restriction is syntactic or semantic. The format is based on the work of Simon (1979) and encompasses characteristics of form, function, and style. It illustrates how these ten sentences would be coded for specific features, though in reality, the language practitioner would be examining a much larger sample of utterances.

Exhibit 3-3 Language Sample Analysis

Name _____ Age _____ Date _____

Conditions for Administration _____

Utterance	MLU	Semantic Restriction	Syntactic Restriction	Comments
1. One little pig was making the (straw) of the house.	11		X	
2. ⌒Was so happy because it was fixed up [and he was ⌒so happy.]	8		X	Nonspecific referent; omitted subject he; maze,
3. Then he went to 'nother house.	7			redundant information
4. The first pig went to 'nother house.	8			Revision of previous sentence
5. Two pigs [and two]pigs were running, singing, dancing.	10	X		Verbal maze
6. The fox was hungry, and the third little pig was so busy.	12	X		Incoherent sequencing
7. OOOOh, he was so busy.	5			Repetition
8. The little pigs—they talking to him.	9		X	Nonspecific referent; omitted verb
9. And say, "Want to play with us?"	7		X	Omitted subject; used present tense verb
10. He was so busy.	4		X	

MLU $= \dfrac{81}{10} = 8.1$

Percentage of restricted sentences $= \dfrac{6}{10} = 60\%$

[	Not included in MLU	___	Words run together
X	Restricted sentence	M	Verbal maze in sentence
O	Substituted form	[ ]	Words within maze
⌒	Omitted form	∼	Reversal, word order

Table 3-3 Organization of Problem Behaviors under Grice's Categories in Clinical Discourse Analysis

Category	Behaviors
Quantity	Failure to provide significant information to listeners
	Use of nonspecific vocabulary
	Informational redundancy
	Need for repetition
Quality	Message inaccuracy
Relation	Poor topic maintenance
	Inappropriate response
	Failure to ask relevant questions
	Situational inappropriateness
	Inappropriate speech style
Manner	Linguistic nonfluency
	Revision
	Delays before responding
	Failure to structure discourse
	Turn-taking difficulty
	Gaze inefficiency
	Inappropriate intonational contour

Source: From *Communication Skills and Classroom Success* by C.S. Simon (Ed.), 1985, San Diego, CA: College Hill Press. Copyright 1985 by College Hill Press.

From this form the language practitioner may compute the child's MLU and the total percentage of restricted utterances. A space for comments enables the language practitioner to review the child's pragmatic use of language and to make specific observations about the constructions produced. From Exhibit 3-3, we can determine that the child Julie omitted many crucial constructions, such as subjects and verbs. She also made several revisions with mazes and used nonspecific referents. In noting trends, we can see that this child would benefit from intervention stressing syntactic use of subjects and verbs. In addition, she should receive pragmatic instructions, helping her learn to provide specific referents for information, and helping her plan conversation before speaking.

With another method for evaluating a language sample, Damico (1985) established a procedure for evaluating discourse or interaction between the language practitioner and the child. Damico based his procedure on the theoretical framework of Grice (1975). Using Grice's four categories or rules of conversation—quantity, quality, relation, and manner—Damico identified 17 problem areas and described error patterns of communication in disordered children. From this framework, Damico established a process for coding conversational interaction to assess communication skills.

Table 3-3 represents the specific items observed in conversation by Damico. Using clinical discourse analysis, the language practitioner can code these 17 problems from a language sample taken from conversation between the language practitioner and the child.

The format in Exhibit 3-4 has been adapted for use by language practitioners in the Las Cruces Public Schools, Las Cruces, New Mexico, to assess discourse skills. It provides space for the language practitioner's utterances so that the child's response to questions and comments may be analyzed in relation to the context of the conversation. The code from clinical discourse analysis is utilized. Utterances are coded specifically for the 17 errors within the four categories of quantity, quality, relation, and manner. In addition, the language practitioner may calculate MLU and determine whether there are any grammatical errors and whether the student switches codes at any time during the interaction.

Information from this format may be summarized on the language sample analysis summary in Exhibit 3-5.

The use of language sampling procedures coupled with information gained from more standardized procedures will enable the language practitioner to observe and assess the child's language. The authors have provided a glossary and description of some of the current assessment measures available to the language practitioner.

ASSESSMENT INSTRUMENTS FOR EVALUATING LANGUAGE

There are many language tests and inventories commercially available to evaluate the language skills of children. Those included in this section on assessment instruments have been found to represent some of the more commonly used language instruments. For purposes of organization these instruments fall into five categories.

1. instruments assessing receptive language
2. instruments assessing expressive language
3. multifaceted instruments assessing several language components
4. language dominance tests or tests of bilingualism
5. computer software to assess language

These tests were examined and compared according to

- name
- author
- publisher
- focus of language measured
- age
- administration
  group or individual
  administration time
  presence of alternate forms
- description
- scoring and interpretation

Exhibit 3-4 Analysis of Children's Language

Language Practitioner's Utterances	Child's Utterances	Grammar	Quantity	Quality	Relation	Manner	Code Switch	MLU

Note:

FSI	Failure to provide significant information to listener	SI	Situational inappropriateness
NSV	Nonspecific vocabulary	ISS	Inappropriate speech style
RED	Informational redundancy	LNF	Linguistic nonfluency
NR	Need for repetition	R	Revision behavior
MI	Message inaccuracy	DR	Delays before responding
PTM	Poor topic maintenance	DS	Failure to structure discourse
IR	Inappropriate response	TTD	Turn-taking difficulty
FRQ	Failure to ask relevant questions	GI	Gaze inefficiency
		IIC	Inappropriate intonational contour

Source: Courtesy of Las Cruces Public Schools.

Exhibit 3-5 Language Sample Analysis Summary

Student's name _____

Date of Birth _____

Chronological Age _____

Date of Sample _____

Speech/Language Pathologist _____

Context(s) of Sample _____

Percent of Restricted Utterances _____

Total Scored Utterances _____

Total Restricted Utterances _____

Mean Length of Utterance _____

Markings within text

< >   Code switching (not an error)

[ ]   Any pragmatic error

0   Grammatical error—substituted form

^   Grammatical error—omitted form

~   Grammatical error—word order

DR   Delayed response—longer than 3 seconds

Analysis Codes

I. Grammatical Restrictions (tally marks)

II. Pragmatic Restrictions

Quantity

Informational Redundancy (RED)

Failure To Provide Significant Information (FSI)

Nonspecific Vocabulary (NSV)

Need for Repetition (NR)

Quality

Message Inaccuracy (MI)

Relation

Poor Topic Maintenance (PTM)

Inappropriate Response (IR)

Failure To Ask Relevant Questions (FRQ)

Situational Inappropriateness (SI)

Inappropriate Speech Style (ISS)

Manner

Linguistic Nonfluency (LNF)

Revision Behavior (R)

Delays Before Responding (DR)

Failure To Structure Discourse (DS)

Turn-taking Difficulty (TTD)

Gaze Inefficiency (GI)

Inappropriate Intonational Contour (IIC)

Source: Courtesy of Las Cruces Public Schools.

Receptive Language Tests

Assessment Instrument   Assessment of Children's Language Comprehension, c. 1972

Authors   Rochana Foster, Jane J. Giddan, and Joel Stark

Publisher   Consulting Psychologists Press, Inc., Palo Alto, California

Language Assessed   Receptive language

Age   3.0 to 6.11 years

Administration   Individual. A shortened form for rapid screening of groups is also available.

Description   Included in this test are 50 items, categorized into four parts. The test measures the comprehension of increasingly complex relations or critical elements. The child is presented with a word or phrase and is asked to mark or point to the correct one out of five choices. Part A checks the understanding of verbs, nouns, prepositions, and modifiers. Part B, the two critical element component, measures the understanding of agent-action, attribute-object, or attribute-agent relationships. Part C measures three critical element relationships and includes attribute-agent-action, agent-action-object, and object-relation-object constructions. Part D measures the understanding of four critical elements. It includes noun-verb-preposition-noun, noun-verb-modifier-noun, and modifier-noun-preposition-noun relationships.

Scoring   Total scores are converted to percentile scores. The language practitioner is able to determine the level of receptive functioning by categorizing errors.

Assessment Instrument   Boehme Test of Basic Concepts (BTBC), c. 1969

Author   Ann E. Boehme

Publisher   The Psychological Corporation, 304 East 45th Street, New York, New York 10017

Language Assessed   Receptive language

Age   5 to 8 years

Administration   Groups of 8 to 12, if the children being tested are not familiar with testing procedures. Or, the BTBC can be administered individually and in groups of regular class size. The BTBC has two forms, A and B. The total test takes approximately 30 to 40 minutes to administer.

Description The BTBC consists of 50 items, measuring the child's comprehension of concepts such as quantity, space, and time. The BTBC is designed to determine whether the child chooses the correct stimulus picture from three choices. The response is made by marking with pencil or crayon. A sample item is included for information. "Look at the car and the boys. Mark the boy at the *side* of the car."

Scoring Raw scores may be converted to percentile equivalents so that comparison to children of the same chronological age and socioeconomic level can be made. The BTBC can also be used as a criterion referenced measure, giving the language practitioner information on the nature and extent of the child's concept deficit. A remediation program may be planned to teach concepts in which the student is deficient.

Assessment Instrument Screening Test for Auditory Comprehension of Language (STACL), c. 1973

Author Elizabeth Carrow

Publisher Teaching Resources Corporation, 50 Pond Park Road, Hingham, Massachusetts 02043

Language Assessed Receptive language

Age 3 to 7 years

Administration Group. The STACL contains Spanish and English forms.

Description This screening test is intended to measure the receptive understanding of linguistic forms. The forms represented in the STACL include prepositional placement, ordinal and other quantity concepts, modifiers, passive actions, and others. The STACL consists of 25 items. The language practitioner presents a word, phrase, or sentence. The child responds by selecting one picture out of three choices.

Scoring Total scores can be converted to percentile rank. Cutoff scores are available to suggest further language diagnosis.

Assessment Instrument Test for Auditory Comprehension of Language (TACL), c. 1973

Author Elizabeth Carrow

Publisher Teaching Resources Corporation, 50 Pond Park Road, Hingham, Massachusetts 02043

Language Assessed   Receptive language

Age   3.0 to 6.11 years

Administration   Individual. The TACL takes approximately 20 minutes to administer. It can be administered in English or Spanish.

Description   The TACL measures how well the child comprehends the word classes of nouns, verbs, adjectives, adverbs, and prepositions. It determines whether the child understands morphological endings such as "er" and "ist." Grammatical categories of tense, number, case, status, voice, and mood are also represented among the items. In the test, the child is presented with three stimuli for each of the 101 items. The child is asked to respond by pointing to the correct picture.

Scoring   Once a total raw score is obtained, it can be converted to age scores, or the child's score may be compared to the mean scores for children of the same age. An analysis section gives the language practitioner a method of categorizing the errors so that specific problem areas may be identified. Assessing problem areas will facilitate writing and selecting an appropriate instructional program for the child.

Assessment Instrument   The Token Test for Children, c. 1978

Author   Frank DiSimoni

Publisher   Teaching Resources Corporation, 50 Pond Park Road, Hingham, Massachusetts 02043

Language Assessed   Receptive language

Age   3.0 to 12.5 years

Administration   Individual

Description   A set of colored tokens is provided for the child to manipulate. The language practitioner gives the student verbal directions to manipulate the tokens. Sixty-one commands of increasing complexity and length are presented. For example, the first section requires the child to perform directions such as "Touch the white square," whereas the fifth section uses commands such as "After picking up the green square, touch the white circle."

Scoring   Responses are scored + or −. A raw score for each of the five sections and a total raw score may be obtained. In addition, age and grade scaled scores may be obtained. Because the token is considered a quick screen, guidelines are given for further assessment.

Expressive Language Tests

Assessment Instrument   Bankson Language Screening Test, c. 1977

Author   Nicholas W. Bankson

Publisher   University Park Press, Chamber of Commerce Building, Baltimore, Maryland 21202

Language Assessed   Expressive language

Age   4.1 to 8.0 years

Administration   Individual. The Bankson takes approximately 25 minutes to administer.

Description   This screening test includes 153 items in five general areas.
Semantic knowledge includes expressive understanding of body parts, nouns, verbs, categories, functions, prepositions, colors/quantity, and opposites.
Morphological rules include items on pronouns, verb tense, plurals, and comparatives/superlatives.
Syntactic rules include subject-verb agreement/negation and sentence repetition/judgment.
Visual perception includes items on visual matching/discrimination and visual association/sequencing.
Auditory perception includes items on auditory memory and auditory sequencing/discrimination.

Responses are obtained after the child is presented colored picture stimuli and a verbal question. A sample item measuring subject-verb agreement is included. The language practitioner shows a picture and says "The cow is eating. The cows _____" (are eating).

Scoring   Responses are scored as correct or incorrect. Raw scores may be converted to percentiles and standard deviations. It is suggested that if scores fall below the 30th percentile, the child be referred for further testing. If scores fall below the 15th percentile, the child may need language intervention. A language profile is included for error analysis.

Assessment Instrument   Carrow Elicited Language Inventory (CELI), c. 1974

Author   Elizabeth Carrow

Publisher   Learning Concepts, Inc., 2501 North Lamar, Austin, Texas 78705

Language Assessed   Expressive language

Age   3.0 to 7.11 years

Administration   Individual

Description   The CELI is designed to evaluate language that has been elicited by the repetition of a core of 52 stimuli. After the child's responses are taped and written on the response form, the child's errors may be analyzed. Several grammatical categories are represented for analysis: articles, adjectives, nouns, plurals, pronouns, verbs, negatives, contractions, adverbs, prepositions, demonstratives, and conjunctions. The CELI also contains a measure of verb usage for children whose scores fall below the tenth percentile for their age.

Scoring   Correct and incorrect responses, as well as the errors made, are recorded. Raw scores may be converted to percentiles for comparison to age peers. Compiling information on the types of errors the child makes within each category may give data useful in prescribing a language treatment program.

Assessment Instrument   Expressive Vocabulary Inventory, c. 1968

Author   Carolyn Stern, Director

Publisher   UCLA Research Projects in Early Childhood Learning

Language Assessed   Expressive language

Age   3.0 to 5.11 years

Administration   Individual

Description   The Expressive Vocabulary Inventory samples vocabulary classes including nouns, progressive verbs, pronouns, adjectives, adverbs, and collective nouns. In presenting the items, the language practitioner shows the child a picture and asks a question such as "Where is the cat?" The child may respond with "in" or "in box."

Scoring   One point is given for each correct answer. Raw scores may be converted to percentile ranks for comparison to age peers.

Assessment Instrument   Preschool Language Assessment Instrument (PLAI)

Author   Marion Blank, Susan Rose, and Laura Berlin

Publisher   Grune & Stratton, Inc., 111 Fifth Avenue, New York, New York 10003

Language Assessed   Expressive language, discourse skills of varying levels of abstraction

Age   3 to 6 years, or with children whose language skills are in question, up to ten years of age.

Administration   Individual. This test takes approximately 20 minutes to administer.

Description   The PLAI consists of 60 items and measures four varying levels of abstraction skills used in discourse.

1. matching perception
2. selective analysis of perception
3. reordering perception
4. reasoning about perception

Scoring   The language practitioner rates each response on the 60 items from 3 to 0. A score of 3 is considered fully adequate, 2 is acceptable, 1 is ambiguous, and 0 means no credit given. After the items are scored, a mean score in each of the four levels of discourse skills is obtained. Scores with a mean of 1 or less indicate weakness. Mean scores between 1.0 and 1.5 indicate moderate weakness. Mean scores between 1.5 and 2.0 indicate moderate strength. A mean score above 2 indicates a strength for that child. The numerical score may also be used to compare discourse abilities of performance.

Multifaceted Assessment Instruments

Assessment Instrument   Clinical Evaluations of Language Fundamentals Revised (CELF-R), c. 1987

Authors   Eleanor Messing Semel and Elizabeth H. Wiig

Publisher   The Psychological Corporation, Harcourt Brace Jovanovich, P.O. Box 9954, San Antonio, Texas 78204-0954

Language Assessed   Receptive and expressive language

Age   5.3 to 15.10 years

Administration   Individual. The test takes approximately 75 minutes to administer.

Description   The CELF-R consists of 11 subtests.

1. Word structure
2. Sentence structure
3. Word classes

4. Linguistic concepts
5. Semantic relationships
6. Oral directions
7. Listening to paragraphs
8. Word associations
9. Recalling sentences
10. Sentence assembly
11. Formulated sentences

From this test the language practitioner may determine the student's oral language in relation to age peers.

Scoring   Scores obtained on the CELF-R include a raw score, which can be converted to a language age and a percentile rank.

Assessment Instrument   Joliet 3-Minute Speech and Language Screen, c. 1983

Authors   Mary Kinzler and Constance Cowing Johnson

Publisher   Communication Skill Builders, 3130 North Dodge Blvd., P.O. Box 42050, Tucson, Arizona 85733

Language Assessed   Receptive and expressive language

Age   5 to approximately 11 years

Administration   Individual. This is a quick screen to be administered in approximately three minutes.

Description   A set of 24 picture plates at each of three grade levels is provided: kindergarten, second grade, and fifth grade. The child is asked to respond to picture stimuli designed to measure receptive vocabulary and grammar by eliciting imitative sentences. Articulation, voice, and fluency are also observed during administration.

Scoring   Each response is marked correct or incorrect. The number of errors is compared with cutoff scores at each grade level, and a determination is made as to whether the child passes or fails the section. If the child fails a significant number of sections on this quick screen, further testing is suggested.

Assessment Instrument   Michigan Picture Language Inventory, c. 1958

Author   W. Wolski

Publisher   University of Michigan, Ann Arbor, Michigan 48109

Language Assessed   Receptive and expressive language

Age   4 to 6 years

Administration   Individual

Description   The test consists of two major components, vocabulary and language structures. The vocabulary section contains 35 picture vocabulary items, measuring comprehension and expression. First, the child is asked to name the item (expressive). Then the language practitioner names an item, and the child responds by pointing (receptive). The language structure component consists of 50 cards testing 69 language structures, including singular and plural nouns, personal pronouns, possessives, adjectives, demonstratives, articles, adverbs, prepositions, and verbs and auxiliaries.

Scoring   Scores on the vocabulary and language structure components are the sums of both comprehension and expression scores. One point is given for each correct response. Expression and comprehension scores in vocabulary and language structure may be compared to mean scores of four, five, and six year old boys and girls.

Assessment Instrument   Northwestern Syntax Screening Test (NSST), c. 1969, 1971

Author   Laura L. Lee

Publisher   Northwestern University Press, 1735 Benson Avenue, Evanston, Illinois 60201

Language Assessed   Receptive and expressive language

Age   3 to 8 years

Administration   Individual

Description   The NSST is intended for use as a general screening test of receptive and expressive use of syntax. It consists of 20 receptive items and 20 expressive items, each containing pairs of sentences. On the receptive component, the language practitioner shows the child four black and white pictures. As the examiner reads a sentence, such as ''Show me: The cat is behind the chair,'' the child is to point to the item that best illustrates the sentence. On the expressive component, the language practitioner shows the child two black and white pictures and presents two model sentences together. For example, the language practitioner may show the child two pictures of a baby, in which one is sleeping and one is not. The language practitioner says to the child: ''The baby is sleeping. The baby is not sleeping. Now what's this picture?'' (points). The child is to repeat the sentence appropriate to the picture being identified. The NSST includes items representing plurals, the passive voice, personal and possessive pronouns, prepositions, verb tenses, demonstratives, and others.

Scoring   Scoring this test results in two types of information: a total raw score and a percentile score. The author suggests that, should the child fall two standard deviations below the mean for that age group in either or both receptive and expressive syntax, the child should certainly be evaluated further to determine the extent of the language delay.

Assessment Instrument   Test of Language Competence (TLC), c. 1985

Authors   Elizabeth H. Wiig and Wayne Secord

Publisher   The Psychological Corporation, Harcourt Brace Jovanovich, P.O. Box 9954, San Antonio, Texas 78204-0954

Language Assessed   Receptive and expressive language

Age   9 to 18 years

Administration   Individual

Description   This test has been developed to assess the use of language by adolescents. It measures four areas.

1. understanding ambiguous sentences
2. making inferences
3. recreating sentences
4. understanding metaphoric expressions

Scoring   This test provides the language practitioner with national norms and percentile ranks. In addition, it contains a task analysis of each subtest, making the transition to the development of the language IEP.

Assessment Instrument   Test of Language Development (TOLD), c. 1977

Authors   Donald D. Hammill and Phyllis L. Newcomer

Publisher   Empiric Press, Austin, Texas

Language Assessed   Receptive and expressive language

Age   4.0 to 8.11 years

Administration   Individual. The TOLD takes approximately 40 minutes to administer.

Description   The TOLD tests two general areas of language: semantics and syntax. Supplemental tests for word discrimination and word articulation are also included. Sample items within the areas of semantics and syntax are included.

Semantics:
- Picture vocabulary—the language practitioner shows the child a group of pictures and says "Show me baby."
- Oral vocabulary—"Will you tell me what each word means?"

Syntax:
- Grammatical understanding—measures ability to comprehend syntactic forms and grammatical markers. The language practitioner shows pictures to the child and makes a statement, "The ball is round." The child chooses one of four choices and responds by pointing to the correct picture.
- Sentence imitation—the child is required to repeat increasingly longer sentences. This measures correct word order and grammatical markers such as plurals and past tenses.
- Grammatical completion—the child completes a missing portion of a sentence. This tests plurals, possessives, verb tenses, comparative and superlative adjectives, and others.

Scoring   The language practitioner discontinues testing after five consecutive failures. Points are awarded for correct answers. Each subtest has a total score, and these are added to give raw scores. From the raw scores a general measure of ability in each subtest can be determined, arriving at a language age. A scaled score can be obtained by transforming raw scores into subtest means and standard deviations. In addition, a language quotient may be obtained by adding scaled scores on the principal subtests. A profile may be graphed from scaled scores.

The authors state that the test only indicates broad areas, measuring deficits and strengths in five areas. They suggest further testing and observation for more specific information needed for language programming.

Assessment Instrument   Utah Test of Language Development, c. 1967

Authors   Merlin J. Mecham, J. Lorin Jex, and J. Dean Jones

Publisher   Communication Research Associates, Inc., P.O. Box 11012, Salt Lake City, Utah 84147

Language Assessed   Receptive and expressive language

Age   1.5 to 14.5 years

Administration   Individual. The Utah takes approximately 30 to 45 minutes to complete.

Description   The Utah includes measures of vocabulary; following directions; rhyming; writing figures, words, and numbers; repeating digits given auditorily; and imitating sentences. A sample item in following simple directions goes as follows.

"Give me the ball," "Put the marble in the cup," "Put the pencil by the gun," and "Hand me the ball and the gun."

Scoring   Scores on the Utah may be converted to language age equivalents. There is no provision for categorizing errors.

Tests of Language Dominance/Bilingualism

Assessment Instrument   Del Rio Language Screening Test, c. 1975

Authors   Allen S. Toronto, D. Leverman, Cornelia Hanna, Peggy Rosenzweig, and Antoneta Maldonado

Publisher   National Educational Laboratory Publishers, Inc., P.O. Box 1003, Austin, Texas 78767

Language Assessed   Receptive and expressive language in English and Spanish

Age   3.0 to 6.11 years

Administration   Individual

Description   The Del Rio consists of five subtests:
1. Receptive vocabulary: measures whether the child can understand single nouns and verbs.
2. Sentence repetition, length: measures memory for words in a sentence.
3. Sentence repetition, complexity: tests the child's ability to repeat sentences of increasing syntactical complexity.
4. Oral commands: child must follow one to four phase tasks.
5. Story comprehension: measures memory of story details.

Scoring   After all five subtests are administered, the language practitioner may determine how the child compares to peers of the same functional language group. This comparison is based on percentiles. Also of relevance is the fact that both Spanish and English forms may be administered, resulting in a determination of language proficiency in both languages. Thus, the extent to which the child has learned either language can be discerned and a determination made as to whether the child should be considered for inclusion in a bilingual program or a program for children with deviant language development.

Assessment Instrument   James Language Dominance Test, c. 1974

Author   Peter James

Publisher   Learning Concepts, Inc., 2501 North Lamar, Austin, Texas 78705

Language Assessed   Language dominance, Spanish and English

Age   Kindergarten and first grade Mexican-Americans

Administration   Individual. The James Language Dominance Test takes approximately seven to ten minutes to administer.

Description   This test measures comprehension and production in both English and Spanish. The child is shown a group of pictures and asked to find the items named. This measures comprehension of vocabulary. In the production component, the child is shown pictures and asked to name them.

Scoring   Counting correct answers gives comprehension and production scores in both English and Spanish. Totaling these scores will give a total English score and a total Spanish score, from which language dominance may be determined. Criteria are used to determine in which of five categories a child belongs.
Category 1—Spanish dominant
Category 2—Bilingual with Spanish as a home language
Category 3—Bilingual with English and Spanish as home languages
Category 4—English dominant but bilingual in comprehension
Category 5—English dominant

Assessment Instrument   Language Assessment Scales (LAS), Level 1, c. 1975, 1977

Authors   Edward A. DeAvila and Sharon E. Duncan

Publisher   Linguametrics Group, Inc., P.O. Box 454, Corte Madera, California 94925

Language Assessed   Language proficiency in English and Spanish; Language dominance

Age   5 to 12 years plus

Administration   Individual. The LAS takes approximately 20 minutes to administer.

Description   The LAS consists of five subtests:

1. Minimal sound pairs—The child must listen to the presentation of two words and determine whether they are the same or different.
2. Lexical—This tests vocabulary acquisition. The language practitioner points to a picture, and the child identifies the item by naming the word.
3. Phonemes—This subtest measures the child's ability to imitate words. The language practitioner listens for phonemic content.
4. Sentence comprehension—This consists of having the child listen to taped sentences. The child is then asked to point to a picture that best summarizes the verbal description.
5. Production—This measures the child's ability to retell a story using his or her own words. The level of proficiency in production is rated with emphasis on fluency, meaning, and syntax.

The LAS should be administered in both English and Spanish for comparison of language proficiency.

Scoring   Raw scores in English and Spanish may be compared in all subtests. Totaling these scores in both languages and transforming them into a ratio gives the relative linguistic proficiency (RLP) in English and Spanish. This provides a method for determining language dominance as well as proficiency in both languages. Considerations for placement in programs can be made from this information.

The results of the LAS are also interfaced with the LAS language arts supplement, which provides instructional activities for problem areas.

Assessment Instrument   The Pictorial Test of Bilingualism and Language Dominance, c. 1975

Authors   Darwin Nelson, Michael J. Fellner, and C.L. Norrell

Publisher   Stoelting Company, 1350 South Kostner Avenue, Chicago, Illinois 60623

Language Assessed   Language dominance in English and Spanish, language development in English and Spanish

Age   Mexican-American children, ages 5 to 8 years

Administration   Individual

Description   Part I tests oral vocabulary in both languages. The child is shown 40 pictures and asked to name them in both English and Spanish.

Part II measures production or expression in both languages. The child is shown two large pictures and asked to describe what is happening. Part II is administered when

- a measure of accuracy in expression and syntax is needed,
- results from part I are inconclusive, or
- the child's ability to function bilingually is not known.

Scoring Part I is scored using one point for each correct answer. Part II is scored according to the level of proficiency of grammar in each language. A raw score for part I can be converted to a language quotient for each grade level and each language and plotted on a grid. This grid can help determine classification of dominance and can be used for placement in bilingual programs. Part II information can help the language practitioner determine whether the child exhibits language problems in either language.

Assessment Instrument Screening Test of Spanish Grammar, c. 1973

Author Allen S. Toronto

Publisher Northwestern University Press, 1735 Benson Avenue, Evanston, Illinois 60201

Language Assessed A screening test to identify Spanish speaking children who do not have syntactic skills commensurate with their chronological age

Age 3.0 to 6.11 years

Administration Individual

Description The Screening Test of Spanish Grammar contains 23 receptive items and 23 expressive items. In the receptive portion, the language practitioner reads two sentences. One sentence is repeated, and the child is asked to point to one of four pictures. In the expressive portion, the language practitioner also produces two sentences, points to one of two pictures, then asks the child to produce the appropriate sentence. The sentences test for comprehension and production of linguistic forms such as negatives, prepositions, pronouns, plurals, and present, past, and future tenses.

Scoring Two points are given for each item, making a possible total of 46 on each subtest. Raw scores are converted to standard deviations. It is suggested that if a child obtains a score at or below the second standard deviation from the mean, there may be a need for language intervention, and further testing should be administered.

Computer Software Programs to Assess Children's Language

Assessment Instrument   Computerized Language Sample Analysis (CLSA), c. 1984

Author   F. Weiner

Publisher   Parrot Software, 190 Sandy Ridge Road, State College, Pennsylvania 16803

Language Assessed   Expressive language

Age   Children of any age for whom a language sample may be obtained

Administration   Individual. A language sample is administered, then analyzed. Entering data takes 20 minutes. Computer analysis of data takes five minutes.

Description   Using a language sample obtained from the student, the language practitioner transcribes and codes the child's utterances for entry. The child's utterances are analyzed for frequency and accuracy in the following categories:

- nouns
- verbs
- sentence types
- mean length of response, number of utterances, number of words in sample
- demonstratives and locatives
- pronoun usage
- articles and conjunctions
- prepositions
- possessive forms
- comparatives and superlatives
- plurals
- copula "be"
- auxiliary plus verb
- modals, past tense markers, present and present progressive markers

Scoring   Fifteen tables, including the transcript, may be generated from the analysis of data.

Assessment Instrument   Lingquest 1: Language Sample Analysis, c. 1982

Author   D.R. Mordecai, M.W. Palin, and C.B. Palmer

Publisher   Lingquest Software, Napa, California 94558

Age   Children of any age from whom a language sample may be obtained

Administration   Individual. A language sample is administered, then analyzed. It takes approximately 30 minutes to enter the data and 20 minutes for the computer to analyze it.

Description   The language practitioner first obtains a language sample. The form analysis generated from this instrument includes these categories.

- nouns
- verbs
- modifiers
- prepositions
- conjunctions
- negation
- interjections
- ''wh'' questions

Scoring   Computer analysis of the language sample includes several types of information. A lexical component, which shows the number of times the expanded version of a vocabulary item correlates with the child's use of the word, is included. A lexical analysis summary includes information on the child's diversity of vocabulary by calculating the number of different words used in the language sample. A form analysis error profile calculates substitutions and omission errors for the eight above-mentioned categories. MLU can be obtained for morphemes and words, and structure analysis gives expanded information on the percentages of phrase structure errors, sentence types, questions, and complex sentence structures. Verb tense analysis is also included.

Assessment Instrument   Systematic Analysis of Language Transcripts (SALT), c. 1983

Author   J.F. Miller and R.S. Chapman

Publisher   Madison Language Analysis Laboratory, Waisman Center on Mental Retardation and Human Development, University of Wisconsin, Madison, Wisconsin 53706

Language Assessed   Expressive language—language sample

Age   Children of any age for whom a language sample may be obtained

Administration   A language sample is administered, then analyzed. This program can code utterances of two speakers. It requires 45 minutes to enter the data and 20 minutes for the computer to analyze it.

Description   The language practitioner obtains a language sample and codes the data for entry. The program offers five functions for analysis of data.

Scoring   Computer analysis of the language sample includes several types of information.
SALT 0: provides a transcript of utterances into 31 categories.
SALT 1: prints a transcript and checks errors.
SALT 2: provides the following information.

- Total number and percentage of complete and incomplete utterances
- Summary of word and morpheme use
- Distributional analysis of the number of utterances of both speakers
- Table providing a frequency count of key structures
- Morpheme analysis of both speakers

SALT 3: provides the frequency of specific items within the transcript.
SALT 4: categorizes the speakers' utterances into structure or function and provides a list of words in each category.

Selecting the Right Test

On many occasions the language practitioner is not sufficiently familiar with the child to determine where to start in assessing language. And frequently, the language practitioner is not able to identify an area for further language assessment. Consequently, much time is wasted in giving tests inappropriate to the abilities of the child. For example, the language practitioner may use a test that is too easy for the child, one that is far below the child's current level of language functioning. Or, the language practitioner may select a test far beyond the child's level of language competence.

It is important, for the sake of efficiency, to make an informed choice in the selection of a test or battery of tests so that appropriate measures are used to assess the child's language, and so that test results yield information useful for programming purposes. The checklist in Exhibit 3-1 facilitates selection of the proper test. In addition, the authors have provided language descriptors that may be used to determine a starting point for assessment. Table 3-4 is intended as a reference for

Table 3-4 Selection of Language Tests According to Behavior Characteristic

Behavior Characteristic	Test To Be Used	Rationale
June, a 6-year-old female, is referred by her 1st-grade teacher for not following directions and "tuning out" in class. After teacher gives directions on an activity or task, June often does things backwards. She expresses herself in complete 6- to 7-word sentences and appears to have normal expressive language.	Boehme Test of Basic Concepts	Determines understanding of directional and relational concepts.
	Test for Auditory Comprehension of Language	Checks for comprehension of word classes: nouns, verbs, adjectives, adverbs, prepositions.
Ronny, a 6-year-old male, comes to public schools from a regular preschool program. He uses 1- or 2-word phrases, seems to be in constant motion, and has an extremely short attention span.	Screening Test for Auditory Comprehension of Language (STACL)	Screens receptive language abilities. Appropriate for student with short attention span, but a measure of understanding concepts.
	Utah Test of Language Development	Informs on functioning in other cognitive areas.
	Expressive Vocabulary Inventory	Requires only 1- or 2-word responses, as appropriate for this student.
	Assessment of Children's Language Comprehension	Determines understanding of 2- and 3-word critical elements.
Juan, a 7-year-old Hispanic male, comes from a family of 5 brothers and sisters; all speak English. However, the parents and grandparents speak Spanish. Juan is being considered for placement in a bilingual program.	James Language Dominance Test	Checks comprehension and production and categorizes child according to 5 classifications for language dominance. This helps determine whether child is eligible for a bilingual program, as well as what kind of bilingual program would best suit his needs.
	Pictorial Test of Bilingualism and Language Dominance	Helps determine dominance and measures development in both languages.

Table 3-4 continued

Behavior Characteristic	Test To Be Used	Rationale
Maria, a 6-year-old Hispanic female, seems to have deficit language skills in English and Spanish. She is being considered for placement in a class for the language delayed.	Del Rio Language Screening Test Screening Test of Spanish Grammar Language Assessment Scales, Level 1 -or- Test for Auditory Comprehension of Language	Measures language proficiency in English and Spanish by providing 2 forms. This tool may also be used, because it identifies children whose syntactic skills are not commensurate with their age. Determines whether child is deficient in one or both languages, providing information valuable for placement decisions. Gives a comparison of receptive language in both English and Spanish.
Robbie, a 6-year-old male, has been identified as language delayed. His language is characterized by immature morphological forms, though he speaks in complete kernel sentences. Language practitioner must prescribe a program to remediate his specific deficits.	Carrow Elicited Language Inventory Developmental Sentence Scoring	Analyzes specific error patterns in use of adjectives, nouns, plurals, verbs, negatives, contractions, adverbs, prepositions, pronouns, demonstrations, conjunctions. Gives language practitioner functioning level of child in 8 grammatical categories: indefinite pronouns, personal pronouns, main verbs, secondary verbs, conjunctions, interrogative reversals, "wh" questions, negatives; pinpoints areas for remediation.

the language practitioner desiring to initiate language assessment. It consists of brief behavioral characteristics of children, along with suggested tests for assessing each particular problem and the rationale for choosing the particular tests selected.

SUMMARY

The assessment portion of any language training program is fundamental to its success. There are two basic types of language assessment instruments: norm referenced tests and criterion referenced tests. Although norm referenced tests are ideally suited for decisions about program placement, criterion referenced tests identify the specific language deficits that a child has, and they are used in the day-to-day operation of the language program.

The language practitioner must be especially sensitive to the possibility of cultural bias in the use of any assessment instrument. Too often, children have been identified as having language problems when, in fact, the situation involved language dominance.

The language assessment tool can provide the language practitioner with valuable information, if selected carefully. The initial measurement of a child's language can aid the language practitioner in

- seeking further information about the child's specific needs
- providing a detailed analysis of the child's specific deficits and strengths

Furthermore, if the theoretical framework of the assessment measure matches that of the language problem, the process of determining goals for language intervention will be facilitated. More specifically, the goals for language programming will be directly related to the skills assessed by the instrument.

A number of language assessment systems and instruments have been reviewed in this chapter to assist the language practitioner in selecting the most appropriate instrument for any given language program.

REFERENCES

Bateman, B. (1967). Three approaches to diagnosis and educational planning for children with learning disabilities. *Academic Therapy, 2*, 215–222.

Brown, R. (1973). *A first language, the early stages*. Cambridge, MA: Harvard University Press.

Carroll, J. (1972). A review of the Illinois test of psycholinguistic abilities. In O.K. Buros (Ed.), *Seventh mental measurement yearbook* (p. 819). Highland Park, NJ: Gryphon.

Cassidy, R.D., Koller, D.E., & Schwartz, A.H. (1984). The uses of word processing for clinical report writing: Part I applications, characteristics, and requirements. *Journal of Childhood Communication Disorders,8*, 7–23.

Damico, J.S. (1985). Clinical discourse analysis. In C.S. Simon (Ed.), *Communication skills and classroom success* (pp. 165–203). San Diego, CA: College Hill Press.

Emerick, L., & Hatten, J. (1979). *Diagnosis and evaluation in speech pathology.* Englewood Cliffs, NJ: Prentice Hall.

Garrett, E. (1973). Programmed articulation therapy. In W.D. Wolfe & D. Goulding (Eds.), *Articulation and learning* (p. 107). Springfield, IL: Charles C. Thomas.

Grice, H.P. (1975). Logic and conversation. In P. Cole & J. Morgan (Eds.) *Studies in syntax and semantics: Speech acts* (Vol. 3). New York: Academic Press.

Hammill, D. (1975). Assessing and teaching perceptual motor processes. In D. Hammill & N. Bartel (Eds.), *Teaching children with learning and behavior problems* (p. 341). Boston, MA: Allyn & Bacon.

Larry P. *vs.* Riles, 343 F. Supp. 1306; 502 F 2d 963 (N.S. Cal. 1979).

Lee, L. (1971). *Northwestern Syntax Screening Test.* Evanston, IL: Northwestern University Press.

Lee, L. (1974). *Developmental sentence analysis.* Evanston, IL: Northwestern University Press.

Lovitt, T. (1977). *In spite of my resistance . . . I've learned from children.* Columbus, OH: Charles E. Merrill.

Mercer, J. (1975). Psychological assessment and the rights of children. In N. Hobbs (Ed.), *Issues in the classification of children* (p. 130). San Francisco, CA: Jossey-Bass.

Miller, J.F., & Chapman, R.S. (1983). *Systematic analysis of language transcripts* [Computer program]. Madison, WI: University of Wisconsin, Madison Language Analysis Laboratory, Waisman Center on Mental Retardation and Human Development.

Mordecai, D.R., Palin, M.W., & Palmer, C.B. (1982). *Lingquest 1: Language sample analysis* [Computer program]. Napa, CA: Lingquest Software.

Muma, J.R. (1981). Language: A new era. *Journal of Childhood Communication Disorders, 5,* 83–89.

Muma, J.R. (1983). Speech-language pathology: Emerging clinical expertise in language. In T.M. Gallagher & C.A. Prutting (Eds.), *Pragmatic assessment and intervention issues in language* (pp. 195–214). San Diego, CA: College Hill Press.

Newcomer, P. & Hammill, D. (1976). *Psycholinguistics in the schools.* Columbus, OH: Charles E. Merrill.

Payne, P.D. (1984). The use of interactive video and videodisc for pre-service and in-service education. *Journal of Childhood Communication Disorders, 8,* 63–79.

Rosenberg, S. (1970). Problems of language development in the retarded. In H.C. Haywood (Ed.), *Social-cultural aspects of mental retardation* (p. 209). New York: Appleton-Century-Crofts.

Rushakoff, G.E. (1984). Microcomputer assisted instruction in communication disorders. *Journal of Childhood Communication Disorders, 8,* 51–61.

Saunders, F., Blake, R., & Decker, C. (1977). *Unbiased assessment: Guidelines, procedures, and forms for the SEA's implementation of 94-142* (p. 22). Salt Lake City: Southwest Regional Resource Center.

Schwartz, A.H. (1984). Microcomputer applications: Facts, functions, fads, and fallacies. *Journal of Childhood Communication Disorders, 8,* 89–111.

Schwartz, A.H. (1985). Microcomputer assisted assessment of linguistic and phonological processes. *Topics in Language Disorders, 6,* 26–40.

Schwartz, A.H., Koller, D.E., & Cassidy, R.D. (1984). The uses of word processing for clinical report writing. Part II—Program features for developing report formats. *Journal of Childhood Communication Disorders, 8,* 23–37.

Simon. C.S. (1979). *Communicative competence: A functional-pragmatic approach to language therapy*. Tucson, AZ: Communication Skill Builders.

Weiner, F. (1984). *Computerized language sample analysis (CLSA)* [Computer program]. University Park, PA: Parrot Software.

Wiig, E.L., & Bray, C.M. (1983). *Let's talk inventory for children*. Columbus, OH: Charles E. Merrill.

Chapter 4

Developing and Implementing the Language Intervention Program

INSTRUCTIONAL PROCESS MODEL FOR LANGUAGE TRAINING

Effective language training must follow a logical series of steps. This chapter will present the reader with an instructional process model for language training consisting of seven steps in an ordered sequence. Each step serves as a prerequisite for the following one.

1. identifying the child
2. assessing the child
3. establishing the instructional objectives
4. developing the language intervention program
5. implementing the language intervention program
6. reassessing the child
7. reteaching if necessary

The process begins with identification of the child with language difficulties. It proceeds through the development and implementation of instruction and ends with the evaluation of the child and subsequent reteaching based on the results of evaluation.

This instructional process model will serve as a structure for initiating language training. It will assist the language practitioner in organizing the language program, which will provide logical order and continuity to the instructional process.

Identifying the Child

There are a number of ways that a child with a language delay might be identified. Before the child is of school age, the most likely persons to spot the problem are the child's parents. In some cases an alert physician is capable of identifying a child with language development problems.

Since the advent of Public Law 94-142, states have been required to develop and implement a "child find" system to identify children with handicapping conditions who will need special services in the public schools. These child find efforts have been successful in finding handicapped children who were not previously being served. Inevitably, some of these children have had language development problems as the primary or secondary referral characteristic.

If the child with language problems is not identified before attending school, it is likely that the child's teacher will observe the problem and refer the child to the appropriate personnel for help. In most cases, by the time the language practitioner receives the child, the educational diagnostician or the school psychologist will have already diagnosed the child as language delayed. In fact, the language practitioner may have been called on to assist with the diagnosis.

Once the child with a possible language delay has been identified, the language practitioner must determine the nature and extent of the language deficit. The next step in the instructional process, assessing the child, will accomplish this purpose.

Assessing the Child

Once the child is deemed qualified for a language training program, assessment is implemented. This evaluation is done by the language practitioner for the purpose of identifying the child's specific language strengths and deficits. (Assessment procedures are discussed at length in Chapter 3.) Basic to the assessment step is determining the language problem so that the language practitioner may begin to set instructional objectives for the child. This process is facilitated when the assessment process specifically defines what the child can or cannot do in terms of receptive and expressive language. Therefore, the more criterion based the assessment tool, the more able the language practitioner will be at translating test results into an intervention program for the child.

Establishing Instructional Objectives

The data from the assessment step are used to develop the instructional objectives for the child's individualized language program.

Instructional objectives should be stated clearly and concisely in behavioral terms. They should leave no doubt about the writer's intent and, therefore, they must be measurable. Poorly written or vague instructional objectives are hardly worth the effort required to write them, because they rarely convey the information needed to carry out a proper instructional program.

The authors suggest the following *ABCD* format, which is easy to remember and contains all the components of a well written instructional objective.

A: represents the *audience* that is to perform the objective. More specifically, who will be doing the learning?

B: represents the desired *behavior* that will be exhibited by the child. The behavior should be stated in clear observable terms.

C: represents the *conditions* under which the audience will perform the desired behavior. This segment is sometimes called the "given" and represents the setting in which the child will perform the learning task. The resources needed are also commonly stated as a condition.

D: represents the *degree of mastery* required to meet an acceptable level of performance on the objective. Mastery statements are frequently stated with one or both of the following components: the number or percentage correct and the specific time limitations required for the child to complete the objective.

The following examples of language objectives have been presented and labeled to illustrate the *ABCD* format. It should be noted that the objective format need not be written in alphabetical order. In fact, the authors recommend starting the objective with the statement of *conditions*.

The following represents an objective in the area of prespeech behavior.

Given the sound of a buzzer, bell, or clap, Alice will turn her head toward the source of the sound nine of ten times.

> **Audience:** Alice
> **Behavior:** will turn her head toward the source of the sound
> **Condition:** given the sound of a buzzer, bell, or clap
> **Degree of mastery:** nine of ten times

An objective in the area of receptive language may be written in this manner. Given three pictures of agents in action and the verbal cue "Show me the . . .," William will select the appropriate picture five of six times, within five seconds, on each trial.

> **Audience:** William
> **Behavior:** will select the appropriate picture
> **Conditions:** given three pictures of agents in action and the verbal cue, "Show me the . . ."
> **Degree of mastery:** five of six times, within five seconds on each trial

The following illustrates an objective in the area of expressive language. Given a verbal cue, Felicia will correctly imitate the appropriate consonant-vowel combination (mă, mē, bōō) 90 percent of the time.

> Audience: Felicia
> Behavior: will correctly imitate the appropriate consonant-vowel combination
> Conditions: given a verbal cue
> Degree of mastery: 90 percent of the time

Writing instructional objectives in a clear concise manner facilitates identification of the target language behavior required of the child. It initiates subsequent development and implementation of the activities and exercises designed to teach the desired language skills.

Developing the Language Intervention Program

Developing an appropriate language intervention program is a process of determining priorities. The language practitioner must be aware of the needs of the child to select the appropriate content and sequence of language intervention. The language practitioner may elect to use a commercially marketed language program. However, the individual needs of the child must be kept in mind at all times. One should never select a language program solely because "it looks good" and proceed to instruct the child in every step, phase, or lesson of that program. Too often, children have been forced to fit the program; identifying a program to fit the child is much more productive. The specific language problem(s) of the child should be listed according to priority. Then, and only then, should materials and resources be chosen to teach those language constructions targeted for instruction. Individualizing intervention training for the child is the key to successful program development.

Implementing the Language Intervention Program

Implementation of language training, the instructional phase, must be accomplished using techniques proven to be successful in the development of language. Techniques such as imitation, modeling, and expansion (reviewed in detail in Chapter 5) should be attempted and compared for their relative effectiveness. The language practitioner must determine which procedures maximize the expressive production of each child.

The overall goal of the instructional process is to help the child develop the ability to understand and communicate through language. The instructional exercises and activities, therefore, should give the child opportunities to learn through experience and to practice language in an interactive process with the environment. Language activities should be chosen on the basis of functional value. The child should gain direct reinforcement from the use of language. More specifically, the child should see a reason for communicating and should experience the direct results of oral expression and its effects on others.

Programming should stress not only the imitation and production of target constructions but also the generalized use of them in the child's spontaneous language. Only when the child uses language in daily life will the goals of the instructional process be realized.

Reassessing the Child

Planned periodic reassessment is absolutely necessary to accurately determine the child's progress. In addition, the reassessment step provides the needed information for modifying existing instructional objectives and establishing new objectives. Reassessment data also allow the language practitioner to evaluate the overall effectiveness of the language program.

Reteaching if Necessary

Through reassessment it may be determined that the child has not met the required objectives and may need additional language instruction. At this point, the child should be cycled back through an instructional loop comprised of step five "implementation of the language intervention program" and step six "reassessing the child" until the objectives have been met. The recycling process may require modifications in the instructional program itself. Simply recycling the child will have few positive results if the instructional program is inappropriate or inadequate for the needs of the child.

INDIVIDUALIZED LANGUAGE PLAN

Vital to the implementation of a language training program is the development of a plan for individualizing language instruction. It is critical that assessment data be interpreted, that the child's specific problems be pinpointed, and that target behaviors be identified. Once the child's language deficit is specified, the objectives for instruction are set and the treatment program is prescribed.

One means of gathering and recording the necessary elements of a language program is the Individualized Language Plan (ILP). The use of this written document will help the language practitioner to organize materials and determine procedures in an effort to maximize the instructional time allotted to each child.

The components of the ILP include

- annual goal
- objectives
- resources to be used in teaching the objectives
- method of evaluation
- date initiated
- date completed
- results of the generalization check

Table 4-1 is a sample ILP to be referred to during the following discussion of the development of the ILP.

Annual Goal

The annual or long range goal is a statement of what the child will be able to accomplish in the span of the treatment period. In most cases, especially if the student is in a public school setting, this period is one year. This does not imply that one should wait the full year before evaluating progress or appraising the effectiveness of the treatment procedure. On the contrary, the process of assessment is continual. Estimating how much the child will be able to accomplish during the treatment period is dependent on knowing the child, the child's rate of learning, and the number of hours the language practitioner can devote to the goal. In the absence of these details the language practitioner must make an informed decision based on what is known about the development of language in children. The goal should be appropriate to the child's developmental age and performance level.

The long range goal need not be stated in specific behavioral terms, but it should be a general description of the target area. The long range goal gives the reader information about the target area pinpointed for instruction, and additionally, it communicates to the reader what the outcome of the instruction will be.

The long range goal is derived from analyzing assessment information that identifies target areas or target constructions to be developed. The more direct the relationship between assessment data and goals for language intervention, the more useful the ILP will be to the language practitioner.

If, for example, the language practitioner takes a language sample and analyzes it for morphological constructions, specific deficits may be revealed. It may be determined that the child inappropriately uses plurals, past tense verb endings, and present progressive verbs. In this case, the language practitioner may see the

Table 4-1 Individualized Language Plan

Student _____

Long Range Goal _____ Student will increase comprehension of language concepts.

Objective	Resources	Evaluation	Date Initiated	Date Completed	Generalization Check
Given 2 objects depicting polar characteristics and verbal cue "Show me the one that is <u>short</u>" (long, etc.), child will point to the appropriate choice within 5 seconds, 4 of 5 trials. The following opposites will be used:	Curriculum and Monitoring System receptive language program objects, e.g., pencils, big and little balls, full and empty cups, blocks, etc.	Curriculum and Monitoring System daily monitoring sheets. When 90% accuracy is achieved, child may be introduced to next pair of opposites.			
long - short			9-11	9-19	Checked 10-1 90% accuracy maintained; probed again 10-10 and 11-24 accuracy maintained.
full - empty			9-20		
big - little					

Given a picture card depicting placement of objects at top, middle, and bottom and verbal cue "Point to the one at the top" (middle, bottom), child will respond correctly with 90% accuracy.

Concept formation
p. 28–30

Data sheets record correct/incorrect responses.

necessity of assigning morphology as a priority target area for that particular child. The child's annual goal should read

The child will increase the appropriate use of morphological inflections.

This goal can then be broken down into specific objectives that will concentrate on the exact target constructions: plurals, past tense verb endings, and present progressive verbs.

Objectives

The objectives of the individual's language program, in contrast to the long range goal, should be very specific—directly observable behaviors that the child will accomplish in the target area. As previously stated, each objective should contain the audience, the behavior, the conditions of the instructional task, and the degree of mastery. In the goal "The child will increase the appropriate use of morphological inflections," the relevant constructions identified for instruction were plurals, regular past tense verb endings, and present progressive verb endings (ing). The language practitioner may then write objectives specifically designed to develop these constructions. The following objectives were selected for this child's language intervention program.

- Given pictures representing plural objects and the verbal cue "Tell me what you see," the child will name the picture, using the correct forms of the plural allomorphs (/s/, /z/, and /ɪs/) with 100 percent accuracy.
- Given a verbal cue "What did you play yesterday?" "What did you watch on TV last night?" "Where did you sleep last night?" or similar questions requiring regular past tense verb inflections (/d/, /t/, and /ɪd/), the child will respond with the appropriate allomorph in ten of ten trials.
- Given an action picture and a verbal cue "What is the boy (girl, man, etc.) doing?" the child will respond using the present progressive form of the verb in ten of ten trials.

Writing the objectives in behavioral terms leaves no doubt about the exact target behavior required. It clarifies for the language practitioner exactly what the child must do to master the skill. Furthermore, should any paraprofessionals be employed to help with language training, it is helpful to have the terminal behavior, as well as the conditions for mastering the skill, clearly specified.

Resources

Resources are the materials the language practitioner will use to accomplish the objective. The resources used to teach the skill may be a commercial language program, teacher devised instructional materials, or objects and pictures used for visual stimuli. The name of the program or description of the materials should be specific enough to communicate to the reader what phase, step, or lesson number will be used in teaching the objective.

Evaluation

The evaluation section of the ILP describes the method used to determine whether the child has met the criterion for mastery stated in the objective. Evaluation can be achieved using formal measures such as the instruments described in Chapter 3 as pre- and postmeasures of progress. Other more informal measures can also be used, including recording data, placement tests, continuous monitoring checks such as those provided in some commercial programs, and teacher devised graphs and charts. The properant, also described in Chapter 3, can be invaluable if the practitioner desires a relatively simple measure of the appropriate use of a particular construction.

The subject of data collection and program monitoring will be dealt with in some depth later in this chapter.

Date Initiated/Date Completed

The date initiated and the date completed are self-explanatory. The day, month, and year are entered at the time instruction on the objective actually begins. The date completed is entered when the child meets the criterion for mastery as stated in the objective or when evaluation determines that the child has completed the objective at the level of proficiency described.

Generalization Check

The column for generalization check is left incomplete until the language practitioner plans to see whether the child has retained appropriate use of the construction or plans to determine whether the child has generalized to spontaneous language what has been learned in the training sessions.

Although the sample ILP in Table 4-1 represents only one area—receptive language—a child may be working on more than one target area. Consequently, an individual's ILP may be several pages in length.

IMPLEMENTING THE LANGUAGE TRAINING PROGRAM

Inherent in the language training process is an organizing structure that will ensure that the instructional time is spent more efficiently and effectively. This structure has three considerations.

1. control of the physical environment
2. implementation of the S→R→S paradigm
3. a system of monitoring and evaluating progress

Control of the Physical Environment

It is very important that the child directly attends to the stimulus the language practitioner uses to elicit verbal responses in a language training session. It is suggested, therefore, that the language practitioner be seated directly in front of the child, in a face-to-face position. The child's chair must be of correct size, allowing the feet to touch the floor. Data sheets should be within easy reach of the language practitioner's dominant hand so that each response can be recorded immediately. The language practitioner should not rely on memory for recording the child's responses. If edible or activity reinforcers are to be used, they must be kept out of the child's reach. The room must be as quiet as possible so extraneous noise does not cause a distraction. Also, if the child is easily distracted by visual stimuli, a folding cardboard screen may be of use in eliminating interfering scenes and activities.

The language practitioner should be able to easily collect and store materials. A rubber dishpan is useful for storing concrete objects, ensuring that they are always in the same place. Recording sheets for monitoring responses should also be readily at hand. One easy means of keeping these materials organized is a folder system wherein a folder for each child contains picture cards, data sheets, and other materials needed for the lesson. The folders are filed together and kept in a central location so that the language practitioner can pick up a child's folder and continue where the lesson was discontinued the previous day.

It is suggested that each language session runs approximately 30 minutes daily, depending on the child's age and ability to attend to a task. During the language lesson the child should be given the maximum number of opportunities to respond and to use the target construction in verbal expression. In many language programs the time the lesson starts is noted, as well as the time the session ends. These data, when compared with the information on percentage of correct responses, can help the language practitioner determine the effectiveness of instruction, the potency of the reinforcers, and whether time is being utilized efficiently. For example, if the child works for 30 minutes in a language session and the language practitioner has only presented 20 trials of the target construction, this is probably not a very efficient teaching session. If on other days the child has been able to complete 50 trials in the same time period, better use has been made of the time available. The language practitioner must also evaluate whether the reinforcers used are effective or whether alternative reinforcers are necessary to increase the rate of response.

S→R→S Paradigm

The S→R→S paradigm lends structure to the language intervention program. Inherent in the S→R→S paradigm is the principle that behavior is controlled by the stimulus events that follow a response. It borrows from behavior theory a three-step learning process.

First, the child is presented with a stimulus (S), sometimes called the preceding stimulus. This stimulus can be auditory, as in the case of a verbal direction, or visual, as when a picture or concrete object is used to elicit a response from the individual. The response (R) from the child can be either a motor response, such as an action or written response, or a verbal answer to the stimulus. The consequent stimulus (S) following the response is the controlling factor. By varying the consequent stimulus, the response can be strengthened, decreased, or eliminated.

In language training, this three-step learning process can be illustrated in the following manner (see Figure 4-1).

Reinforcers are consequent stimuli that follow the child's response and can be separated into several types. In fact, they even exist in a hierarchy (Stile, Cole & Cole, 1978; Lovitt, 1977). At the lower end of the hierarchy are the primary reinforcers, which fulfill certain basic needs such as hunger, thirst, etc. In language training, children just beginning to learn language may perform better using a primary reinforcer such as cereal, cheese, juice, popcorn, or other snacks that are readily consumed. One note of caution should be mentioned here, however. Edibles can cause salivation, which may interfere with the production of sounds and words. If the individual is able to wait for a reinforcer, the language practitioner should delay the consumption of the reinforcer until the language lesson is finished.

Activity reinforcers, the next level of reinforcement in the hierarchy, can also be used to strengthen desired behaviors. An activity reinforcer may be a game, a manipulative toy, or an object that the individual finds interesting to see, touch, hear, or play with. One enterprising university student in special education, whose

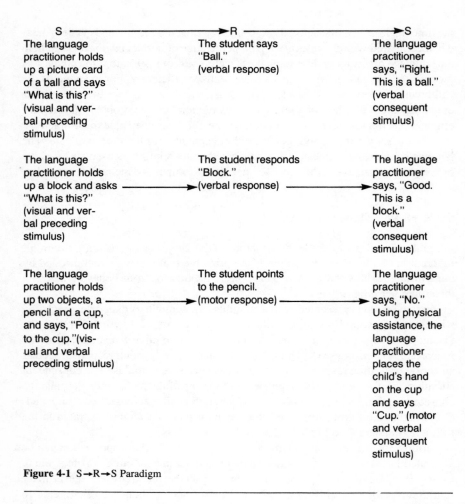

Figure 4-1 S→R→S Paradigm

practicum experience included daily visits to a classroom, worked with a child on an expressive language program. She always brought with her a sack that she called her "bag of tricks," containing several activity reinforcers—a pair of rose colored sunglasses that her assigned child loved to use to view the world, a sand hourglass, a lump of clay, a plastic window filled with colored sand that made interesting designs when shaken, some soap bubbles, and various other small toys. The university trainee would present several trials of the target language construction, sufficient to enable the child to meet criterion on one step of the program. If a specified accuracy level was achieved by the child, he could choose an activity from the bag of tricks and play with it for one or two minutes. The child always gave up the toy willingly at the end of that time, knowing that if he performed well and met the criterion on the next step of the program, he would have another opportunity to play. This creative use of reinforcers illustrates the principle that learning can be an enjoyable process for the child and that appropriate use of reinforcers can strengthen the desired response.

The next highest level of reinforcement is social. Social reinforcers may be comprised of verbal praise such as "You're right," "Super, you said it the right way," or "Good talking." Social reinforcers can also include a pat of approval, a smile, a handshake, or the more to-date greeting "Give me ten."

A social reinforcer serves to let children know that their responses or behaviors are appropriate and even desired. When a higher level social reinforcer such as verbal praise is paired with a lower level reinforcer such as something to eat, the higher level reinforcer may eventually replace the lower level reinforcer. This represents for the child a transition away from reliance on edibles to a more acceptable form of reinforcement, social value.

The highest level of reinforcement is self-evaluation, where knowledge of doing the task provides the individual with inner satisfaction. At this level the child is learning for the sheer pleasure of learning.

The language practitioner must constantly be aware of the levels of reinforcement and the appropriate use of reinforcers in the language intervention program. The language practitioner must skillfully use the relationships between levels of reinforcement to help the child attain increased proficiency and independence from external consequences.

Within the S→R→S process there are other techniques that the language practitioner may employ to elicit the child's responses.

Nonverbal children beginning to approximate sound production and elementary sound blending must be instructed with techniques that maximize the success rate in learning these new sounds. These techniques include modeling, prompting, shaping, and branching.

Modeling

Modeling, providing the child with the target construction, is important in letting the child know what response is expected. Though modeling has its limits in facilitating spontaneous language and generalization of the linguistic code, it is an essential first step in learning language. It is important to use modeling in the first stages of a language training program or when the child is first learning a new task or target construction. However, if one relies too heavily on modeling, it may jeopardize the progress of internalizing the structure into spontaneous language.

The language practitioner must systematically "fade" the model so that the child produces the construction more and more independently. Figure 4-2 illustrates how modeling can be used to initiate the individual's response.

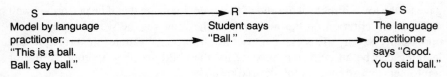

Figure 4-2 Modeling Using S→R→S Paradigm

Prompting

Prompts are additional cues given to the individual to initiate a response. They may be previously taught stimuli that can be used to start the response or to begin a new stimulus. A prompt is represented in Figure 4-3.

The language practitioner can use prompting as an effective means of getting the child to respond. Prompts, like modeling, should eventually be faded so that the child initiates the response with no assistance. Otherwise, the child may continue to rely on prompts to respond and will seldom initiate responses independently.

Shaping

In language training, shaping refers to the systematic process of requiring the individual to make closer and closer approximations of the target response through the use of selective reinforcement. At the beginning of language training the language practitioner may be satisfied with the response ''ba'' for ball, especially if the child has only uttered ''b'' before in response to the object or picture. Once the ''ba'' response has been consistently established, however, the language practitioner may discontinue reinforcement of that response to gain the full phonemic content in the word ball. The shaping of closer approximations to the target sound or construction can lead to systematic successes for the severely language delayed child. Although these successive steps may seem minute to the average observer, they nevertheless mean that the child is producing responses more independently and is thus closer to mastering the target construction.

Branching

When a child is not achieving the level of proficiency required of a particular language program or instructional objective, the method or sequence of instruction must be modified. This modification of steps is called branching, for it suggests a transitional step from one point to another. It implies that the learning task should be analyzed and sequenced in smaller alternative steps to ensure success for the individual. Take, for example, a child who is responding incorrectly to pictures of objects for the prepositional placements *in* and *on*. Given a picture of a ball *on* a table and asked ''Where is the ball?'' the child responded ''In table.'' Succeeding trials with an object placed *in* a container revealed that the child was also

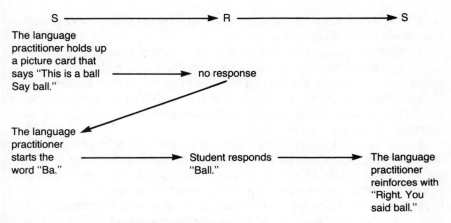

Figure 4-3 Prompting Using S→R→S Paradigm

responding incorrectly with *on* instead of *in*. In this instance, branching steps will need to be implemented. One method of branching or modifying the instructional sequence in teaching prepositional placement is to make sure the child distinguishes between *in* and *on* receptively. This could be accomplished by teaching *in* using successive discrimination choices with real objects until 100 percent accuracy is attained. The child would be asked to select the toy *in* the container. Once criterion is attained the concept *on* would be taught in the same manner, using multiple discrimination tasks with objects. Once criterion is met with *on* the two concepts may be combined and alternated until the child can select the appropriate object when both prepositional placements are represented. Once criterion is met alternating *in* and *on* the child may then be asked to respond verbally to a series of stimuli by responding randomly that a picture of a toy is "in" or "on" a container.

In this manner, sequences of steps that originally were too difficult for the child can be analyzed to provide for branching from one step to another. Branching allows for modifications of instructional programming, ensuring success for the learner.

A System of Monitoring Progress

To measure attainment of a target construction, it is necessary to collect data directly linked to the instructional objective. As the child works on a particular instructional objective in the language intervention program, the language practitioner must present numerous trials of the target construction. The results of these trials must be recorded so that the language practitioner can determine when the child has met the criterion for mastery. There are various techniques for recording this information in a continuous manner.

The simplest way is to record correct and incorrect responses. Exhibit 4-1 represents one type of data collection form used to record each response as the child makes it, using the C column for a correct response and the I column for an incorrect response. Space is also provided for the date, the construction being taught, the reinforcers used, and the level of accuracy to be calculated when the language session has been completed.

The notation of reinforcers is important in determining the relative effectiveness of different consequent stimuli. If, for example, the child had achieved 70 percent accuracy when allowed to blow soap bubbles after correct responses, yet accuracy dropped to 40 percent when social praise was used as a consequence, this would imply that the child functions more effectively with an activity reinforcer. Data, then, can be analyzed to assess the strength of the reinforcer.

Other language programs, such as the *Fokes Sentence Builder Program* (1976), provide response sheets that allow the language practitioner to specify in which grammatical element of the sentence the learner made errors. This program also provides a response form for graphing percentage of errors.

The *Language Acquisition Program for the Retarded or Multiply Impaired* (LAP), authored by Louise Kent (1974), provides an extensive data sheet for monitoring responses. It is designed to monitor responses in the initial inventory, the training session, the final inventory, or in a retention check, all elements specific to the program. Its value as a recording system is indicated by the variety of information that can be obtained through its use. Not only are correct and incorrect responses recorded, but the number of times the child approximates the response is also noted. In the language training session this is extremely valuable information, because it indicates when the child attempts to form the word, sound, or phrase. It can guide the language practitioner in deciding when to initiate and fade prompts or when to reinforce closer approximations of the construction, and it can help determine when to demand the full and correct articulation of the phoneme, word, or phrase from the child.

The data sheet from the LAP also helps the language practitioner monitor the times the child makes no response, as well as the times the child makes extraneous remarks during the training session. Also included is a space for recording what the child "buys" with exchange tokens if a token economy system of reinforcement is used.

Exhibit 4-2 is a data sheet taken from the LAP. It represents a sophisticated method of collecting data, one that yields information valuable for interpreting the progress of the child in the language intervention program.

These represent only two of the many types of response forms that can be utilized to monitor the development of the child along the language continuum. The language practitioner is encouraged to determine what information is most

Exhibit 4-1 Response Form

Student _____

Date _____	Date _____
Construction _____	Construction _____
CI CI CI CI	CI CI CI CI
CI CI CI CI	CI CI CI CI
CI CI CI CI	CI CI CI CI
CI CI CI CI	CI CI CI CI
CI CI CI CI	CI CI CI CI
CI CI CI CI	CI CI CI CI
Reinforcer _____	Reinforcer _____
% Correct _____	% Correct _____
Date _____	Date _____
Construction _____	Construction _____
CI CI CI CI	CI CI CI CI
CI CI CI CI	CI CI CI CI
CI CI CI CI	CI CI CI CI
CI CI CI CI	CI CI CI CI
CI CI CI CI	CI CI CI CI
CI CI CI CI	CI CI CI CI
Reinforcer _____	Reinforcer _____
% Correct _____	% Correct _____
Date _____	Date _____
Construction _____	Construction _____
CI CI CI CI	CI CI CI CI
CI CI CI CI	CI CI CI CI
CI CI CI CI	CI CI CI CI
CI CI CI CI	CI CI CI CI
CI CI CI CI	CI CI CI CI
CI CI CI CI	CI CI CI CI
Reinforcer _____	Reinforcer _____
% Correct _____	% Correct _____

Exhibit 4-2 Data Sheet

Child's name _____   Date _____

Trainer's name _____   Session number _____

Trial	1	2	3	4	5	6	7	8	9	10
1										
2										
3										
4										
5										
6										
7										
8										
9										
10										
11										
12										
13										
14										
15										
16										
17										
18										
19										
20										
21										
22										
23										
24										
No.										
C										
A										
I										
NR										

Phase _____

Part _____

No. Sessions completed on part

_____

Check One:

I-I _____

Training Session

   Test-step _____

   Teach-step _____

F-I _____

Retention Check _____

Data Summary Totals

No. Trials presented _____ (a)

No. Correct R's _____ (b)

No. Approximations _____

No. Incorrect R's _____

No. NR's _____

% Correct _____

$$\left(\frac{b}{a} \times 100 \right)$$

Exhibit 4-2 continued

Token Exchange Behavior
_____
_____
_____

Extraneous Responses
　　　　Response　　　　　　　　　　　　Comment
_____
_____
_____
_____
_____
_____
_____
_____

Source: From *Language Acquisition Program for the Retarded or Multiply Impaired* (p. 6) by Louise R. Kent, 1974, Champaign, Ill.: Research Press Company. Reprinted by permission of author.

applicable to the program being used, to the language construction being taught, and to the individual child. The language practitioner must then select a response form or method of collecting data that meets these needs. It is suggested that if the response forms or data sheets provided by a language program are not suitable, the language practitioner may create one that does meet the specific needs of the child.

Generalization Checks

It is important to determine whether a construction trained in a language session has generalized to spontaneous language acquisition and whether the response has been maintained over a period of time. For this reason, the language practitioner will need to periodically and systematically check generalization and/or retention. Chapter 5 covers this issue in greater detail and offers training suggestions for ensuring generalization. Important to our discussion here is the technique of recording generalization with the use of a monitoring system. For recording generalization checks or probes, the same type of data form used in the training session may be used if it contains a place for a retention check to be recorded. If it does not, the language practitioner will need to devise a form that can be used as a probe to monitor maintenance of a skill learned in the training sessions. Exhibit 4-3 presents such a form. It contains a place for the child's name, the date, and the construction being probed. For example, if the child had achieved mastery of plural nouns in training, and the language practitioner intended to determine whether the child was still using plurals correctly, the practitioner would enter the term ''plurals'' in the space titled ''Construction.'' In the space labeled ''Set-

Exhibit 4-3 Generalization Check

Date _____ Student _____

Construction _____

_____

Setting _____

_____

Observation Time _____

Correct Responses _____

Incorrect Responses _____

Total Responses _____

Accuracy = $\frac{\text{Correct Responses}}{\text{Total Responses}}$ = _____

ting,'' the language practitioner would record the environmental events surrounding the generalization check. For example, if the language practitioner observed the child in free play to determine whether the child used the construction spontaneously, the free play situation would be described. Observation time should also be noted, both the initial starting time as well as the time the observation is finished. Correct and incorrect responses can be marked with a simple tally for easy computation later. To determine accuracy level, the language practitioner should divide the number of correct responses by the total number of responses possible. This will give a percentage of accuracy for the child's use of the particular construction.

Information on generalization checks can be of use in determining the effectiveness of program training and whether subsequent reteaching is necessary to facilitate maintenance of the skill.

MAXIMIZING INSTRUCTIONAL TIME

The learner must be provided with the maximum time possible to practice language and gain experience in language patterns.

Fredericks, Anderson, and Baldwin (1978) sought to identify the instructional practices used by teachers who most effectively influenced student performance. One of the relevant factors they found was called "length of the instructional day." This term referred to maximizing the instructional time for each student by organizing and scheduling personnel and materials. They determined that teachers whose students made positive gains had a system for structuring and managing the learning process.

There are several ways in which the language practitioner can organize time spent in the instructional process to attain the maximum amount of language practice for the language delayed child.

Scheduling Time and Materials for Instruction

In a self-contained setting, the language practitioner must manage materials and children's time so that instructional activities are orchestrated smoothly and children are functioning productively every moment of the day. One way of achieving this is by making a master schedule that functions as the language practitioner's daily plan. Once the children's needs are assessed and known, the language practitioner may initiate scheduling by completing a grid detailing what each child does during the day. To accomplish this, the language practitioner should segment the day into 15- or 30-minute sessions and assign materials and personnel to each child. If the language practitioner is fortunate enough to have an instructional aide, the duties and responsibilities of that person should also be included on the schedule. If there is a university education program that provides practicum students, or if volunteers have been solicited, this schedule is even more necessary. Auxiliary personnel providing ancillary services such as speech therapy, occupational therapy, and physical therapy should also be represented on the schedule. In addition, current efforts to "mainstream" or integrate the child with normal age peers in academic, social, or physical areas should be reflected on the schedule. The schedule can provide an organized plan for each child and enhance the smooth functioning of the program. Table 4-2 illustrates a typical morning schedule for a self-contained setting of seven language delayed children.

As can be seen in the schedule, the persons responsible for working with each child are included in the schedule. The initials L.P. refer to the language practitioner. The word "aide" underneath the lesson area indicates a responsibility of the instructional aide. A practicum student was working in the classroom during the period that this schedule was implemented, so those responsibilities for instructing individuals were also included.

It is extremely important to adhere to the daily schedule. Maintaining this schedule and organization will provide consistency and structure in the language intervention process.

Table 4-2 Class Schedule

Student	9:00–9:30 A.M.	9:30–10:00 A.M.	10:00–10:30 A.M.	10:30–11:00 A.M.	11:00–11:30 A.M.
John	Reading - Aide	Expressive Language - L.P.	Integration with 3rd-Grade P.E.		Articulation - Speech Pathologist
Becky	Reading - Aide	Cursive Writing - Aide	Expressive Language - L.P.	Integration with 3rd-Grade Math	
Charles		Cursive Writing - Aide	Integration with 3rd-Grade P.E.	Expressive Language - L.P.	Reading - L.P.
Ronny	Expressive Language - L.P.	Receptive Language - Aide		Integration with 4th-Grade P.E.	Reading - Aide
Sue	Expressive Language - L.P.		Receptive Language - Aide	Fine Motor - Practicum Student	Integration for Socialization in Kindergarten
Andy		Gross Motor - Physical Therapist	Number Skills - Practicum Student	Articulation - Speech Pathologist	Expressive Language - Aide
Vicky		Gross Motor - Physical Therapist	Fine Motor - Aide	Expressive Language - Aide	Handwriting - Practicum Student

Each child cannot be instructed in individualized lessons 100 percent of the day. Therefore, the child must also be engaged in independent work, allowing the language practitioner to work with other individuals. Programmed materials and taped lessons in math, reading, and other areas of the curriculum will facilitate the organization of each child's time. Audiovisual equipment, such as The Language Master (see Appendix B), can give the child opportunities for language practice during free time. Paper and pencil tasks and workbooks may be used to reinforce reading and math skills previously learned. Children who are functioning at a more independent level may be able to work from an assignment sheet. One successful method used by the authors was developed for nonreading, language delayed children. A color coded assignment sheet was utilized to structure the children's activities so that each day the children picked up their folders and completed the color coded activities assigned for that day. Placed strategically around the room were kits, workbooks, and audiovisual materials that had been marked with a colored construction paper circle. If the child had a red circle and the number 15 on an assignment sheet, the child knew to go to the red circle, in this instance a math kit, find the activity numbered 15, and proceed to complete it independently. This method enabled children to become more self-sufficient in managing their own time and schedules when not participating in an instructional session with an adult.

Grouping

One can easily state a case for the individualization of instruction. Conducting individual lessons is most frequently used by language practitioners as a means of optimizing the child's practice in language. However, another effective means of providing the maximum time for practicing language is grouping. If used appropriately, children can be provided with as much language practice as in an individualized program, especially when children are encouraged to answer in a choral response.

The best means of grouping is according to need. Flexible arrangements combining different children can be achieved for the purpose of working on a common language construction. For example, if three children are inappropriately using personal pronouns, a group may be temporarily formed to work on that specific construction. Once the children have met criterion on using the specified pronouns, the group may be disbanded. This arrangement provides a flexible yet organized method of structuring instructional time.

Managing Personnel

The language practitioner must train all personnel in the use of methods, techniques, and materials used with the language delayed child. Within the field of special education there has recently been an increase in the number of paraprofessionals engaged in the instructional process, which has meant additional help for the language practitioner in providing services to the child. But if the language practitioner is not skillful in organizing and managing these human resources, their use may result more in impeding the organizational structure of the program than in facilitating the instructional process.

The aide or other paraprofessional must be thoroughly familiar with the instructional schedule so that children are in the proper place at the appropriate time. The paraprofessional must be made aware of the need to follow a structured time schedule. Failure to begin and change activities on time will result in children's confusion and further upset the schedules of other adults working in the classroom.

In some cases, the paraprofessional is responsible for providing direct instruction to children. The language practitioner must be responsible for training the paraprofessional in the goals and objectives of the program, as well as in the methods and techniques used with the children. For this reason the language practitioner should make every effort to create a program with detailed lessons, leaving little room for error.

The paraprofessional and the language practitioner must stay on task to ensure that activities blend effortlessly into subsequent activities. Conversations between adults that are not program related should be kept to a minimum in an effort to keep the language training sessions exclusively for the instruction of the children.

Utilization of more than one paraprofessional in the instructional setting at any given time can be organized with proper scheduling. Careful attention should be taken to match assigned duties and responsibilities to personal and professional qualifications and strengths of the individual. If, for example, there are two volunteers working in the program, one a graduate with teaching experience, the other a parent volunteer from the community with no background in education, one would want to assign them classroom responsibilities commensurate with their experiences and education. The parent volunteer might be utilized in preparing instructional materials, supervising snacks and meals, preparation of media, collecting baseline data, or a myriad of other noninstructional tasks. The experienced teacher, on the other hand, may be fully qualified to execute complex lessons and, thus, be assigned more direct teaching contact with children.

The careful management of materials and personnel includes the delineation of the responsibilities and duties of all adults working within the instructional setting. The result will be a highly organized environment that maximizes the children's instructional time.

SUMMARY

The instructional process model provides a structure by which the language practitioner can develop a language training program. The seven steps constitute the major components of any good language program. It is important to remember that each step serves as a prerequisite to the following step. Therefore, no step can be left out without endangering the quality and continuity of the entire program.

Developing an individualized language plan will aid the language practitioner in setting goals for instructing the language delayed child. Implementation of this plan may be facilitated by an environment conducive to learning. Controlling physical elements of the language lesson and initiating the S→R→S paradigm in instructing the child will structure the language intervention program. Establishing a system of evaluating progress to monitor attainment of the language objectives and maximizing the instructional time for the children will ensure the best utilization of resources and personnel in language training.

REFERENCES

Fokes, J. (1976). *Fokes sentence builder program*. Hingham, MA: Teaching Resources.

Fredericks, H.D., Anderson R., & Baldwin V. (1978). *The identification of competency indicators of teachers of the severely handicapped*. Monmouth, OR: Teaching Research.

Kent, L. (1974). *The language acquisition program for the retarded or multiply impaired* (p. 6). Champaign, IL: Research Press.

Lovitt, T. (1977). *In spite of my resistance . . . I've learned from children*. Columbus, OH: Charles E. Merrill.

Stile, S., Cole, J., & Cole, M. (1978). Reinforcers for handicapped learners. *The Pointer, 23,* 34–39.

Chapter 5

Teaching Language to the Nonverbal Child

Teaching children who have significant language delays, such as nonverbal children, is time consuming and demanding. The language practitioner will meet with failures as well as successes. The language intervention process requires great commitment from the language practitioner, including efforts in motivating the child and consistency in initiating and maintaining a daily systematic training procedure to remediate the child's language deficit. Furthermore, the language practitioner must be aware of specific program goals that further determine and describe the parameters of language instruction and provide a basis for planning remediation.

PROGRAM GOALS

Early Intervention

As soon as a language delay is suspected, the language intervention process should be initiated. Vital to the success of any language training program is the initiation of the intervention process early enough to positively affect the child's development of linguistic structures.

The notion that there are critical periods for learning language has been suggested by Lennenberg (1967), who presented evidence that the greatest period of language learning takes place between the age of two and puberty. This has implications for determining when to initiate instruction. Bricker and Bricker (1974) indicated that early language intervention should begin with stimulation activities at birth, when "high risk" infants are identified. Apgar (1953) developed a method to evaluate the newborn infant that allowed for identification of risk infants. Subsequent development of behavioral assessment procedures for observing infants led to significant progress in neonatal evaluation. The identification of infants exhibiting developmental difficulties has, in many cases, helped identify children with language delays and has facilitated the initiation of early intervention in language.

Developing Prespeech Behaviors

Prerequisite to language learning, and indeed to the learning process in general, is the development of attention span. Nonverbal children, especially those with little or no formal training, exhibit characteristics that may interfere with learning. The child may not be able to focus on an object for more than a fleeting second, may not be able to establish eye contact with another person, or may not be capable of listening to or following auditory instructions. It is clear that the child will maintain these characteristics that obstruct the learning process unless the characteristics are dealt with specifically.

Some of the prespeech behaviors that the language practitioner must teach to increase the child's attention span are

- attending to sound
- responding to name
- attending to objects
- accomplishing motor imitation
- matching to sample

Establishing these skills will facilitate progress when the nonverbal child is later presented with vocal imitation.

Attending to Sound

Attending to sound means that the child is alerted to a sound such as a ringing bell or a clap for a period of time. On receiving the sound auditorily, the child should be able to turn head or eyes toward the source of the sound. This skill requires the child to focus for a brief period of time only. Longer sustained attention may be required and differentially reinforced in later training phases.

Responding to Name

This skill is initiated when the language practitioner says the child's name during the training session. The child is required to respond by initiating and maintaining brief eye contact with the trainer.

Attending to Objects

Attending to objects requires the child to respond with sustained eye contact to the command "Look," paired with a visual stimulus such as an object or a picture.

The child should be required to maintain eye contact with the object or picture for increasingly longer periods of time. Once a sustained focus is attained, it can be assumed that the child will be able to attend to the stimulus for a time period sufficient to initiate instruction in motor imitation.

Motor Imitation

Striefel (1974) established a rationale for developing imitation before beginning language training. Implied is the assumption that the child must be able to follow or imitate motor stimuli as a prerequisite to following verbal commands or responding verbally. Striefel stated that

> Speech training for a child who does not imitate is at very best a slow process in comparison with teaching a child who does imitate. The combination of imitation and comprehension helps a child learn to use speech in social situations. It is through imitation that a child increases his verbal and nonverbal skills in new situations. (p. 1)

Implicit in the process of motor imitation is bringing the behavior of the child under control and managing that behavior so that the language practitioner can later elicit verbal responses from the child. The steps of attending to sound, attending to name, attending to objects, and accomplishing motor imitation set the $S \rightarrow R \rightarrow S$ paradigm into action. They prepare the child for sitting in a language training session and working for a sustained period of time.

Motor imitation consists of an auditory command such as "Touch your head" or "Do this," paired with the visual model of the motor response to be learned. In this instance, the language practitioner would touch his/her own head. The child would be expected to imitate this motor response within a short time period—five seconds, for example. If the child does not respond with the appropriate response, the language practitioner would physically assist by holding the child's hand and placing it on top of the child's head. Proper reinforcement will increase the likelihood of the response occurring again. This process may need to be repeated until the child is able to make the motor response without assistance. Furthermore, the visual model should be faded until the child can respond and perform the motor task after only the auditory command. This establishes a pattern of response to auditory stimuli without a visual model.

Some typical motor imitation tasks include clapping, standing up, sitting down, dropping an object, and picking up an object. The language practitioner should make sure that these motor responses are clearly visible to the child. For this reason, the motor stimuli should be exaggerated movements so that the child can see the stimulus being modeled.

One problem the language practitioner may encounter in the motor imitation phase of language training is that of self-stimulatory behaviors. These behaviors, which serve as a stimulation to the child, may interfere with learning other motor responses. Motions such as exaggerated rocking, hand waving, and finger movements may inhibit or prevent the child from attending. Azrin, Kaplan, and Foxx (1973) have described methods for teaching specific appropriate motor responses that are incompatible with specific self-stimulatory behaviors.

In the process of teaching a repertoire of motor responses, the primary effect will be in establishing the readiness to imitate verbal language. The child will have learned to respond on request, will be able to attend to visual and auditory stimuli, and will be able to sit for increasingly longer periods of time without being distracted. Maintaining these prerequisite attending skills before the initiation of a program aimed at teaching vocal responses is an important element of language training.

Matching to Sample

The procedure of matching to sample requires the learner to show or point to an object or picture as requested by the language practitioner. Ruder (1978) described the procedure for training the child to match to a sample. The child is first shown a visual sample—an object or picture of an object. The child must first be trained to pick an identical object with no intervening stimuli with only one correct choice possible. After the child succeeds in matching with only the correct choice, other alternatives may be introduced until the child can select a matching object from among several diverse choices. Ruder also describes a process of introducing finer levels of discrimination among choices. For example, if the child were asked to match a ball, the objects first presented might include distractors with a physical appearance quite unlike the ball, such as a boat or a table. An identical ball would also be used as a choice for response, which in this case represents the correct selection. After the child matches objects using unlike distractors, the child may be presented with distractors more alike in size, shape, color, etc. An apple, a ball the same color but slightly smaller in size, and an identical ball might be used as choices. The child would have to discriminate between the choices and select the matching object. Figure 5-1 illustrates a four-step procedure in visual matching to sample. In addition, the child may be trained to match nearly identical objects, as well as identical objects, as a step in generalization training.

Matching to sample training can include matching to a visual sample as described above, or matching to an auditory sample, where the child is asked to respond to a verbal cue such as "Touch the ball." This procedure of teaching the child to make a receptive choice to different stimuli is a further refinement before the beginning of language training. It helps manage the behaviors of the child so that attention can be directed toward the language task at hand.

Implementation of a program to train these prespeech behaviors establishes readiness to attend and respond, vital skills needed before the implementation of a program designed to elicit vocal responses.

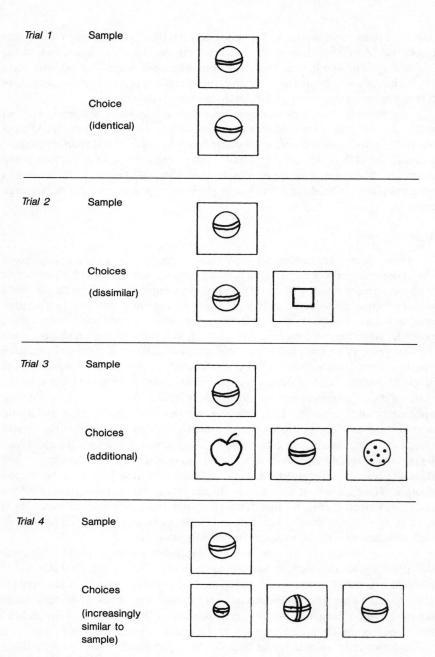

Figure 5-1 Matching to Visual Sample

PRAGMATIC PRESPEECH BEHAVIORS

Also of importance to note in this discussion of prespeech behaviors is the development of pragmatic precursors to speech. In an ecological assessment of communication, MacDonald and Gillette (1982) identified several components of pragmatic language and prelinguistic subskills.

Communicative Mode
The child communicates with

- body language
- sounds
- single words
- two- and four-word combinations
- sentences longer than four words

Interaction Conversation
The child interacts/communicates

- initiates contact
- responds to contact
- maintains contact

The child takes turns with actions for

- one or two turns
- three or more turns

The child takes turns with communication for

- one or two turns
- three or more turns

Communicative Content
The child communicates about

- self
- anything outside of self
- concrete experiences
- abstract experiences

- active experiences
- extends comment to topic

Communicative Use
The child communicates for

- personal reasons
- instrumental reasons
- social reasons

They emphasized that a child's language development occurs in a sequence from interactional to conversational skills, stressing progressive matches between the child's and adult's exchanges.

Sequence and Content

There are varying opinions with regard to the selection of content and sequence of a language training program. Miller and Yoder (1974) have developed a program that is semantically based. They indicated that when semantic intent is taken into account, child grammar approximates adult syntax. They stressed that the child's utterances are dependent on the child's experience and the context of the situation. They suggested that the content of a language intervention program for retarded children should be based on normal language acquisition. Furthermore, they stressed that the sequence of a program should be based on the sequence in which semantic relations are acquired. They advocated structuring the intervention process to provide for pairing a frequently occurring experience with the appropriate lexical marker. Once the child masters this, meaning can be extended to cover experiences expressing the same functions. Finally, they emphasized that expansions should be based on relations previously expressed in one-word relations.

Developmental research has long offered language practitioners a theoretical framework and a structure for instruction. However, when the content and sequence of an intervention program are being developed, one should keep in mind the changing developmental trends based on current research. DeVilliers and deVilliers (1978) caution against the dogmatic acceptance of a single developmental sequence, stating

All too frequently clinicians take a description of the course of normal acquisition as a prescription for the way language must be taught. But trends change, and what was once proposed as a necessary universal stage of development can become just one of several alternative strategies for acquiring language or merely an anachronism in theories of acquisition. (p. 270)

Guess, Sailor, and Baer (1974) advocated another view of content selection, stressing a more pragmatic base for language training. Their main focus was to teach language to the nonverbal retarded child. Consequently, they stressed learning functional words and phrases that would enable the child to operate in the environment. The emphasis was on training the child to label familiar persons and things as well as actions. Furthermore, the program developed expression within areas of possession, color, size, and relation—training useful in helping children specify their wants and needs.

Culatta (1976) took the position that the content of word classes in a language program for the retarded should be based on groups of objects, actions, and attributes familiar to the learner. Culatta stressed that the goal of a language program should be the generalization of skills leading to communication of novel events and that words for recurring similarities as they exist in the natural environment should form the core of words to be taught.

MacDonald and Blott (1974) made a significant contribution in proposing content and techniques of a language program for children with severe language delays. They proposed that language classes should be trained by specifying rules of position rather than traditional grammatical categories. They suggested that these two-word relationships represent the core content of their environmental language intervention strategy. Table 5-1 represents the rules of position in two-word utterances based on the work of MacDonald and Blott. Also included are examples or specific forms of these two-word relationships.

Furthermore, MacDonald and Blott sought to develop a diagnostic procedure based on two phases, first imitation and then conversation, to achieve generalization. They specified techniques for training with demonstration, which they termed the nonlinguistic environment, and verbal cues or the linguistic environment. For example, in teaching an action plus object, such as "throw ball," the language practitioner would provide a demonstration of throwing a ball paired with a verbal cue asking the child to imitate the phrase "throw ball." Then, by fading the verbal model and asking "Tell me what I am doing," the child would spontaneously produce the phrase "throw ball."

Holland (1975) specified what the content of the language intervention should include and how it can be made more meaningful to the child. She suggested that labeling for a child represents more than just object-word correspondence and that it serves as the child's functional way of expressing relationships. She stressed that a program should be child related, using words and activities reflecting the interests of children. She also stressed the egocentricity of children's language, recognizing that at a young age the concept "me" is of utmost importance.

Table 5-1 Rule Governed Relationships in Two-Word Utterances

Rule Governed Relationships	Examples
Agent + action	Mommy sit
Action + object	eat cookie
Agent + object	boy ball
X + locative	
entity + locative	ball table
action + locative	play there
Negation + X	
nonexistence	no milk—when there is none and child expects it
rejection	no bath—when child does not want the object
denial	no car—when child denies that an object is a car
Modifier + head	
attribution	big ball
possession	my book
recurrence	more play
Introducer + X	it train
	see kitty
X + dative	throw me

Holland saw language as reflecting present situations rather than past situations the child cannot relate to, and he noted that by participating in contextual learning situations in symbolic play, the child acquires a relevant vocabulary. She stressed giving the child opportunities to use language by limiting the size of the initial lexicon so that words can function in more than one grammatical slot. She suggested a core lexicon of 35 child centered words that can be combined to make a variety of two- and three-word phrases.

Lahey and Bloom (1977) suggested several considerations in addition to Holland's. They indicated that a first lexicon should include concepts that are easily demonstrated. Concepts like ''slide'' can be experienced firsthand and thus have more meaning to the child. They added that words that can be used in a number of contexts, or that have multiple applications, allow for more frequent use by the child and therefore should be used more by the language practitioner. They proposed that careful attention be given to choosing substantive words and, more importantly, relational words that are least object specific. They suggested that the language practitioner use this first lexicon and add words within classes and contexts.

Pragmatic language intervention places emphasis on increasing interactions of the nonverbal child. Muma (1978) suggested that the intervention goals for the nonverbal child are to

- establish a desire to communicate
- identify and increase the number of vocalizations

- vary the vocalizations or establish a repertoire of alternative vocalizations and functions
- elicit purposeful naming behavior at the one- and two-word levels. (p. 276)

McCormick and Goldman (1984) further specified programming goals for early intervention. Using the work of Dore (1974), Bates (1976), and Dore (1977), they developed a sequence of training objectives for the limited language child.

For the Preverbal Child

1. **Requesting** an object, action, or information
2. **Greeting** someone entering the immediate environment
3. **Giving** an object to another person
4. **Showing** off an action or object to another person
5. **Acknowledging** receipt of another person's message
6. **Responding/Answering** another person's request

For the Single-Word Level Child

1. **Labeling** an object or event with a word or word approximation while looking at it
2. **Repeating** part or all of a previous adult utterance
3. **Answering** adult's questions
4. **Requesting** an object, action, or information with a word or vocalization
5. **Calling** adult's name loudly and waiting for a response
6. **Greeting** an adult or object
7. **Protesting** an adult's action with a word or cry
8. **Practicing** word prosodic patterns (in absence of specific object or event)

For the Multiword Level Child

1. **Requesting** information, action, or acknowledgment
2. **Responding** to requests
3. **Describing** past and present events
4. **Stating** facts, rules, attitudes, feelings, and beliefs; evaluating
5. **Acknowledging** and evaluating responses and nonrequests
6. **Regulating** contact and conversation
7. **Accomplishing** acts (e.g., warning, teasing, protesting) (p. 217)

There is a variety of opinions determining the content of language intervention programs. The language practitioner must assess the relative merits of these programs with their varying sequences and content, keeping in mind the different language problems of the children in the training program. No one program is the answer to the needs of all children. On consideration of the different language deficits, differences in learning modes, and differences in interest levels of children, it would seem more reasonable to draw from several programs to address specific needs.

Ruder and Smith (1974) suggested the adoption of a battery of programs, stressing that individual differences in children provide the basic rationale for selection of several language programs. They stated

> That is, when one considers the diversity and scope of the language problems encountered, it is naive to assume that a single language program has been, or will be, devised which is capable of handling such a diversity of problems and individual differences in as efficient a manner as would a battery of language training programs which are geared and individualized to meet a particular child's language deficiencies and communicative needs. (p. 599)

Generalization

The language practitioner must provide methods to train and evaluate generalization of language learning.

Inherent in any language training program is the problem of ensuring that the child generalizes to spontaneous language what is learned in training. Often, training programs fail to provide for generalization training and for the evaluation of the transfer of language learning. The language practitioner frequently teaches a child a language construction, achieving an acceptable level of competency, and then complacently continues to the next construction the child needs to develop. This error in language training may lead to only short term attainment of the language construction. If the language practitioner were to accept one time only evaluation results as the sole method for determining that the child had indeed achieved the mastery of a language skill, a serious mistake would be made. The language practitioner must build into the language training process a method of training and evaluating long term maintenance of skills.

Siegel and Spradlin (1978) stated the rationale for generalization training

> The therapist or teacher who trains speech or language makes the assumption that his efforts will have an effect on the child's communication outside the training situation; otherwise, there would be no reason to engage in the training since it is usually an artificial intervention into the child's life, with no inherent value. The problem of training speech or language so that its use will generalize into natural settings raises

many issues concerning the nature of teaching and of natural settings. (p. 388)

Guess, Keogh, and Sailor (1978) recognized that there are a number of socioecological variables that affect the individual's ability to generalize language. They stated that the child's ability to generalize language is dependent on the interaction between these environmental variables and the nature of the language competency in the child. They established four basic assumptions that guide and govern generalization of language.

1. Generalization to the natural environment is a function of the child's complement of language. The degree to which a child uses language is heavily influenced by his existing language repertoire. Children with meager language expression have little opportunity to take advantage of environmental events that serve as stimuli for verbal expression. Systematic language training is one avenue for producing generalization by increasing the child's ability to respond to language stimuli when they occur.
2. Generalization is a function of environmental opportunities for verbal expression. Very little is known about what, from the child's point of view, may constitute an appropriate opportunity for verbal expression. It is fairly easy to compare environments with respect to any number of physical properties that serve as stimuli for generalized language use. The term "stimulating" is used frequently to describe various environments. Yet, it is likely that stimulation is defined more from the perspective of adults than from the actual behavior of the child.
3. Generalization is a function of both programmed and natural contingencies in the environment. The extent to which a child uses language depends on the reinforcing consequences that follow. This is an area of analysis with unlimited research opportunities. The central issue is to define and measure reinforcing consequences for language use across environments and as a function of the systematic manipulations of key variables within the same environment. What, indeed, are the major variables within an environment that serve to reinforce language? How do these variables interact with the child's existing level of language competence? What types of language skills need to be taught to increase the probability that a child's utterances will be reinforced?
4. Generalization is a function of the degree of similarity between the training environment and the generalization setting. This assumption must take into consideration both the similarity between the physical

> properties of the training environment and the generalization setting, as well as the similarity between the content taught and the frequency with which that same content is present in the generalization setting. (p. 392)

With these assumptions in mind, several programming techniques for generalization may now be examined.

Whitney and Striefel (1980) provided a rationale and plan for including generalization training as an integral part of the instructional procedure. They stated

> In a recently completed comprehensive review of some 270 studies concerning generalization, over half of the studies reviewed focused on the observation of generalization but did nothing to program its occurrence. The review concluded that generalization could not be expected unless procedures were implemented during training to program its occurrence. One of the methods of programming generalization, identified in this review, involves the training of sufficient examples. When acquisition of a skill occurs in a training setting, a number of examples of the skill (e.g., the presentation of the skill in different settings, with different persons, and/or responses) are trained in order to produce generalization across all of the settings, persons, and/or responses that were identified prior to training. Training can be terminated when a "sufficient" number of examples have been trained across identified settings, persons, and/or responses so that correct responding occurs to new settings, persons, and/or responses without any direct training. (p. 3)

They provided a graphic representation of how this generalization can be trained across three settings and three persons. Figure 5-2 represents a generalization matrix and procedure for the teacher, therapist, or parent who is responsible for training in the educational setting, the therapy room, and the child's home.

Other authors have included a generalization component within the language training program. One such example is the *Functional Speech and Language Training for the Severely Handicapped,* by Guess et al. (1977). Each training step in this program contains "programming for generalization" suggestions for the parent or surrogate parent.

Similarly, MacDonald et al. (1978) included generalization training by providing for the transition from imitation to spontaneous language through fading imitative cues. This resulted in the child's production of the target construction in conversation.

Mowery and Replogle (1977) have also provided a systematic way of training for generalization. By differentiating five levels of eliciting response, they sug-

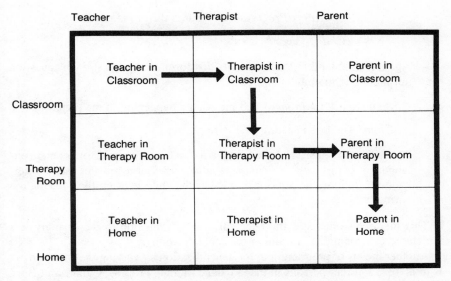

Figure 5-2 Generalization Matrix. *Source:* From "Functionality and Generalization in Training Severely and Profoundly Handicapped Children" by Richard Whitney and Sebastian Striefel, 1980, *Exceptional News, 3*[2]. Copyright 1980 by Utah State University. Reprinted by permission.

gested that there is a hierarchy of steps that lead to generalization of language constructions.

1. At the first step the language practitioner provides an imitative model of the target response, requiring an imitative response from the child.

   Language Practitioner: The boy is eating.

   Child: The boy is eating.

2. In the second step the language practitioner gives the verbal model, but follows it with intervening language so that there is a delay between the model and the child's response.

   Language Practitioner: The boy is eating. Tell me about the boy, or
   The boy is eating. What is the boy doing?

   Child: The boy is eating.

3. In step three, imbedding is used, where the target construction appears in an alternate form, such as a question.

Language Practitioner: What is the boy doing?

Child: The boy is eating.

4. Again the model is not offered in its first form. Instead, a stimulus question not including the model is used.

Language Practitioner: Tell me what's happening in the picture.

Child: The boy is eating.

5. The fifth step consists of providing a natural environment for spontaneous language. In this environment the language practitioner makes use of observation techniques to determine whether the child is using the construction correctly.

This hierarchy illustrates the need for careful transition to increasingly less structured environments in training for generalization.

Another means of programming for generalization by varying the environment is to involve familiar persons in the language training process. Culatta and Horn (1979) developed a process to teach parents to record language samples at home. These samples were designed to check generalization in the natural environment.

Similarly, Cole and Henrich (1980) conducted a three-component program designed to train for and evaluate transfer of language skills by language delayed and hearing impaired students. Their procedure trained for language generalization in the classroom setting, the community, and the home environment.

In addition to programming for generalization, there is some conviction that the content of a language program itself may determine whether language is generalized. Mahoney (1975), in proposing an ethological approach to language programming, suggested that children's rates of acquisition are determined by the nature of their interactions with their environment and that failure to generalize imitative speech into spontaneous utterances may be because the language program and the content of the language curriculum have neglected to represent children's interests and information structure.

Therefore, evidence suggests that generalization training should be an integral component of any language intervention program. Generalization probes, operant techniques, programming for transfer, and careful attention to content all contribute to the effectiveness of the language program. Furthermore, generalization probes should be included in the training process so that an accurate evaluation of mastery of skills can be attained.

Task Analysis in Language Programming

To the greatest extent possible, the language curriculum should be task analyzed to provide for continuous progress along the language continuum.

Task analysis refers to dividing an instructional task into its smaller constituent parts. Implied in this process is the assumption that a complex skill or task can be more easily learned if it is broken down into smaller units.

Several researchers have pointed out the benefits of task analysis. Thiagarajan, Semmel, and Semmel (1974) stressed that task analysis can suggest a sequence for instruction and the materials to be used for instruction, and that it lends itself to measuring entry level skills as well as progress. Gold (1976) reported significant results in the use of task analysis to break down complex skills for retarded blind children. Fredericks, Anderson, and Baldwin (1978) likewise pointed to task analysis as a factor in the achievement of severely handicapped students.

Similarly, task analysis holds a promise for language intervention programs for the nonverbal child. It provides a procedure to miniaturize the learning task into "learnable" units. There are two types of task analysis commonly found in language curricula. The first is illustrated by programs that sequence the elements within the language training process. For example, the objectives that form the child's program are sequenced from the least difficult to the most complex, forming a hierarchy of language constructions. Judgment of the complexity of the elements is usually based on developmental sequences. The normal child, for example, first develops one-word responses, then two-word strings of seemingly unrelated words. The normal child then moves to two-word syntactic constructions, where semantic intent is noted. A program for the nonverbal child may be sequenced along this hierarchy, forming a logical order for learning language construction.

Second, a specific language skill may be task analyzed, breaking down the task even further. For example, if the child were working on the syntactical development of a simple declarative sentence using a noun and a present progressive verb, such as "The boy is running," the instructional sequence aimed at teaching the child to elicit that sentence may be further divided into parts.

More specifically, the language practitioner may ask the child to imitate the noun phrase—"the boy" in this sentence—varying the nouns used—"the girl," "the dog," "the cat," "the man," etc. Once imitation of the noun phrase is under control and the child has met criterion, the language practitioner may work on the verb phrase of the sentence "is running." Again, variations may be introduced to produce different verbs such as "is sitting," "is eating," "is walking," etc. It is important to note here that in a task analyzed program, these two elements, the noun phrase and the verb phrase, would have already been taught in previous objectives, perhaps as two-word strings or two-word syntactic constructions.

Once the two elements have been initiated separately and each brought to criterion, phrases may be combined into the target sentence. The child may then be asked to imitate the sentence and required to meet criterion on it.

Next, the child may move through a series of steps, with the language practitioner progressively reducing the verbal model so that the child is able to respond to a question such as "What is the boy doing?"

An example of such a highly task analyzed program is the *Curriculum and Monitoring System Expressive Language Program*, authored by Douglass and Baer (1977).

Data Collection

Language programming for the nonverbal child should provide direct observation and measurement of the attainment of stated objectives. In an effort to provide a systematic orderly progression in the development of language for the nonverbal child, the language practitioner must document and substantiate achievement and learning.

Proper data collection can indicate progress or the lack of progress by the individual. This information has several uses. First, it can lead to a reevaluation of the instructional method used, the relative success of a particular program, or the strengths and weaknesses of specific reinforcers. It can pinpoint the exact place of difficulty for the child so that time is not lost using ineffective intervention strategies. Second, data collection can provide substantiation for communicating progress to parents and other professionals involved in training the child. Third, data can be utilized to substantiate the completion of objectives stated on the Individualized Language Plan (ILP) or the Individualized Education Program (IEP).

Waryas and Stremel-Campbell (1978) provided a focus for analyzing language programming data. They stated

> In deciding if a program is appropriate for a specific student, an ongoing evaluation must be made. The trainer must determine whether each program step is appropriate, if branching steps are needed, or if the student indeed requires each step. To make these decisions, not only must the trainer record data, but that data must also be analyzed. The data analysis and comparative data should provide answers to the following questions.
>
> • Is the student acquiring the behavior in a consistent manner?
> • What is the rate of acquisition?
> • When is the student failing? (p. 185)

Answering these questions by analyzing data would certainly give the language practitioner firm grounds on which to base programming decisions.

Program Format and Strategies

In an effort to help the child achieve maximum language development, the program format and strategies to be used in the instructional process should be chosen on the basis of their proven effectiveness and support by practitioners and researchers in the field.

The use of operant procedures; the relationships between imitation, comprehension, and production; and the techniques of modeling and expansion are all important issues in determining the format to be used in the language intervention process.

Operant Techniques in Language Training

B.F. Skinner, in *Verbal Behavior* (1957), proposed a theoretical framework that initiated an abundance of research on the effects of operant conditioning on language development. Skinner indicated that verbal behavior was a repertoire of responses under the control of environmental variables. These variables included mediation by other persons who selectively reinforce the verbal behaviors of others. He stressed the importance of reinforcing consequences not only as the individual acquires language, but as reinforcement affects verbal behavior after language has been acquired. He stated

> Operant reinforcement, then, is simply a way of controlling the probability of occurrence of a certain class of verbal responses. If we wish to make a response of given form highly probable we arrange for the effective reinforcement of many instances. If we wish to eliminate it from a verbal repertoire, we arrange that reinforcement shall no longer follow. Any information regarding the relative frequency of reinforcement characteristic of a given verbal community is obviously valuable in predicting such behavior. (p. 30)

Many researchers and practitioners have taken this theoretical framework and applied it to research and practice in language training. Operant procedures have been used to determine the effects of reinforcement on acquiring syntax, morphological development, and phonological and semantic acquisition. The efficacy of operant procedures in language training is well documented in the literature. Researchers such as Garcia, Guess, and Byrnes (1973); Rees (1975); Hester and Hendrickson (1976); and Gray and Ryan (1973) have indicated that operant procedures utilizing techniques of imitation, modeling, and reinforcement are effective in helping the child acquire various language constructions.

Ruder and Smith (1974) summarized the concurrence of research in this manner.

> It is sufficient to say that the general consensus of opinion is that the basic operant or behavior modification paradigm segmenting the clinical interaction into three classes of events (antecedent, response, and subsequent events) constitutes a powerful methodology for language intervention. (p. 580)

Therefore, the language practitioner who plans and implements a language intervention program would be wise to include operant techniques to ensure success. Chapter 4 deals more specifically with the S→ R→ S paradigm and how it can be utilized to elicit verbal responses in a language acquisition program.

Imitation, Comprehension, and Production

For the nonverbal child acquiring a first language, the process of imitation provides a vehicle for enabling the child to initiate a response for the first time. Though language researchers have long debated the relative merits of imitation in language training, one finds a variety of views on the definition of imitation. For some, it means the verbatim or echoic repeating of the verbal model immediately preceding it. For others, imitation may be more broadly interpreted, allowing for the partial mirroring of length, order, complexity, and aspects of structure. In such cases, imitation can be interpreted as a process for obtaining behaviors, especially verbal behaviors in which the nonverbal child is being trained.

In the broadest sense, imitation also serves as a technique for managing behavior. It functions as an effective means of training the prespeech behaviors noted earlier in this chapter.

The efficacy of imitation as a training device, therefore, would seem to vary according to the definition one chooses to accept. If imitation is seen in the narrow sense as an exact repetition of a response, then its exclusive use in language training would be limiting. One can readily see the problems that would be incurred in using imitation as the sole methodological tool in language training. Elicited imitation of sounds, words, phrases, and sentences in a language program, if not accompanied by the programmed transfer to spontaneous speech and/ or comprehension training, can result in the child's failure to generalize learning and, in effect, hinder language development.

If, on the other hand, the broader definition of imitation is accepted, i.e., a process of initiating verbal and nonverbal behaviors in training, then its use increases. One cannot deny that, in this sense, imitation is a powerful tool in helping some children acquire a verbal repertoire.

The effectiveness of imitation as a methodological tool in language training increases with the inclusion of comprehension training. Comprehension, according to Chapman (1974), refers to the process by which listeners obtain meaning from utterances. Training to increase the child's receptive base aids the child in understanding the semantic relationships included in verbal expression. Comprehension training, when coupled with imitation, increases the likelihood of production of verbal responses.

Modeling and Expansion

Modeling as a technique in initiating the S → R→ S paradigm is a means of providing the child with an example of the desired appropriate behavior. It specifies for the child what verbal response is required. In modeling, the language practitioner identifies the target construction that the child is required to produce by vocalizing it. For example, if the child is working on two-word phrases using an adjective and a noun in combination, the language practitioner may model the phrase in this manner. "This is a red ball, Billy. Red ball." Red ball, in this instance, is the construction that the language practitioner wishes the child to produce and, thus, constitutes the model for the child.

Expansion refers to enlarging the child's response. Using the child's utterance, the language practitioner develops it into a grammatically complete sentence. For example, if the child says "Cat eat," the language practitioner would expand this two-word phrase into a more grammatically correct sentence by saying "The cat is eating." In this instance, the language practitioner preserves the word order and meaning intended by the child, but expands it into a more complete utterance.

Schumaker and Sherman (1978) pointed to the potential use of expansion, a natural technique available to parents as intervention agents in the language development process.

Ruder and Smith (1974) reported the results of a study in which the technique of expansion to the next level of language construction was found to be successful for aiding the child in producing some linguistic structures. They stated

> Suffice it to say that even if expansion can be utilized effectively for only a limited number of structures, the data seem sufficiently clear to indicate that this is probably a useful technique for language training, at least until further data contradict use of such a procedure. (p. 593)

In summary, there are techniques available to the language practitioner that will enable the child to achieve maximum results from language training. Operant procedures, imitation, modeling, and expansion should be considered as tools for eliciting the production of oral language. The role or extent to which any of these techniques is used in language training should be based on its relative effectiveness in achieving the desired results.

LANGUAGE PROGRAMMING FOR THE NONVERBAL CHILD

It is beyond the scope of this work to provide a complete language program for the nonverbal child. Such a program requires years of development, implementation, and field testing before a final product can claim to achieve the desired results. However, the authors will contribute suggestions for the content of a language intervention program. These suggestions will include a potential outline of the sequence and content as well as a structure for implementation. The intent of this program structure is to provide guidelines for the language practitioner so that

A language intervention sequence for the nonverbal child
and the pragmatic precursors to speech
located in
Teaching the Nonverbal Child
(Chapter 5)

↓

Remediating problems of form, function, and style
located in
Remediating Specific Language Problems
(Chapter 6)

↓

Enhancing the communicative and cognitive
processes through enrichment
located in
Language Activities for Enrichment
(Chapter 7)

Figure 5-3 An Outline for Language Intervention

an individualized program can be tailored to suit the needs of the nonverbal child.

Figure 5-3 represents an outline for language intervention and is designed for the nonverbal child and the language delayed child. It ranges in its scope from preverbal attending skills to simple declarative sentences using primarily present progressive verbs. Teaching transformations and morphological changes in sentence patterns will be included in Chapter 6.

Similarly, remediating specific language problems precedes the extension of language programming into the broader development of language skills. Chapter 7 represents an expansion and refinement of language skills.

This book presents to the reader a three-component hierarchy in developing language skills, as illustrated in Figure 5-3.

A language intervention sequence (Exhibit 5-1) has been included as a suggested base for initiating language instruction. It details a broad sequence of skills based on developmental data. Within each level, the constructions included are not intended to be placed in a rigid sequence. The language practitioner implementing the training should use professional discretion in determining priority areas for any particular child. However, the levels represent a hierarchy of skills arranged in order from the least complex level to the most complex. Training prespeech behaviors is a prerequisite step to the receptive skills (level two) included in the outline, which in turn precedes level three, expressive skills. Similarly, one-word phrase production precedes two- and three-word phrases and sentences.

It is suggested that this sequence be used as a base for teaching the nonverbal child. It is intended as a starting point for instruction along developmental language milestones. Should the language practitioner determine from the data collected that the child is not progressing as rapidly as expected, it may be

Exhibit 5-1 A Language Intervention Sequence for the Nonverbal Child

1. *Training Prespeech Behaviors*
   1.1 Attends to sound
   1.2 Responds to name
   1.3 Attends to object
   1.4 Imitates motor responses
   1.5 Matches to visual sample
   1.6 Matches to auditory sample
2. *Reception*
   2.1 Responds to commands
   2.2 Responds to agents (nouns)
   2.3 Responds to actions (verbs)
   2.4 Responds to objects (nouns)
   2.5 Responds to prepositional placement
3. *Expression*
   3.1 Produces single sounds
   3.2 Produces consonant-vowel combinations
   3.3 Produces one-word phrases
       3.3.1 agents
       3.3.2 actions
       3.3.3 objects
       3.3.4 modifiers
   3.4 Produces two-word combinations
       3.4.1 agent-action (boy fall)
       3.4.2 action-object (eat apple)
       3.4.3 agent-object (boy apple)
       3.4.4 modifier-object (big ball)
       3.4.5 object-locater (book there)
       3.4.6 demonstrator-object (that kitty)
       3.4.7 quantifier-object (more juice)
       3.4.8 article-agent or object (a ball)
       3.4.9 possessive-object (my milk)
       3.4.10 preposition-object (on table)
   3.5 Produces three-word combinations
       3.5.1 agent-action-object (boy hit ball)
       3.5.2 action-modifier-object (ride big bike)
       3.5.3 article-modifier-object (the big dog)
       3.5.4 possessive-modifier-object (my blue bus)
       3.5.5 preposition-article-object (on the chair)
       3.5.6 pronoun agent-action-object (she hit ball)
       3.5.7 agent-action-pronoun as object (girl see him)
   3.6 Produces simple declarative sentences
       3.6.1 article-agent-auxiliary is-present progressive action (The boy is eating.)
       3.6.2 pronoun-auxiliary is-present progressive action (He is running.)
       3.6.3 article-agent-copula is-modifier (The man is happy.)
       3.6.4 article-agent-copula is-locater (The girl is here.)
       3.6.5 pronoun-action-article-object (I eat the cookie.)
       3.6.6 article-agent-auxiliary is-present progressive action-article-object (The man is writing a letter.)
       3.6.7 article-agent-auxiliary is-present progressive action-preposition-article-object (The man is walking on the road.)

necessary to provide branching steps to bridge the gap between the steps and/or levels.

The structure for conducting a language program is also provided to facilitate language instruction. Exhibit 5-2 provides the program structure.

The structure for language intervention places great emphasis on a functional format to be used in actual language training as a system for monitoring all relevant instructional information. It includes space for the objectives, the stimulus to be provided by the language practitioner, the responses required from the child, a place for monitoring the accuracy level for each step of the program, modifications necessary in training, and space for the environmental conditions and/or dates of generalization probes. The language practitioner is encouraged to use it as a working document for intervention and evaluation.

In the structure for language intervention, the level of language training is entered at the top of the page. Likewise, the reinforcer is included so that the language practitioner can monitor the reinforcers used in each step of the program. This gives information on the relative strength or effectiveness of reinforcers used with the child.

The "Objective" column is included so that the language practitioner knows the specific observable behavior sought. It represents the terminal step in the elicitation of a response and should be task analyzed to provide for mastery at each step. The criterion for mastery is included in the objective. It represents the number of correct responses required to consider the language objective completed. It is usually stated in a percentage of accuracy, for rapid comparison with the column "Percentage Correct." "Stimulus" refers to the specific event, either auditory, visual, or both, which the language practitioner must use to elicit a response.

The "Response" column refers to the exact motor or verbal behavior required of the child. It may be considered a behavior necessary for continuation to the next objective.

The "Percentage Correct" column is summarized from daily data sheets used to monitor progress continuously. (For a discussion of methods of collecting data, see Chapter 4.) The date the objective is passed may be noted under this column, along with the final percentage of correct responses attained by the child on that step.

Included under the column labeled "Modifications" is space for the language practitioner to record changes made in the child's program. Modifications to be noted in this column may include (1) branching steps necessary for the child's transition to the next, more complex step; (2) changes in reinforcers; (3) elimination of steps found to be unnecessary for a particular child; and (4) changes in the stimulus presented to the child.

The column labeled "Generalization Probes" is included so that the language practitioner can determine at later dates whether the child has maintained the skills

Exhibit 5-2 A Structure for Language Intervention

Level			Reinforcer			
Objective	*Stimulus*	*Response*	*Percentage Correct*	*Modifications*	*Generalization Probes*

taught previously. The three spaces provided represent dates and/or a description of the environmental events surrounding the probe.

Appendix 5A, following this chapter, is a suggested language intervention program for the nonverbal child. It combines the sequence of proposed content (Exhibit 5-1) within the structure of training (Exhibit 5-2).

Appendix 5B includes intervention techniques stressing pragmatic use of language. It differs from the intervention program in Appendix 5A in that it provides a less formal structure for eliciting pragmatic precursors to speech. It develops pragmatic subskills within the contextual environment of informal interactions between the child and the language practitioner. The pragmatic intervention program includes two components: the objective and the suggested activities to elicit the pragmatic subskills. The objectives include the use of language for the child's instrumental purposes, for social use, and for the child's personal use.

The authors stress that these programs provide the language practitioner with only an initial base for language training. Additional task analysis of each objective may be necessary to individualize language training for a specific child.

SUMMARY

The process of teaching the nonverbal child requires planning and organization. The language practitioner must consider program goals and guidelines for early intervention, the development of prespeech behavior, the sequence and content of the language intervention, and generalization training. Furthermore, the language practitioner must be aware of the importance of task analysis and data collection in language programming as well as issues in program format and procedures. All of these variables determine the effectiveness of language training for the nonverbal child.

Structure and intervention sequences are provided for the language practitioner. Likewise, two suggested programs are offered for use in teaching language to the nonverbal child. The language practitioner is encouraged to use these programs as a base for initiating language training, modifying them to include priorities for the individual child.

REFERENCES

Apgar, V. (1953). A proposal for a new method of evaluation of the newborn infant. *Current Research in Anesthesia and Analgesia, 32,* 260.

Azrin, N., Kaplan, S.J., & Foxx, R. (1973). Autism reversal: Eliminating stereotyped stimulation of retarded individuals. *American Journal of Mental Deficiency, 78,* 241.

Bates, E. (1976). *Language and context.* New York: Academic Press.

Bricker, W., & Bricker, D. (1974). An early language training strategy. In R.L. Schiefelbusch and L. Lloyd (Eds.), *Language perspectives—acquisition, retardation, and intervention* (p. 444). Baltimore, MD: University Park Press.

Chapman, R. (1974). Discussion summary—developmental relationship between receptive and expressive language. In R.L. Schiefelbusch & L. Lloyd (Eds.), *Language perspectives—acquisition, retardation, and intervention* (p. 336). Baltimore, MD: University Park Press.

Cole, M.L., & Henrich, V. (1980). *Cross categorical programming for the language impaired/ hearing impaired in a rural setting.* Paper presented at the 58th Annual International Convention of the Council for Exceptional Children, Philadelphia, PA.

Culatta, B. (1976). *A conceptually based approach to teaching language to retarded children.* Paper presented at the Kentucky Interdisciplinary Conference on Linguistics, Lexington, KY.

Culatta, V., & Horn, D. (1979). Parent-recorded language samples: A method to analyze communicative ability in language disordered children. *Journal of Childhood Communication Disorders, III,* 16–27.

DeVilliers, J., & deVilliers, P. (1978). *Language acquisition* (p. 270). Cambridge, MA: Harvard University Press.

Dore, J. (1974). A pragmatic description of early language development, *Journal of Psycholinguistic Research, 3,* 343–350.

Dore, J. (1977). Children's illocutionary acts. In R. Freedle (Ed.), *Discourse Relations: Comprehension and production.* Hillsdale, NJ: Lawrence Earlbaum Associates.

Douglass, V., & Baer, R. (1977). *Curriculum and monitoring system expressive language program training manual* (p. 21). New York: Walker Book.

Fredericks, H.D., Anderson, R., & Baldwin, V. (1978). *The identification of competency indicators of teachers of the severely handicapped.* Monmouth, OR: Teaching Research.

Garcia, E., Guess, D., & Byrnes, J. (1973). Development of syntax in a retarded girl using procedures of imitation, reinforcement, and modeling. *Journal of Applied Behavior Analysis, 6,* 299–310.

Gold, M. (1976). Task analysis of a complex assembly task by the retarded blind. *Exceptional Children, 43,* 78–84.

Gray, B., & Ryan, B. (1973). *A language program for the nonlanguage child* (p. 9). Champaign, IL: Research Press.

Guess, D., Keogh, W., & Sailor, W. (1978). Generalization of speech and language behavior. In R.L. Schiefelbusch (Ed.), *Language intervention strategies* (p. 388). Baltimore, MD: University Park Press.

Guess, D., Sailor, W., & Baer, D. (1974). To teach language to retarded children. In R.L. Schiefelbusch & L. Lloyd (Eds.), *Language perspectives—acquisition, retardation and intervention* (p. 550). Baltimore, MD: University Park Press.

Guess, D., Sailor, W., & Baer, D. (1977). *Functional speech and language training for the severely handicapped.* Part I (p. 4). Lawrence, KS: H & H Enterprises.

Hester, P., & Hendrickson, J. (1976). *A language training strategy for teaching young language delayed children—A functional syntactical form.* Paper presented at the 56th International Convention of the Council for Exceptional Children, Chicago, IL.

Holland, A. (1975). Language therapy for children: Some thoughts on context and content. *Journal of Speech and Hearing Disorders, 40,* 514–523.

Lahey, M., & Bloom, L. (1977). Planning a first lexicon: Which words to teach first. *Journal of Speech and Hearing Disorders, 42,* 340–350.

Lennenberg, E. (1967). *Biological foundations of language* (p. 179). New York: John Wiley and Sons.

MacDonald, J.D., & Blott, J. (1974). Environmental language intervention: The rationale for a diagnostic and training strategy through rules, context, and generalization. *Journal of Speech and Hearing Disorders, 39,* 244–256.

MacDonald, J.D., & Gillette, Y. (1982). *ECO Maps. Ecological communication assessment of adult-child conversations*. Columbus, OH: The Nisonger Center.

MacDonald, J.D. et al. (1978). An experimental parent assisted treatment program for preschool language delayed children. In M. Lahey (Ed.), *Readings in childhood language disorders* (p. 327). New York: John Wiley and Sons.

Mahoney, G. (1975). Ethological approach to delayed language acquisition. *American Journal of Mental Deficiency, 80,* 139–148.

McCormick, L., & Goldman, R. (1984). Developing an optimal learning program. In L. McCormick & R.L. Schiefelbusch (Eds.), *Early language intervention* (p. 217). Columbus, OH: Charles E. Merrill Publishing.

Miller, J., & Yoder, D. (1974). An ontogenetic language teaching strategy for retarded children. In R.L. Schiefelbusch & L. Lloyd (Eds.), *Language perspectives—acquisition, retardation, and intervention* (p. 503–528). Baltimore, MD: University Park Press.

Mowery, C., & Replogle, A. (1977). *Developmental language lessons* (p. 19). Boston, MA: Teaching Resources.

Muma, J.R. (1978). *Language handbook: Concepts, assessment, intervention*. Englewood Cliffs, NJ: Prentice-Hall.

Rees, N. (1975). Imitation and language development: Issues and clinical implications. *Journal of Speech and Hearing Disorders, 40,* 339–350.

Ruder, K. (1978). Planning and programming for language intervention. In R.L. Schiefelbusch (Ed.), *Bases of language intervention* (p. 341). Baltimore, MD: University Park Press.

Ruder, K., & Smith, M. (1974). Issues in language training. In R.L. Schiefelbusch & L. Lloyd (Eds.), *Language perspectives—acquisition, retardation, and intervention* (p. 599). Baltimore, MD: University Park Press.

Schumaker, J.B., & Sherman, J. (1978). Parent as intervention agent. In R.L. Schiefelbusch (Ed.), *Language intervention strategies* (p. 301). Baltimore, MD: University Park Press.

Siegel, G., & Spradlin, J. (1978). Programming for language and communication therapy. In R.L. Schiefelbusch (Ed.), *Language intervention strategies* (p. 388). Baltimore, MD: University Park Press.

Skinner, B.F. (1957). *Verbal behavior* (p. 30). New York: Appleton-Century-Crofts.

Striefel, S. (1974). *Behavior modification: Teaching the child to imitate* (p. 1). Lawrence, KS: H & H Enterprises.

Thiagarajan, S., Semmel, D., & Semmel, M. (1974). *Instructional development for training teachers of exceptional children* (p. 31). Bloomington, IN: Center for Innovation in Teaching the Handicapped.

Waryas, C.L., & Stremel-Campbell, K. (1978). Grammatical training for the language delayed child. In R.L. Schiefelbusch (Ed.), *Language intervention strategies* (p. 185). Baltimore, MD: University Park Press.

Whitney, R., & Striefel, S. (1980). Functionality and generalization in training severely and profoundly handicapped children. *Exceptional News, 3,* 2–3.

Language Intervention for the Nonverbal Child

Level 1. Training Prespeech Behaviors

Objective	Stimulus	Response
1.1 *Attends to sound.* Given the sound of a buzzer, bell, or clap, child will turn his head toward the source of the sound in 9 of 10 trials.	1.1 Language Practitioner (L.P.) and child are seated face to face. L.P. uses an object such as a bell to make a sound. L.P. waits 5 seconds for child to turn head and eyes toward source of the sound.	1.1 Child turns head and eyes toward the source of sound. If child does not respond, physical assistance should be given by placing a hand on child's chin and gently turning it toward the source.
1.2 *Responds to name.* Given a verbal stimulus "Look, name," child will turn head and eyes toward person giving the stimulus in 9 of 10 trials.	1.2 Seated facing child, L.P. says "Look, name" (entering child's name in the appropriate place).	1.2 Child turns head and eyes toward L.P. If no response, L.P. should gently turn child's head and give physical assistance.
1.3 *Attends to object.* Given a visual stimulus and the verbal request "Look," child will turn toward the object in 9 of 10 trials.	1.3 A toy car, doll, block, or other interesting object is held up in front of child. L.P. accompanies the visual stimulus with the auditory stimulus "Look." Suggested objects include toy car toy boat doll cookie block juice balloon pencil ball flashlight	1.3 Child should focus on the object within 5 seconds. If child does not respond, L.P. should assist child in turning toward the object.
1.4 *Imitates motor responses.* Given a visual model of a motor skill, child will imitate motor skill in 9 of 10 trials.	1.4 L.P. gives child a model of motor response child is to imitate. L.P. accompanies visual model with a verbal cue "*Child's name*, do	1.4 Child imitates the motor model within 5 seconds. If child does not respond, L.P. should give physical assistance in initiating the motor behavior.

Reinforcer _____

Percentage Correct	Modifications	Generalization Probes
Date _____ % Correct _____		1. 2. 3.
Date _____ % Correct _____		1. 2. 3.
Date _____ % Correct _____		1. 2. 3.
Date _____ % Correct _____		1. 2. 3.

Level 1. Training Prespeech Behaviors

Objective	Stimulus	Response
	this.'' Examples of motor behaviors to be trained are standing up sitting down touching the head opening the mouth hopping on both feet	
1.5 *Matches to visual sample.* Given an object or picture, child will point to an identical object among 3 choices with 100 percent accuracy.	1.5.1 L.P. places 3 objects on table. L.P. holds up a sample object and presents the verbal stimulus "Find one like this." Distractors should first be dissimilar objects. As child masters matching to sample at this level, the visual differences among distracters call for finer discriminations.	1.5.1 Child will point to appropriate object within 5 seconds. If child does not respond, L.P. gives physical assistance by placing child's hand on the correct object.
	1.5.2 L.P. places three pictures on table. L.P. holds up a stimulus picture and says "Find one like this."	1.5.2 Child points to appropriate picture within 5 seconds. If no response, L.P. should physically assist child in finding the correct picture.
1.6 *Matches to auditory sample.* Given 3 objects and an auditory request "Find the _____,'' child will point to correct object with 100 percent accuracy.	1.6.1 L.P. places 3 objects on table. Common objects may be used, such as a ball, block, book, or a cup. L.P. says "Find the ball."	1.6.1 Child points to appropriate object within 5 seconds of request. If child does not respond, or make an incorrect choice, L.P. may place child's hand on the correct object.

Reinforcer _____

Percentage Correct	Modifications	Generalization Probes
Date _____ % Correct _____		1. 2. 3.
Date _____ % Correct _____		1. 2. 3.
Date _____ % Correct _____		1. 2. 3.

Level 1. Training Prespeech Behaviors

Objective	Stimulus	Response
	1.6.2 L.P. places 3 pictures on table. Pictures of familiar items may be used, such as a cookie, a bike, a fork, etc. L.P. says "Find the *cookie*."	1.6.2 Child selects correct picture by pointing. If child responds incorrectly, or if there is no response, L.P. places child's hand on the correct picture.

Level 2. Reception

Objective	Stimulus	Response
2.1 *Responds to commands*. Given a verbal request, child will complete the motor task in 9 of 10 trials.	2.1 L.P. gives a verbal request such as "Stand up." Other actions may include sit down touch your head open your mouth close the door hop run clap	2.1 Child responds by completing the motor task within 5 seconds. If child does not respond or responds incorrectly, L.P. should physically assist child in performing the action.
2.2 *Responds to agents*. Given a choice of 3 pictured agents (nouns) and a verbal cue, child will point to the correct agent with 90 percent accuracy.	2.2 L.P. places 3 pictures of nouns on the table. L.P. gives the verbal stimulus "Find the _____." Suggested agents (nouns) to be trained include boy girl man woman Mommy Daddy dog horse cat cow duck chicken fish rabbit	2.2 Child selects the appropriate pictures within 5 seconds. If child responds incorrectly, L.P. should point to the correct picture and name the agent.

Reinforcer _____

Percentage Correct	Modifications	Generalization Probes
Date _____ % Correct _____		1. 2. 3.

Reinforcer _____

Percentage Correct	Modifications	Generalization Probes
Date _____ % Correct _____		1. 2. 3.
Date _____ % Correct _____		1. 2. 3.

Level 2. Reception

Objective	Stimulus	Response
2.3 *Responds to actions*. Given 3 pictures of agents in action, and the verbal cue "Show me _____," child will select the appropriate picture in 9 of 10 trials.	2.3 L.P. places 3 pictures of actions on the table and says, *"Show me eating."* Pictures included may illustrate these actions. jumping sitting running drinking talking writing playing working hopping sleeping	2.3 Child points to the picture depicting the correct action within 5 seconds. If child responds incorrectly, L.P. should point to the correct action picture and say *"Eating."*
2.4 *Responds to objects*. Given 3 objects and a verbal cue, child will select the appropriate object in 9 of 10 trials.	2.4.1 L.P. places 3 objects on table. L.P. says "Point to the _____." Object names to be taught may include cookie soap ball brush juice water doll towel cup pencil fork shoe spoon shirt	2.4.1 Child points to the appropriate object within 5 seconds. If child does not respond, or responds incorrectly, L.P. places child's hand on the correct object and gives the object's name.
	2.4.2 L.P. places 3 pictures of objects on table. L.P. says "Point to the _____." Use similar pictures to objects previously trained.	2.4.2 Child points to the appropriate picture within 5 seconds. If no response, or if child responds incorrectly, L.P. may point to the correct choice, again repeating the object's name.

Reinforcer _____

Percentage Correct	*Modifications*	*Generalization Probes*
Date _____ % Correct _____		1. 2. 3.
Date _____ % Correct _____		1. 2. 3.
Date _____ % Correct _____		1. 2. 3.

Level 2. Reception

Objective	Stimulus	Response
2.5 *Responds to prepositional placement*. Given an object and a verbal cue, child will place the object in, on, under, between, or beside another object with 100 percent accuracy.	2.5.1 L.P. places 2 boxes and several small objects on table. L.P. places an object on the box and says "On." Verbal cue is then presented to child "Put the block on the box" as the object is handed to child.	2.5.1 Child should respond, placing the block on the box within 5 seconds. If no response, or if child responds incorrectly, L.P. must physically assist child in placing the object correctly and repeats the verbal stimulus "On."
	2.5.2 L.P. places an object in the box and says "In. Put the block in the box" as the block is handed to child.	2.5.2 Child places the object in the box. If child makes no response, or responds incorrectly, L.P. gives physical assistance while repeating the verbal stimulus "In."
	2.5.3 L.P. combines on and in. Verbal stimulus is given "Put the block in (or on) the box." L.P. hands the object to child.	2.5.3 Child responds by placing the block in or on the box. Physically assist child and repeat verbal stimulus "in" or "on" if child does not respond.
	2.5.4 L.P. places an object under the box or table and gives the verbal stimulus "Under. Put the object under." L.P. hands the object to child.	2.5.4 Child responds within 5 seconds by placing the object under the box. If no response, L.P. corrects by using physical assistance, placing the object and child's hand under the box.

Reinforcer _____

Percentage Correct	Modifications	Generalization Probes
Date _____ % Correct _____		1. 2. 3.
Date _____ % Correct _____		1. 2. 3.
Date _____ % Correct _____		1. 2. 3.
Date _____ % Correct _____		1. 2. 3.

Level 2. Reception

Objective	Stimulus	Response
	2.5.5 L.P. combines in, on and under. Varying the verbal cue "Put the object in, on, or under the box." L.P. hands the object to child.	2.5.5 Child responds within 5 seconds by placing the object in the appropriate place. If child makes incorrect responses, L.P. may need to repeat previous steps.
	2.5.6 L.P. places an object beside the box and says "Beside." Child is then presented with the verbal cue "Put the object beside." L.P. hands child the object.	2.5.6 Child responds within 5 seconds by placing the object beside the box. If child responds incorrectly, L.P. should physically assist child in placing the object beside the box.
	2.5.7 L.P. combines placement of objects and presents child with 3 or 4 objects. As L.P. hands child an object, the verbal cue is given "Put it in, on, under, beside, or on top of the box."	2.5.7 Child places the object appropriately. If no response within 5 seconds, or if child responds incorrectly, L.P. may need to repeat steps previously taught.
	2.5.8 L.P. places an object between 2 other objects. L.P. says "Between," as this placement is made. Verbal cue is given "Put the object between." L.P. hands the object to child.	2.5.8 Child should place the object between the 2 others within 5 seconds. If no response, or if child responds incorrectly, L.P. should physically assist child in placing the object between the others.

Reinforcer _____

Percentage Correct	Modifications	Generalization Probes
Date _____ % Correct _____		1. 2. 3.
Date _____ % Correct _____		1. 2. 3.
Date _____ % Correct _____		1. 2. 3.
Date _____ % Correct _____		1. 2. 3.

Level 2. Reception

Objective	Stimulus	Response
	2.5.9 L.P. combines all 5 placements by handing child the object and presenting the verbal stimulus "Put the object in, on, under, beside, or between the box."	2.5.9 Child places object appropriately within 5 seconds. If child responds incorrectly, L.P. should physically assist child in placing the object, or retrace previous teaching steps to achieve mastery.

Level 3. Expression

Objective	Stimulus	Response
3.1 *Produces single sounds.* Given a verbal model, child will produce a single sound in 18 of 20 trials.	3.1 L.P. faces child and gives the verbal stimulus "Say m." The following sounds may be trained m k ŏ b f d ē ŏo ă ōo n g ĭ l p w t s ō r	3.1 Child responds with the correct sound within 5 seconds. On the first 3 sounds, physical assistance may be given in helping child position lips, teeth, and tongue to make the sound, if child does not respond correctly.
3.2 *Produces consonant-vowel combinations.* Given a verbal model, child will imitate consonant-vowel combinations with 90 percent accuracy.	3.2 Facing child, L.P. gives the following verbal stimuli. "Say ŏm." The following c-v, v-c, or c-v-c combinations may be trained	3.2 The child responds within 5 seconds, giving the appropriate consonant-vowel combinations.

Reinforcer _____

Percentage Correct	Modifications	Generalization Probes
Date _____ % Correct _____		1. 2. 3.

Reinforcer _____

Percentage Correct	Modifications	Generalization Probes
Date _____ % Correct _____		1. 2. 3.
Date _____ % Correct _____		1. 2. 3.

Level 3. Expression

Objective	Stimulus	Response
	ăm noō	
	mē ik	
	sē tō	
	ŏf bŏo	
	ēs lŏ	
	ham doōp	
	fēt kŏt	
	rēf wēp	
3.3 *Produces one-word phrases*. Given a picture card and a verbal model, child will name the appropriate agent, action, or object using a one-word response with 90 percent accuracy.	3.3 L.P. presents child with a picture and asks "What is it?" One-word responses in this objective fall into 4 main classes: agent, action, objects, and modifiers. Agents are things or persons who perform an action. Actions refer to the verb component of an event. Objects refer to those nouns receiving an action. Modifiers are those words fulfilling descriptive functions, e.g., adjectives. Suggested examples of words to be trained within these classes include 3.3.1 Agent—may be animate or inanimate.	3.3 Child responds with one word, appropriately corresponding to the picture.
	boy shoe	
	girl juice	
	Mama milk	
	Daddy baby	
	man lady	
	doggie doll	
	kitty water	

Reinforcer _____

Percentage Correct	Modifications	Generalization Probes
Date _____ % Correct _____		1. 2. 3.
Date _____ % Correct _____		1. 2. 3.

Level 3. Expression

Objective	Stimulus	Response
	cookie　　ball	
	child's　　child's	
	siblings　　name	
	3.3.2 Action words may include verbs that take an object or those that do not.	
	sleep　　give	
	walk　　put	
	go　　fall	
	come　　jump	
	hit　　ride	
	throw　　drive	
	eat　　brush	
	run　　comb	
	The present progressive forms of these action words may also be trained. Examples:	
	sleeping　　walking	
	going　　coming	
	3.3.3 Object words	
	table　　house	
	chair　　tree	
	floor　　box	
	couch　　cookie	
	doll　　juice	
	soap　　water	
	hand　　comb	
	leg　　eyes	
	foot　　teeth	
	finger　　hair	
	3.3.4 Modifiers:	
	big　　red	
	little　　blue	
	fat　　green	
	good　　cold	
	pretty　　fast	
	slow　　hot	

Reinforcer _____

Percentage Correct	Modifications	Generalization Probes
Date _____ % Correct _____		1. 2. 3.
Date _____ % Correct _____		1. 2. 3.
Date _____ % Correct _____		1. 2. 3.

Level 3. Expression

Objective	Stimulus	Response
3.4 Produces two-word combinations. Given objects or pictures of objects and events and a verbal cue, child will produce two-word combinations with 90 percent accuracy.		
3.4.1 *Agent-action phrases.*	3.4.1 L.P. points out an existing situation where a person or thing is engaging in an action, or a picture depicting a person in action. L.P. gives the verbal stimulus "What is the *boy* doing?" Examples of agent-action pictures to be elicited may include a boy running a father at work a girl eating a dog sitting a cat sleeping	3.4.1 Child answers in a two-word response using an agent-action phrase. The following agent-action phrases may be elicited in training: doggie sit boy run Daddy work girl eat Mommy go juice spill kitty sleep boy throw baby fall man walk
3.4.2 *Action-object phrases.*	3.4.2 L.P. demonstrates an action to child such as eating, drinking, hitting, etc. L.P. presents the verbal stimulus "What did I do?" Examples of stimuli to be used in eliciting responses include hitting a ball handing the child a cookie	3.4.2 Child responds with 2 words using an action-object phrase. Examples of responses to be elicited include hit ball give cookie eat raisin drink milk put doll throw ball drive car ride bike

Reinforcer _____

Percentage Correct	Modifications	Generalization Probes
Date _____ % Correct _____		1. 2. 3.
Date _____ % Correct _____		1. 2. 3.
Date _____ % Correct _____		1. 2. 3.

Level 3. Expression

Objective	Stimulus	Response
	drinking from a glass eating a raisin throwing a ball	comb hair brush teeth
3.4.3 *Agent-object phrases*.	3.4.3 L.P. shows child a picture of a person or thing in possession of an object. L.P. presents this as "What does the boy have?" or "What did the boy hit?" Examples of pictures to be used include a mother with a comb a father with a fork a baby with a doll a girl eating a cookie a boy hitting a ball a dog with a bone a mother with a baby a cat drinking milk	3.4.3 Child answers using an agent-object relationship using a two-word phrase. Examples of phrases to be elicited may include Mommy comb Daddy fork boy ball baby doll girl cookie man car boy bike dog bone Mama baby kitty milk
3.4.4 *Modifier-object phrases*.	3.4.4 L.P. presents child with a concrete object or a picture of an object and gives the verbal stimulus "What is the *object* like?" Examples of stimuli to be trained may include a picture of a big dog a picture of a red bike a cookie a picture of a baby a blue ball a picture of a racing car a picture of hot soup a glass of juice a fat bug	3.4.4 Child responds using a two-word phrase illustrating the modifier-object relationship. Child may respond using the reverse order object-modifier in his phrases. This is acceptable. Examples: big dog red bike good cookie little baby blue ball fast car hot soup cold juice fat bug

Reinforcer _____

Percentage Correct	Modifications	Generalization Probes
Date _____ % Correct _____		1. 2. 3.
Date _____ % Correct _____		1. 2. 3.

Level 3. Expression

Objective	Stimulus	Response
3.4.5 *Object-locater phrases*.	3.4.5 L.P. places a concrete object on the floor, a nearby chair, or the table or shows a picture of an object and its position relative to another object. L.P. gives the verbal stimulus "Where is the object?" Suggested objects to be used include ball doll pillow shoe book toy boy man cookie dog	3.4.5 Child responds using a two-word object-locater phrase. If child responds in a locator-object sequence, e.g., "there boy," it is acceptable. Suggested responses to be elicited may include shoe floor ball chair doll floor book table dog here boy there cookie plate man car pillow bed
3.4.6 *Demonstrator-object phrases*.	3.4.6 L.P. presents a concrete object or a picture of an object to child and asks "What is that?" or "What is it?"	3.4.6 Child responds using 2 words in expressing a demonstrator-object relationship. Examples of phrases that may be trained include that ball it tree thatsa block itsa cup
3.4.7 *Quantifier-object phrases*.	3.4.7 L.P. presents child with a favorite snack food—chips, cookies, juice, etc. L.P. asks "What do you want?"	3.4.7 Child responds using a quantifier-object phrase. Examples of phrases to be trained include more juice two cookies some chips

Reinforcer _____

Percentage Correct	Modifications	Generalization Probes
Date _____ % Correct _____		1. 2. 3.
Date _____ % Correct _____		1. 2. 3.
Date _____ % Correct _____		1. 2. 3.

Level 3. Expression

Objective	Stimulus	Response
3.4.8 *Article-agent or article-object phrases.*	3.4.8 L.P. presents child with a concrete object and the verbal stimulus "What is it?"	3.4.8 Child responds using an article and an agent or object in a two-word phrase. Examples: a ball the car a boy a train the man an apple
3.4.9 *Possessive-object phrases.*	3.4.9 L.P. presents a concrete object belonging to someone child knows, or a picture of an agent in possession of an object. L.P. asks "Whose *object* is this?"	3.4.9 Child responds using a two-word phrase containing a possessive and an object. Examples: Daddy's car my ball Mommy's dress baby's milk
3.4.10 *Preposition-object phrases.*	3.4.10 L.P. presents child with a concrete object or picture of an object placed in, on, under, beside, or between other objects. L.P. presents the verbal stimulus "Where is the object?"	3.4.10 Child responds using a preposition and an object. Examples: in cup on floor beside chair between boxes under table
3.5 *Produces three-word combinations.* Given a concrete object or a picture and a verbal cue, child will respond using three-word phrases with 90 percent accuracy.		
3.5.1 *Agent-action-object phrases.*	3.5.1 L.P. presents child with a picture of a person or thing performing an action.	3.5.1 Child responds with a three-word phrase illustrating the agent-action-object

Reinforcer _____

Percentage Correct	Modifications	Generalization Probes
Date _____ % Correct _____		1. 2. 3.
Date _____ % Correct _____		1. 2. 3.
Date _____ % Correct _____		1. 2. 3.
Date _____ % Correct _____		1. 2. 3.
Date _____ % Correct _____		1. 2.

Level 3. Expression

Objective	Stimulus	Response
	L.P. gives the verbal stimulus "What is the man doing?" or "What did the boy *eat?*"	relationship; e.g., man hit ball boy eat apple dog drink water girl feed doll Mama give juice cat eat food horse jump fence baby drink milk boy ride bike doctor give shot
3.5.2 *Action-modifier-object phrases.*	3.5.2 L.P. shows child a picture of a person performing an action, preferably one that illustrates an exaggerated size, color, or temperature to be described. L.P. gives the verbal stimulus "What do you see the *agent* doing?"	3.5.2 Child responds in a three-word phrase using the agent-modifier-object relationship, e.g., hit red ball climb big tree fly blue kite drink cold milk touch hot stove eat big cookie smell pretty flower ride green bike ride brown horse drive red car
3.5.3 *Article-modifier-object phrases.*	3.5.3 L.P. presents a concrete object or a picture to the child and says "What is this?"	3.5.3 Child responds in a three-word phrase using the article-modifier-object sequence, e.g., a red apple a blue ball an orange carrot a green tree the big house

Reinforcer _____

Percentage Correct	Modifications	Generalization Probes
		3.
Date _____ % Correct _____		1. 2. 3.
Date _____ % Correct _____		1. 2. 3.

Level 3. Expression

Objective	Stimulus	Response
3.5.4 *Possessive-modifier-object phrases.*	3.5.4 L.P. selects and presents objects belonging to child as well as pictures depicting agents in possession of objects. L.P. says "What is it?"	3.5.4 Child responds with a three-word phrase illustrating the possessive-modifier-object construction, e.g., my red pencil my blue shirt my brown desk man's blue car Daddy's little baby girl's brown dog doggie's big bone boy's green bike Mommy's little girl man's big hat
3.5.5 *Preposition article-object phrases.*	3.5.5 L.P. places an object on, in, under, beside, or between other objects or presents a picture of an object depicting prepositional placement. L.P. gives the verbal stimulus "What is the *object*?"	3.5.5 Child responds in a three-word phrase illustrating the prepositional-article-object construction, e.g., on the table on the chair on the bed in a cup under a table beside the plate between the boys in the box beside the bike between the blocks
3.5.6 *Pronoun agent-action-object phrases.*	3.5.6 L.P. presents child with pictures of people performing actions with objects. L.P. asks "What is he (she) doing?"	3.5.6 Child responds in a three-word phrase exemplifying the pronoun-agent-object construction, e.g., he eat soup

Reinforcer _____

Percentage Correct	Modifications	Generalization Probes
Date _____ % Correct _____		1. 2. 3.
Date _____ % Correct _____		1. 2. 3.
Date _____ % Correct _____		1. 2. 3.

Level 3. Expression

Objective	Stimulus	Response
		she drink pop
		he ride horse
		she jump rope
		he bounce ball
		it catch frisbee
		it drink milk
		she feed baby
		she iron shirt
		he throw ball
3.5.7 *Agent-action-pronoun as-object phrases.*	3.5.7 L.P. presents a picture of a person performing an action with, or to, another. L.P. asks "What does the girl (agent) do?"	3.5.7 Child responds with a three-word phrase illustrating the agent-action-pronoun construction, e.g.,
		girl throw it
		man watch him
		baby pet it
		boy hit him
		Mother kiss him
		Mother hold her
		cat lick it
		boy ride it
		man chop it
		Mother feed her
3.6 *Produces simple declarative sentences.* Given a concrete object or a picture and a verbal stimulus, child will respond using a complete sentence with 90 percent accuracy.		
3.6.1 *Article-agent-auxiliary is-present progressive action.*	3.6.1 L.P. presents child with a concrete situation or a picture of a person in action. L.P. gives the verbal stimulus "What is the *boy* doing?"	3.6.1 Child responds with a minimum of 4 words in a sentence, including the following constructions in the appropriate sequence: article-agent-auxiliary is-

Reinforcer _____

Percentage Correct	Modifications	Generalization Probes
Date _____ % Correct _____		1. 2. 3.
Date _____ % Correct _____		1. 2. 3.
Date _____ % Correct _____		1. 2. 3.

Level 3. Expression

Objective	Stimulus	Response
		present progressive action, e.g., The boy is swimming. The man is working. The lady is sweeping. The baby is sleeping. The dog is running. The girl is playing. The boy is painting. The mother is cooking. The girl is dancing.
3.6.2 *Pronoun-auxiliary is-present progressive action.*	3.6.2 L.P. presents child with a concrete situation or a picture depicting a person or animal in action. L.P. asks "What is she/he (it) doing?"	3.6.2 Child responds with a minimum of a three-word sentence utilizing the pronoun-auxiliary is-present progressive action. Examples: He is fishing. She is eating. He is sweeping. He is writing. It is jumping. He is playing. She is typing. She is sewing. It is chewing. He is cooking.
3.6.3 *Article-agent-copula is-modifier.*	3.6.3 L.P. presents child with an object or a picture of an object. L.P. asks "What is the *object* like?"	3.6.3 Child responds with a minimum of 4 words in a complete sentence, using an article-agent-copula is-modifier sequence. Examples: The elephant is big. The boat is blue.

Reinforcer _____

Percentage Correct	Modifications	Generalization Probes
Date _____		1.
% Correct _____		2.
		3.
Date _____		1.
% Correct _____		2.
		3.

Level 3. Expression

Objective	Stimulus	Response
		The girl is sad. The boy is happy. The dog is little. The house is brown. The tire is flat. The bike is broken. The dress is pretty. The door is open.
3.6.4 *Article-agent-copula is-locater*.	3.6.4 L.P. presents child with a concrete object. L.P. points and gives the verbal cue "Where is the *agent*?"	3.6.4 Child points to the object and responds in a four-word sentence using the article-agent-copula is-locater. Examples: The book is here. The flag is there. The paper is here. The ball is here. The pencil is here. The boy is there. The clock is there. The girl is here.
3.6.5 *Pronoun-action-article-object*.	3.6.5 L.P. points to a person or to the student who is performing an action with an object. L.P. asks "What does she/he do?" or "What are you doing?"	3.6.5 Child responds in a sentence using a minimum of 4 words: pronoun-action-article-object. Examples: I eat the apple. He eats a sandwich. I cut the meat. She jumps the fence. He waters the grass. He hammers the nail. He chops the wood. She fixes the car. He builds a house. She buys a present.

Reinforcer _____

Percentage Correct	Modifications	Generalization Probes
Date _____ % Correct _____		1. 2. 3.
Date _____ % Correct _____		1. 2. 3.

Level 3. Expression

Objective	Stimulus	Response
3.6.6 *Article-agent-auxiliary is-present progressive action-article-object.*	3.6.6 L.P. presents child with a concrete situation depicting a person performing an action on an object. L.P. asks "What is the *agent* doing?"	3.6.6 Child responds with a minimum of 6 words in a sentence, using an article-agent-auxiliary is-present progressive action-article-object sequence; e.g., The boy is hitting the ball. The girl is eating the hamburger. The man is cooking the food. The woman is sewing a dress. The dog is eating a bone. The horse is jumping a fence.
3.6.7 *Article-agent-auxiliary is-present progressive action-preposition-article-object.*	3.6.7 L.P. presents child with a concrete situation or a picture depicting a person performing an action and asks "Where is the *agent action*?" Examples: "Where is the girl jumping?" or "Where is the boy eating?"	3.6.7 Child responds in a seven-word sentence utilizing these constructions: Article-agent-auxiliary is-present progressive action-preposition-article-object. Examples: The boy is swimming in the pool. The girl is jumping in the water. The man is standing on a ladder. The dog is sitting under the tree. The girl is playing on the swing.

Reinforcer _____

Percentage Correct	Modifications	Generalization Probes
Date _____ % Correct _____		1. 2. 3.
Date _____ % Correct _____		1. 2. 3.

Appendix 5-B

Training Pragmatic Precursors to Speech

Objective	Activity
1. Given a play situation, the child will take turns with actions four of five times.	The language practitioner (L.P.) and child should be seated on the floor. Several toys should be placed about the floor. The L.P. observes the child in play, noting which objects or toys the child manipulates. After an object has been put down by the child, the L.P. may pick it up and perform an action with it. The L.P. then gives it back to the child and praises the child for acceptance. If the child performs an action and returns the toy to the L.P., praise should again be given. Repeat this procedure for successive turn taking.
2. Given a play situation, the child will take turns with vocalizations four of five times.	The L.P. and child should be seated on the floor, surrounded by interesting objects/toys. As the child vocalizes while playing, the L.P. should imitate each of the child's utterances. After several trials the child should begin to make utterances in response to those of the L.P. If this occurs, the L.P. should praise and perform an action based on the supposed intent of the child's utterance. In this manner the child begins to internalize the notion that utterances have a subsequent effect on the other person.

3. Given a play situation, the child will give an object when requested four of five times.

The L.P. and child are seated on the floor, surrounded by interesting objects and toys. After the child has had ample opportunity to play with several objects, the L.P. says "Give me the ___object___." When the child complies, the L.P. should praise the child and then return the object.

4. Given a play situation, the child will show an object or action to another person four of five times.

The L.P. and child are seated on the floor amidst toys and objects. During the play situation the L.P. picks up a toy, shows it to the child, demonstrating an action. The L.P. uses the verbal stimulus "Look" simultaneously with the action. This should be repeated several times during the play session. If the child likewise holds up an object for demonstration, the L.P. should affirm the action and make a short verbal comment on it, such as "Yes, see it go around."

5. Given a play situation, where the child is faced with three choices, the child will indicate by gesture the choices wanted four of five times.

The L.P. and child are seated at a table. The L.P. places three toys just out of the child's reach. The L.P. asks "Which one do you want?" The child should respond by pointing to the toy of choice, and be reinforced with the awarding of the toy and time to play with it. Repeat the procedure several times, varying the toy choices.

6. Given a situation where a person enters the immediate environment, the child will acknowledge by facial cues, gesture, or verbally four of five times.

The L.P. and child are seated on the floor, surrounded by interesting objects and toys. Arrangements should be made for a third person to enter the room. The L.P. should model acknowledgment of the person by waving, smiling, or saying hello. This should be repeated several times. If the L.P. wishes to obtain acknowledgment, the L.P. may step out of the room for 3–5 seconds, then return, greeting the child. If the child responds with eye contact, gesture, smile, or verbal response, the L.P. should praise. (A natural elicitor in the first stages of acknowledgment would be the child's mother or other person familiar to the child, such as a peer.) The third party would then enter the play situation and wait for acknowledgment.

7. Given a play situation, along with a verbal and visual cue, the child will perform a requested action four of five times.

The L.P. and child are seated on the floor amidst toys and other interesting objects. The L.P. picks up a toy, such as a doll, performs an action, such as patting the doll, and says "Here, you pat the doll." The doll is then handed to the child. If the child performs the requested action, the L.P. should praise and affirm the action. "Good, you patted the doll." This can be repeated for the following actions.

Rock the doll.
Feed the doll.
Walk the doll.

8. Given a play situation, the child will label familiar play objects 18 of 20 times.

The L.P. and child are seated on the floor amidst toys and other objects. During play sessions, as the child picks up and plays with a toy, the L.P. labels the toy with a single word. Each time the child changes toys, a new label should be given. The child may attempt to repeat the name for the toy. If so, the L.P. should affirm the name and praise. "Yes, a ball." or "Yes, it's a doll." Gradually, the child will label these toys as she/he reaches for them.

9. Given a play situation where the child is faced with three toy choices, the child will indicate by naming which choice is wanted four of five times.

The L.P. and child are seated at a table. The L.P. places three toys just out of the child's reach. The L.P. asks "Which one do you want, the ball, the doll, or the book?" (pointing to each one as it is named). If the child points, require the child to verbalize or approximate a verbal name for the object of choice.

10. Given a play situation, the child will answer with one-word responses to an adult's questions about an object four of five times.

The L.P. and the child are seated on the floor amidst toys. (One good toy for this purpose is a playhouse, with several items: furniture, family members, etc.) As the L.P. and child engage in physically moving the objects and people around the playhouse, the L.P. asks questions that may be answered with one word, such as

"Where is the mother?" (kitchen)
"What is she fixing?" (supper)
"Who is on the bed?" (boy)
"What color is the car?" (red)

Chapter 6

Remediating Specific Language Problems

Beyond the scope of providing a developmental program for the nonverbal child, the practitioner must be aware of specific language difficulties that are common among language delayed children. In the language hierarchy, remediation of these problems may be seen as an extension of programming efforts in teaching the nonverbal child.

The terminal behavior in the instructional program for nonverbal children presented in Chapter 5 consists of enabling the child to speak in six- or seven-word simple declarative sentences. A logical outgrowth of this terminal behavior is skills that increase the child's ability to make refinements in the use of morphological rules. Furthermore, the child must be instructed in making transformations that are changes in the basic structure of the simple sentence. This extension of instructional programming is consistent with the developmental hierarchy in language acquisition. It may be implemented on achievement of the six- or seven-word simple declarative sentence.

Decisions on what specific elements to cover in this chapter were based on the typical errors of form, function, and style described in Chapter 2.

Remediating problems of form includes the types of morphological and syntactical errors commonly made by children with language difficulties. Remediating problems of function and style includes intervention activities designed to develop and refine pragmatic skills of children.

REMEDIATING PROBLEMS OF FORM

Problems of form involve the inability of the child to transform sentences through the use of morphological markers and syntactical changes. The specific problems include

191

- inappropriate word order or syntax
- omission of articles
- difficulty with verb tenses
- failure to generalize rules governing plurality of nouns
- subject/verb agreement
- difficulty with first and third person pronouns
- use of "wh" questions
- use of conjunctions

This chapter provides techniques, materials, and instructional activities designed to remediate these language problems.

INAPPROPRIATE WORD ORDER

Use of a developmental, task analyzed approach to teaching language to the nonverbal child, as illustrated in Chapter 5, should result in the acquisition of correct syntax. In addition to the program content, however, another method may be employed to increase the development of correct word order in simple sentences. One such method is the use of a "slot filler" program.

Based on tagmemic theory, a slot refers to the grammatical function in a sentence, such as subject, predicate, and object. Fillers are any class or structure that fulfills the grammatical functions of the slots represented in the sentence. Distinguishing a slot filler program is the fact that all elements of the sentence are represented by something tangible, such as a picture or card with words or symbols acting as the place holder of that element. This visual presentation reinforces word order and gives the child a graphic illustration of the correct word order in sentences in a left to right progression. Slot filler programs, it is theorized, help the child generalize the rules of word order by providing many opportunities to use the target construction. For example, if the target construction being stressed is a declarative sentence using a subject, the auxiliary verb "is," and the present progressive form of an action verb, the pictures and sentence elements might resemble this arrangement.

The   boy   is   walking.

Verb changes can be made by changing the last card frequently so that the student is given practice using several fillers in the same sentence pattern. For example, the following sentences could be developed.

The boy is eating.	The boy is running.
The boy is swimming.	The boy is jumping.

Or if the emphasis is to be placed on the subject slot of the sentence, different subject fillers could be presented by rearranging the cards.

The girl is walking.	The doctor is walking.
The man is walking.	The baby is walking.
The woman is walking.	

Through techniques of expansion and reduction and fading visual cues, the child should be able to generalize the rules governing the word order of sentences.

OMISSION OF ARTICLES

The problem of omission of articles can be dealt with in much the same manner. If the child can see that each element of a sentence is represented, including articles, then the child will be able to visualize correct word order. This may facilitate the internalization of the rule that governs articles preceding nouns.

Examples such as these sentence patterns reinforce the visualization of articles and their place in phrases and sentences.

The	apple

| The | ball |

Further practice may be given by reviewing steps 3.4.7, 3.5.3, 3.5.6, 3.6.1, 3.6.3, 3.6.4, 3.6.6, and 3.6.7 from the language program for the nonverbal child in Chapter 5. These steps emphasize the use of articles in phrases and sentences in various degrees of complexity.

DIFFICULTY WITH VERB TENSES

Regular Past Tense Verbs

A method provided by Mowery and Replogle (1977) is often used to elicit regular past tense verbs through the use of questioning. For example, the language practitioner may ask the child to perform several regular verb actions, such as clapping, smiling, closing the eyes, pointing, and jumping. As each one is performed the language practitioner may ask the child "What did you do?" The child may respond

I jumped.	I smiled.
I clapped.	I pointed.
I closed my eyes.	

The child should be given practice using all three allomorphs, or alternative forms of the morpheme, /d/, /t/, and /ɪd/. By presenting several trials, the child should generalize which allomorph fits the particular verb. Listed for the convenience of the language practitioner are examples that may be used in teaching differentiation of the three past tense allomorphs.

/d/	/t/	/ɪd/
played	jumped	shouted
closed	walked	parted
smiled	hopped	waded
opened	talked	painted

Irregular Past Tense Verbs

Irregular forms of past tense verbs may be practiced in much the same way. The following common irregular verbs may present priority verbs for initial coverage in language programs.

ate	went	had	made
saw	gave	fell	ran
wrote	came	got	rode
slid	swung	caught	threw
drank	heard	sang	slept

Again, the language practitioner may elicit appropriate practice of these verbs by asking questions.

Language Practitioner: What did you eat for dinner last night?
Child: I ate _____.

Language Practitioner: What did you drink for breakfast?
Child: I drank _____.

Confusing Past and Future Tense Verbs

Children often incorrectly use present tense verbs when past or future tense verbs would be more appropriate. This problem may stem from the inability to understand concepts of time. One technique for developing the concept of time and its application to past and future events is the use of a calendar chart. A large laminated calendar chart can be used to visually represent past events and anticipated events. The chart may be constructed of heavy tagboard and should measure approximately four feet by three feet. Like a calendar, it is marked off vertically in seven sections, corresponding with the seven days of the week. Horizontally, it contains five sections, the maximum number of weeks any month may contain. The chart must be laminated to enable the language practitioner and children to write and erase on it. Once the chart has been posted in the room, a daily exercise provides the practice needed for developing verb tenses.

At the beginning of each day the language practitioner may gather the group of children together for a discussion of their experiences. Sharing an event will enable the children to practice their use of past tense verbs. As children relate events, the language practitioner writes them on the laminated calendar chart with a grease pencil, using the proper form of the past tense verb. For example, in Monday's sharing session, John tells the group that on the previous Sunday his family went to the park for a picnic lunch. The language practitioner writes the sentence on the chart in this manner. ''Yesterday John *went* to the park.'' Children hear the correct use of the past tense verb ''went'' and see it in writing on the chart. Future tenses may also be taught in this manner. If the children are told at their discussion time in the morning that they will see a movie that afternoon, it may be written on the chart this way. ''This afternoon, we *will see* a movie.'' The following morning the same event may be stated in the past tense. "Yesterday, we *saw* the movie *Insect World*."

The chart for the month may be full of events. At the end of the week or month, discussion may center on the summary of the events, giving the students additional practice in relating events using correct usage of past tense verbs. Table 6-1 illustrates a chart that has been completed for a month.

PLURALS

Regular Plurals

Regular plural nouns may first be taught using concrete objects and manipulative toys and then pictures. In teaching regular plurals, one must keep in mind that when nouns change in number, they may change in three ways. Regular nouns have three allomorphs or alternate forms of a morpheme. These are /s/, /z/, and /ɪs/. Children should be given several trials to help them generalize a particular allomorph changing a noun.

When using concrete objects to illustrate the singular and plural forms of the same noun, the language practitioner must demonstrate that when the number of the noun changes, it adds another sound, /s/, /ɪs/, or /z/. The child should be provided with several objects illustrating the target allomorph to gain verbal practice in making changes in inflections as the nouns change in number.

Once this is mastered, paired pictures of objects can be used in the same manner, again giving the child opportunities to use each of the three allomorphs.

Once children reach criterion on this skill, they may be requested to name nouns and identify their plural forms without the use of visual cues.

The following lists of examples of the three alternative allomorphs may be helpful in providing practice in plurals.

/s/	/ɪs/	/z/
cat-cats	witch-witches	dog-dogs
shirt-shirts	watch-watches	table-tables
hat-hats	stitch-stitches	shoe-shoes
plate-plates	wish-wishes	toy-toys
mop-mops	dish-dishes	boy-boys
fork-forks	bus-buses	girl-girls

Irregular Plurals

Irregular plurals may be taught using specific instances, because the rules governing changes vary. Children should be provided with practice in learning how each of these words changes with the transition from singular to plural.

Table 6-1 Developing Tenses with a Calendar

December

Sunday	Monday	Tuesday	Wednesday	Thursday	Friday	Saturday
		1 Yesterday we *played* in the snow.	2 Becky *went* to the doctor today.	3 We *will play* Bingo tomorrow.	4 On Monday we *will have* a math contest.	5
6	7 Yesterday John *went* skiing. Mary *ate* at her Grandmother's.	8 Sam *won* the math contest yesterday. Sue *was* second.	9 Today we *will* practice for the Christmas program.	10 Charles *did not come* to school today.	11 Charles *will have* an operation on his tonsils during vacation.	12
13	14 We *saw* Christmas decorations in town yesterday.	15 Today we *will* have science. We *will* work with magnets.	16 Yesterday we *picked* up iron objects with magnets.	17 Tonight is the Christmas program. We *will all come.*	18 Last night we *sang* in the Christmas program.	19
20	21 On Wednesday we *will have a* Christmas party.	22 Tomorrow we *will get* out of school early for vacation.	23 When we come back to school it *will be* a new year.	24	25	26
27	28	29	30	31		

leaf-leaves   deer-deer   calf-calves
child-children   fish-fish   man-men
woman-women   person-people   half-halves

SUBJECT/VERB AGREEMENT

For children beginning to use language, it is difficult to explain the rule that when a subject is singular, the verb contains an -s ending and when the subject is plural, the verb has no -s ending.

> The dog eats.
> The dogs eat.

One way of teaching the -s ending is by the "Sneaky -s" game. The child can be presented with picture cards, one showing a singular noun and one showing the plural of the same noun. The child is also given two sentence patterns, as in a slot filler program, and an -s card. The sentence patterns may consist of pictures, symbols, or words for the various slots to be represented. The arrangement of pictures and cards may resemble this example.

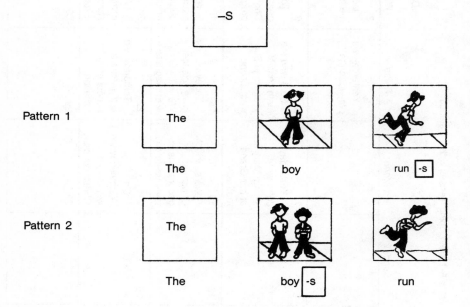

The child is told that the -s sound is sneaky and that it moves from place to place when a sentence changes. The shift from the verb when a noun is singular, as in pattern 1, to the plural noun, as in pattern 2, should be demonstrated. The child should then be given the -s card and given practice through several trials using the same sentence patterns but varying the verbs and regular nouns. The following list of examples is suggested for use in the "Sneaky -s" game.

The girl plays.   The mother sews.
The girls play.   The mothers sew.

The cat eats.   The tiger jumps.
The cats eat.   The tigers jump.

To teach the -s shift with irregular plurals, the following activity may be used. Using the same basic format for teaching -s verbs with regular plurals gives the child the opportunity to shift the sneaky -s. The child is told that in these types of sentences the sneaky -s hides when the sentence changes and that it is not necessary to use the -s in the second sentence pattern. For example

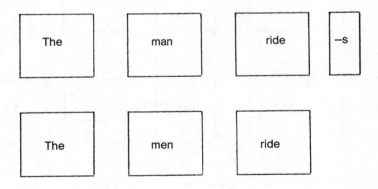

Giving the child the opportunity of removing the sneaky -s and hiding it gives the concrete experience of visualizing the change in verbs when nouns change in number. Numerous trials of this shift reinforce the concept of -s verbs and help the individual internalize the rule.

Sentence patterns can also help teach the rule that copular verbs and auxiliary verbs—is, was, am, and has—change to are, were, are, and have when the noun or pronoun changes in number. For example, in the arrangement of these sentence patterns the auxiliary verb changes in this manner. The slots represented here by words may also be illustrated in pictures or symbols.

| The | boy | is | running. |

| The | boys | are | running. |

Other examples may include

| The | girl | has | a | ball. |

| The | girls | have | a | ball. |

| I | am | happy. |

| You | are | happy. |

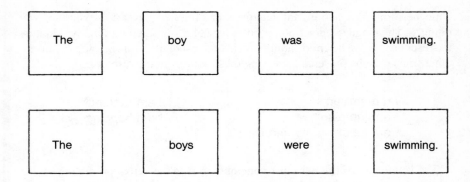

Fading the visual stimulus of the sentence patterns will make it necessary for the child to remember the patterns and, thus, generalize the rule.

PRONOUNS

Children make errors in using pronouns by incorrectly substituting one for another. For example, the child may use the dative or objective case pronoun "me" instead of the nominative "I." The child may say a sentence such as "Me want a cookie." Or the child may use the dative or objective case pronoun "him" or "her" in place of the nominative case pronouns "he" and "she."

> Him play with me.
> Her went home.

The child may also incorrectly use the nominative case "she" with an -s ending added instead of using the genitive or possessive pronoun "her."

> I see shes pencil.

Another common problem that children have with pronouns is in confusing the masculine and feminine genders. To give appropriate practice in the correct usage of pronouns, several exercises may be employed.

Nominative I

To develop the correct use of the nominative case pronoun "I," the language practitioner may have the child perform an action, such as clapping hands. As the child performs this action, the language practitioner may ask "What are you doing?" The language practitioner gives the child verbal prompting by initiating the response "I." The child should join in and respond "I am clapping." Several other trials may be presented stressing these actions in the response

I am smiling.	I am running.
I am jumping.	I am hopping.
I am touching my head.	

The language practitioner must remember to fade the verbal prompting so that the child independently initiates sentences with "I."

Reinforcement of this skill may be achieved during the day. At periodic intervals, the language practitioner may walk up to the child who is busy at an activity and ask "What are you doing?" The child should respond "I am _____."

Another activity to reinforce the use of "I" in the nominative case would be to show the child pictures of different foods. The language practitioner says to the child "Tell me which foods you like." The child is required to respond in complete sentences, "I like _____." Similarly, showing the child a picture of a playground and asking "What can you do outside at recess time?" can elicit sentence responses such as "I can swing," "I can climb," "I can play ball."

Nominative He/She

To teach correct usage of the nominative case third person pronouns he and she, the language practitioner may use pictures of females and males performing different actions. The language practitioner shows the child a picture and asks "What is she doing?" The child should respond "She is _____ _____." Once the child has mastered the feminine gender, the same procedure can be used to teach the masculine gender and the response "He is _____." Only when both are brought to criterion should they be combined. Alternating pictures of male and female subjects can be presented to determine whether the child is using them appropriately.

Once the child correctly uses he/she pronouns with pictures, this skill may be generalized by taking the child for a walk around the premises or home setting. The language practitioner may instruct a child to observe a male or female performing an action and then may ask the child "What is s/he doing?" The child should respond "S/he is _____."

Dative and Accusative Her/Him

To develop correct usage of the dative and accusative case pronouns her and him, the language practitioner will need to find pictures illustrating males and females receiving an action, such as a mother giving a boy a cookie, a girl receiving a book from her teacher, a woman holding a letter given to her by the mailman, or other similar scenes. The language practitioner asks "Who did the mother give the cookie to?" "Who did the teacher give the book to?" or "What did the mailman give to her?" Responses may need to be modeled first by the language practitioner. The child should begin to respond in sentences such as this.

The mother gave him a cookie.	The mailman gave her a letter.
or	or
The mother gave the cookie to him.	The mailman gave a letter to her.
The teacher gave the book to her.	
or	
The teacher gave her a book.	

As an activity to develop the genitive or possessive pronouns her/his or hers/his, the language practitioner may show the child an object belonging to another child or adult. The language practitioner points and says "Whose book is that?" "Whose pencil is this?" The child should be encouraged to respond in complete sentences "It is her book," "It is hers," "It is his pencil," or "It is his."

"WH" QUESTIONS

A "wh" question is an interrogative sentence, usually beginning with the letters "wh." Responding to and being able to ask "wh" questions are important processes in the development of language. Appropriate use of questions enables the child to obtain information about the environment and about concepts. Furthermore, the use of questions in a child's language development is a manifestation of the process of transforming sentences and indicates a higher stage in the developmental hierarchy.

The acquisition of "wh" questions generally follows this order.

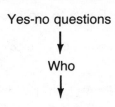

Yes-no questions

Who

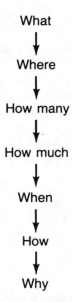

The language practitioner should observe the child in spontaneous language or use a language sample to determine what level of questions the child uses and use that level as a starting point for initiating instruction.

Yes/No Questions

The first step in developing questions is the understanding of yes/no questions. To develop this skill, the language practitioner may use objects familiar to the child—a ball, a doll, a block, colored objects, a cookie, a cup, or similar items. The language practitioner makes a declarative sentence and then transforms it into a yes/no question, to which the child is asked to respond.

> *Language Practitioner:* Points to the cup and says, This is a cup.
> Transformation to question: Is this a cup?
> *Child:* Yes.

> *Language Practitioner:* Points to the book and says, This is a block.
> Transformation to question: Is this a block?
> *Child:* Yes.

> *Language Practitioner:* Points to the ball and says, This ball is red.
> Transformation to question: Is this ball red?
> *Child:* Yes.

Language Practitioner: Points to the doll and says, This is a cookie.
Transformation question: Is this a cookie?
Child: No.

The language practitioner must be certain that the child understands the task in responding to yes/no questions and that the child achieves a high degree of accuracy. Mastering yes/no questions is a necessary prerequisite step in responding to and asking "wh" questions.

"Who" Questions

To develop "who" questions in the child's repertoire, the following four-step process can be employed.

Step 1. The language practitioner may use small figurines depicting different family members—mother, father, girl, boy, baby—or other plastic figures representing people familiar to the child. Also suggested for use in this activity is a dollhouse so that characters may be placed in different parts of the house and identified by the child. If a dollhouse is not available, the language practitioner may place the figures on a chair, a table, or in another location. The language practitioner places a figure such as the mother inside the dollhouse or on a chair and says to the child

Language Practitioner: The mother is in the house.
Transformation to question: Who is in the house?
Child: The mother, or
Mother.

The language practitioner places the boy in the house.

Language Practitioner: The boy is in the house.
Transformation to question: Who is in the house?
Child: Boy, or
The boy.

This procedure should be followed for several trials until the child can respond correctly to the statement transformed into a question.

Step 2. The language practitioner fades the statement and only asks the transformed question.

Transformation to question: Who is in the house?
Child: The girl.

Step 3. The next step in this process is changing roles so that the child initiates the question. The child places the figure in the dollhouse.

> *Child:* Who is in the house?
> *Language Practitioner:* The baby.

Step 4. This activity may be extended with the use of picture cards that depict people in action. The language practitioner first asks the child "Who is working?" The child responds "The man." Again, roles should be changed so that the child has the opportunity to ask "who" questions.

The child may be given more practice in asking and responding to "who" questions by using pictures and the following target constructions.

> Who is that?
> Who is happy?
> Who ran?

"What" Questions

"What" questions may first be taught using concrete objects.

Step 1. The language practitioner points to or picks up an object.

> *Language Practitioner:* This is a ball.
> Transformation to question: What is it?
> *Child:* A ball.

The language practitioner picks up a pencil and points.

> *Language Practitioner:* This is a pencil.
> Transformation to question: What is this?
> *Child:* A pencil.

This procedure may be followed until criterion is met with the language practitioner giving the verbal model in the form of a statement, then a question.

Step 2. Next the child must meet criterion with only the transformation to question as the verbal stimulus.

> The language practitioner picks up a cup.
> *Language Practitioner:* What is this?
> *Child:* A cup.

Step 3. After ample trials responding to questions provided by the language practitioner, children should be given opportunities to ask the questions themselves, again achieving a satisfactory percentage of accuracy.

Child: What is that?

Step 4. To vary the exercise, pictures may be used with the verbal stimulus. Other question patterns may also be added.

What is in the box?
What is there?
What is he doing?
What do you want?

"Where" Questions

Understanding and responding to "where" questions may also be accomplished with the use of the dollhouse, plastic human figures, or other objects.

Step 1. By placing one of the figures in a room of the house such as the kitchen, the language practitioner makes the statement first, then transforms it into the question format.

Language Practitioner: The girl is in the kitchen.
Transformation to question: Where is the girl?
Child: Kitchen, or
In the kitchen.

Step 2. When criterion is met, the language practitioner fades the statement and gives only the question stimulus.

Language Practitioner: Where is the boy?
Child: In the bedroom, or
Bedroom.

Step 3. Once criterion is met, the child should be given several trials in placing the figures and asking the questions.

Child: Where is the baby?
Language Practitioner: In the living room.

Step 4. This activity may be extended by using the following question patterns.

> **Where is he sitting?**
> **Where is the cat?**
> **Where is he going?**
> **Where do we get clothing? (food, gas, etc.)**

"How Many" Questions

"How many" questions concern quantity and are usually the next to develop in the child's repertoire. They may be taught using a similar four-step procedure that gradually enables the child to ask questions.

Step 1. Using a number of blocks or other objects, the language practitioner places a certain number (three, for example) on the table.

> *Language Practitioner:* **I have three blocks.**
> **Transformation to question: How many blocks do I have?**
> *Child:* **Three.**

Several trials are presented and brought to criterion.

Step 2. The language practitioner fades the statement and uses only the question format.

> *Language Practitioner:* **How many blocks do I have?**
> *Child:* **Two.**

Step 3. Roles are now changed and the child is given practice in asking questions.

> *Child:* **How many blocks do I have?**
> *Language Practitioner:* **Five.**

Step 4. Variations of this include the following question patterns.

> **How many _____ do you want?**
> **How many _____ do you have?**
> **How many _____ are there?**

"How Much" Questions

Practice in asking questions concerning "how much" can refer to specific quantities such as one-half, and all, or specific monetary values such as twenty-nine cents. To learn how to ask questions concerning how much a particular item costs, a game of "store" may be played with the child. In this game the child is given the opportunity to request the costs of items in the store following this process.

Step 1. The language practitioner shows the child an item.

> *Language Practitioner:* Cookies cost seventy-nine cents.
> Transformation to question: How much do cookies cost?
> *Child:* Seventy-nine cents.

Many trials of step 1 should be presented and brought to criterion.

Step 2. The language practitioner fades the statement and presents only the question.

> *Language Practitioner:* How much does ice cream cost?
> *Child:* Twenty-five cents.

Similarly, many trials should be presented and brought to criterion.

Step 3. Roles are changed so that the child asks the question.

> *Child:* How much does a candy bar cost?
> *Language Practitioner:* Thirty cents.

Step 4. The following question formats may be used to extend the child's opportunities to respond to and ask questions.

> How much _____ do you want?
> How much _____ do you have?

"When" Questions

Abstract time concepts such as the time of day and seasons of the year often confuse children, especially if they must respond to questions requiring them to relate an incident occurring at a specific time. The familiar four-step method of teaching questions can also be used in developing these abstract concepts of time.

Step 1. The language practitioner initiates the lesson by stating events familiar to the child's school activities, home schedule, or daily routine.

> *Language Practitioner:* At night we sleep.
> Transformation to question: When do we sleep?
> *Child:* At night.

Step 2. Once the child is responding appropriately to the transformation, the statement modeled may be faded.

> *Language Practitioner:* When do we eat breakfast?
> *Child:* In the morning.

Step 3. When the child meets criterion on responding to questions the child must be given the opportunity to initiate the question.

> *Child:* When do you eat dinner?
> *Language Practitioner:* At 6:30.

Step 4. These alternative sentence patterns may be used in reinforcing the ability to respond to and use "when" questions.

> When is Christmas?
> When is your birthday?
> When do we wear warm clothes?

"How" Questions

"How" questions first involve asking how something is performed, which requires a descriptive answer. Questions such as "How do you _____?" exemplify this type of "how" question. They also include question patterns such as "how" coupled with a modifier. "How old are you?" and "How tall is it?" are examples of this type of question. For the latter type of "how" question the four-step procedure may again be used.

Step 1. The language practitioner first makes a statement, then uses the transformation.

> *Language Practitioner:* You are seven years old.
> Transformation to question: How old are you?
> *Child:* Seven.

Step 2. Fade the statement in the verbal stimulus, leaving only the question.

> *Language Practitioner:* How tall is a giraffe?
> *Child:* As tall as a tree, or
> Very tall.

Step 3. The child assumes the role of asking the questions.

> *Child:* How tall are you?
> *Language Practitioner:* I am five feet, three inches tall.

Step 4. Using these varied patterns, the skill of asking ''how'' questions is reinforced.

> How big is it?
> How _____ are they?

A technique for teaching descriptive responses to ''how'' questions can also enhance the child's skill in this area. The child may be encouraged to describe the process for making something or performing an activity. For example, the language practitioner may ask the child to describe how to make a sandwich, how to brush teeth, or any number of familiar activities. Once the child can describe the event, roles may again be changed and the child may be encouraged to ask the questions. These examples may be used to elicit responses and to teach the child to initiate ''how'' questions.

> How do you make chocolate milk?
> How do you fry an egg?
> How can I find out?
> How is he going to get there?

''Why'' Questions

Abstract reasoning is necessary for the child to be able to respond to ''why'' questions. One way of teaching the child to respond to the use of ''why'' questions is accomplished through the use of picture stimuli. Pictures showing a sequence of events lend themselves to describing causal events. For example, in one set of commercially produced cards, the *Why?-Because Cards* (1976), a man wearing street clothes is shown diving into a pond. A corresponding picture shows a girl in a pond drowning. The child is shown both pictures simultaneously. The language practitioner asks ''Why is the man jumping in the water?'' The child should respond ''To save the girl'' or ''To get the girl.'' Thus, a two-picture sequence completes for the child a cause and effect relationship. Furthermore, the child gains practice in responding to ''why'' questions.

The child may also be given the opportunity to initiate the questions, giving practice in using several different sentence patterns beginning with the question ''why.''

USE OF CONJUNCTIONS

To enable the child to increase the complexity of sentences, practice may be provided in expanding sentences with the use of conjunctions. Simple sentences may be compounded with the use of ''and,'' ''but,'' and ''because.'' This provides another means of transforming sentences and utilizing more complex utterances.

The Conjunction "And"

Children can be encouraged to expand sentences with ''and'' in the following exercise. The language practitioner presents a child with a set of pictures or plastic models of fruits or other familiar foods. The child is asked to name two items that he or she likes to eat, using ''and'' to make a compound sentence. For example, the language practitioner may use these sentences to model the expanded constructions.

> I like bananas and apples.
> I like corn and peas.
> I like potatoes and beans.

To extend this activity, a child may be asked to name enjoyable games.

> I like to play baseball and soccer.
> I like to run and jump.

To develop the use of ''and'' in eliciting two or more different subjects, the language practitioner may ask the child to name a friend and then to state what they do when they play together.

John and I like to ride bikes.
Dick and Sue play marbles.

The Conjunction "But"

To conjoin sentences with the conjunction "but," the child may be asked to discriminate between liked and disliked foods. With picture stimuli or plastic foods, the child may be asked to name a favorite food and then a disliked food. The child must use the two in the same sentence using the conjunction "but" to combine thoughts.

I like tomatoes, but I don't like onions.
I like popcorn, but I don't like peanuts.

Similarly, the child can describe likes and dislikes in games or school activities.

I like to play baseball, but I don't like to jog.
I like reading, but I don't like spelling.

Children may also gain practice in using the conjunction "but" by completing sentences initiated by the language practitioner.

I want to go, but _____.
I can sew, but _____.
Mary would go with us, but _____.

The Conjunction "Because"

The conjoining of clauses with the conjunction "because" is similar to the process described for teaching the use of "why" questions. Children must be able to connect two events illustrating a cause and effect relationship. Picture cards depicting the event may be used, stressing the use of phrases conjoined by "because."

The curtains caught on fire because the boy was playing with matches.
The man was mad because his dog ran away.

Similar sentences may be elicited if the language practitioner skillfully asks questions drawing out a causal relationship.

Language practitioner: Why do we eat food?
Child: We eat food because we're hungry, or
   We eat food because our bodies need food to grow.

Language practitioner: Why do we wear coats in the winter?
Child: We wear coats because we need to keep warm.

REMEDIATING PROBLEMS OF FUNCTION

Included in the area of language function are these specific pragmatic problems.

- Wanders from the conversational topic
- Has difficulty describing what is needed (instrumental function)
- Has difficulty giving directions and commands (regulatory function)
- Has difficulty answering questions and inappropriately uses social greetings (interactional function)
- Has difficulty expressing opinions (personal function)
- Has difficulty asking questions to gain information (heuristic function)
- Has difficulty relating a sequence of details (imaginative function)
- Has difficulty describing common objects and events (informative function)
- Has difficulty using specific vocabulary (restricted code)
- Uses tactless statements

Wanders from Conversational Topic

One suggestion for enhancing topic maintenance is to help the child expand simple sentences around a predefined theme. The language practitioner writes a declarative sentence on the board and encourages the child to expand the thought by adding more specific information. The language practitioner may need to direct the child by asking specific questions.

The girl walked.
Language Practitioner: Where did the girl walk?
Child: The girl walked to her friend's house.

Language Practitioner: Why?
Child: The girl walked to her friend's house to play.

The language practitioner may continue to encourage expansion of the following sentences.

The boy ran.	I went to the movie.
I went to town.	We had a picnic.

Another exercise to enhance topic maintenance is the utilization of visual stimuli to maintain a story plot. Commercially produced sequence cards may be used to help the child develop a plot in a step-by-step sequence. This helps the child internalize an order and cohesion of thoughts.

A round robin story telling activity may also encourage topic maintenance. The language practitioner can paste an interesting picture inside a manila folder. One child gets the folder, and without showing the picture to the other students, begins to tell a story. After a few sentences the folder is passed to the next child, who continues the story.

In informal conversation with a child who has difficulty maintaining the topic of conversation, the language practitioner should ignore utterances extraneous to the conversation and direct the child back to the topic at hand.

Difficulty Describing What Is Needed

The instrumental function of language enables the child to express needs, wants, and desires. The most obvious way to develop this expression is to provide choices for decision making, encouraging the child to express needs and wants.

The language practitioner may first develop this skill by offering the child two or three choices of toys. The language practitioner should ask the child "Which toy do you want, the doll, the ball, or the blocks?" The language practitioner should encourage the child to verbalize a response.

The child can also be encouraged to make desires known using picture stimuli. The child may be asked to decide among two or three choices.

- a favorite food, such as hamburger or pizza
- a favorite game, such as baseball or soccer
- the event the child would like to attend, a movie or the circus
- a favorite color, blue or red

For very young nonverbal children, a communication board with several pictorial choices may provide the child with the opportunity to make needs known. Pictures depicting water, milk, juice, a toilet, food items, and other vital needs will encourage the child to communicate desires to an adult.

Meal time is an excellent opportunity to reinforce choice making. Adults should require the child to request a particular food item on the dinner table. Receiving the item is a natural reinforcer of the request. At school the same requests might be required at snack time, when the child is encouraged to ask for a particular food.

During an art activity the child may be required to request supplies. The language practitioner needs to be aware of the many spontaneous opportunities to require the child's expression of needs and wants for a specific purpose.

Difficulty Giving Directions and Commands

The regulatory function of language is the child's use of expression to persuade or direct someone in a task. Work on this skill might include giving the child opportunities to direct others in an activity. The language practitioner may give the child an opportunity to give directions on how to perform a task, such as folding a paper airplane. The other children in class would follow the oral directions given by the child. This may be extended to include having the child explain the following actions.

- making a peanut butter sandwich
- brushing teeth
- fixing a bowl of cereal
- feeding the dog
- playing checkers

Another activity might utilize a school floor plan. Each child would be asked to outline the route a person would take to go from the classroom to the office or from the office to the cafeteria. The child would then verbally explain the route chosen. This could be expanded to include explanations of how to get to specific locations in the child's immediate neighborhood.

Difficulty Answering Questions and Using Social Greetings

The interactional function of language enables the child to verbally exchange with another person. This interaction requires that the child reciprocate in social greetings, as well as respond appropriately to another person's statements and questions.

Role playing provides an opportunity for the child to learn appropriate social greetings. The language practitioner may provide the following role playing activities in which the child may use social language.

- meeting a person for the first time
- offering another child a toy

- accidentally bumping a person
- asking for a favor
- asking for a toy
- spilling a glass of milk
- asking permission to leave the room

Another role playing activity for practice of social interaction phrases is to have children pretend they are in a restaurant. The language practitioner may provide menus from a local restaurant. One child is appointed to be the waiter or waitress. The children each order their meals, using appropriate social language.

Another dramatic activity designed to elicit appropriate social language involves presenting the following hypothetical situations that pairs and groups of children may dramatize.

- Pretend to see a child take something belonging to another.
- Pretend to be on the playground playing ball. A child comes up and kicks the ball away.
- Pretend to be choosing teams for a baseball game, and one child is left out.
- Pretend to disagree with a friend on a choice of game.
- Pretend someone is teasing another child.

Practicing telephone etiquette is another means of using social language. The language practitioner may use toy telephones to have the children dramatize the following situations.

- Call a friend to come over to play.
- Call to order a pizza to be delivered.
- Call your mom and ask her to pick you up after school.
- Call the fire department to report a fire.
- Call the movie theater to find out what movie is playing and the time it starts.
- Call the hairdresser for an appointment to get a haircut.

For children to be helped in answering conversational questions appropriately, they must first be able to answer factual questions with a visual cue stimulus. It is suggested that children be given the opportunity to respond to questions on the detail contained in pictures, filmstrips, storybooks, and movies.

Teaching specific use of "wh" questions is discussed earlier in this chapter.

Difficulty Expressing Opinions

Often children with language delays have difficulty expressing opinions, or more specifically, expressing opinions in a tactful manner. This personal function of language is important in interactions with others.

One way of getting the child to identify and express feelings and opinions is to provide experiences in identifying opinions of others. The language practitioner should collect pictures from magazines depicting people in various types of interactions and with a variety of facial expressions. As the picture is shown, encourage the child to identify

- how the person in the picture is feeling
- what the person in the picture is saying

As the child identifies a verbal quotation, the language practitioner may encapsulate it in a balloon, much like a cartoon.

Another activity designed to enable the child to express personal opinions is to give choices. Picture cards can be used to encourage the child to state preferences between foods, family activities, and chores that the child is responsible for in the home, asking the child for a rationale for the choice.

Difficulty Asking Questions To Gain Information

The heuristic function of language is that which enables the child to find out more about the environment. Without the ability to ask questions to gain information, a child's natural curiosity may go unreinforced. The language practitioner can help the child learn to ask appropriate questions using a spinner board. The circular spinner board, made of cardboard, should have the following words printed around the perimeter of the circle: Who, What, Why, When, Where, and How much. As the child spins the spinner, the child must think of a question beginning with that word. Sample questions are included for illustrative purposes.

Where is the girl going?   *When* do you go to bed?
Why was the girl sad?   *How much* does a bike cost?
Who ate the pie?   *What* is your mother's name?

Another activity to encourage the child to seek information is a variation of the 20 questions game. The language practitioner tells the child that he/she is thinking of an animal. The child must ask questions to gain information.

Can it be found in a zoo?   Does it eat meat?
Is it a wild animal?   Does it have four legs?

Other categories to expand this game include

- movies
- foods
- games

- countries
- sports
- famous people

The language practitioner may also encourage the use of questions to gain information by asking the child to interview an older person, or a person who worked within the child's environment. The child may tape record the interview and share the information with other children in the class. When interviewing the senior citizen, the child may focus on questions that

- indicate what life was like "back then"
- tell how the houses were different
- relate how family activities were different

When interviewing people working in the community, such as the cook, the principal, or the nurse, the child may focus on questions such as

- What are the duties and responsibilities of the job?
- Why do they like or dislike their work?
- What kind of education or training does the job require?

The tape recording of the interview will help the language practitioner determine if the child is using appropriate questions.

Difficulty Relating a Sequence of Details

The imaginative function enables a child to form mental images of abstract events and to express them. It is an important language process because it takes the child from the concrete to the conceptual.

To develop this skill, the language practitioner can provide opportunities for the child to pretend and dramatize the following hypothetical events.

- Imagine you are an animal.
- Pretend you can fly. Where would you go? What would you do?
- If you had a magic pebble to make you invisible, what would you do?
- I have a magic carpet. Let's go somewhere.
- The funniest thing happened to me today . . .
- I heard a scary noise . . .
- If you were principal for a day, what would you do?
- Pretend you are an inventor. What would you invent?

At a later stage of development the child may be unable to relate a sequence of events. To develop this skill, the language practitioner should first give the child practice in ordering events. The language practitioner first reads a short story consisting of no more than four events. After discussing the story with the child, the practitioner should have the child number the four parts according to their occurrence in the story.

Another activity that lends itself to the expression of fantasy events is the use of human interest headlines taken from the local newspaper, such as "Shipwrecked Pair Escapes" or "Bear Raids Camp." The child should be encouraged to relate events that happened in the story. The child may role play as the story unfolds.

Difficulty Describing Common Objects and Events

The informative function of language enables the child to describe common objects and events in a factual manner. It may involve explanation, demonstration, and illustration. Expressively, it involves a clear accounting or description of objects and events.

To develop this skill, the language practitioner may ask the child to place hands on a familiar object, while blindfolded, and describe it.

Another activity to develop the ability to describe utilizes three to five picture cards, placed in full view of a small group of children. One child is asked to mentally select a picture and verbally describe it. The task of the other children in the group is to correctly identify the picture that was described.

The language practitioner may provide another opportunity for the child to describe and inform by utilizing objects commonly found around the home such as

a paper clip	ice tongs
a hammer	an eggbeater
a screwdriver	a shoehorn

The child must describe the function of the object to classmates.

The use of an instant developing camera enables a hands-on approach to describing events. The child should be encouraged to take pictures of activities and events around the school. After the pictures are developed, the child must show the picture(s) to classmates and describe the events.

A peekbox or diorama provides another object for description. Using a shoebox, the practitioner can create a dioramic scene out of clay, paper, cardboard, or natural materials. The peekbox is closed, and a small hole is made for viewing. The child may describe the scene and/or develop a story about it, which is related on a tape recording that may be used later for evaluation.

Difficulty Using Specific Vocabulary

To develop the child's ability to increase vocabulary, the language practitioner should provide many opportunities to learn specific names for objects, items, and events. The language practitioner may bring objects or pictures to the language session and point out the names of their respective parts.

> chair—legs, seat, back, cushion
> coat—collar, sleeve, pockets, buttons, buttonholes, snaps
> house—windows, door, roof, stairs, chimney, rooms
> flower—leaves, stem, petals
> car—steering wheel, tires, roof, trunk, hood

This activity may be varied in game form, where the language practitioner provides pictures of the separate parts on cards and lays them face down on the table. The child selects a card and tries to identify the part, giving its specific name. Points may be awarded for correct responses.

Using a feltboard and felt cutouts of persons in different occupations, along with clothing, tools, and instruments of their trade, the language practitioner may stress specific vocabulary in discussion. As pieces of tools and clothing are placed on the board, the child must identify them by giving their specific names.

> police officer   police car, badge, uniform, siren
> firefighter   ladder, hose, hat, boots, oxygen
> doctor   medicine, stethoscope, x-ray

To develop specific vocabulary for action words, the language practitioner may provide an activity that requires the child to match a picture of an object with a verbal representation of the sound it makes. For example, the language practitioner may place three pictures on the table, such as a soda being poured, a hammer pounding a nail, and a person beating a drum. The language practitioner may say to the child "Find the one that goes *fizz*." The child should pick the picture of the soda being poured. Other pictures may illustrate the following descriptive words.

band	ring	slurp
crunch	sizzle	whistle
buzz	thump	creak

The child should also be exposed to vocabulary that describes different textures. The language practitioner should provide opportunities for tactile experiences with objects that illustrate the following characteristics.

bumpy	smooth
squishy	sticky
silky	soft
rough	hard
scratchy	

Several games may reinforce the new vocabulary learned.

- Match a small textured object with a larger sample.
- Find a picture of something exhibiting the above characteristics.
- Have a blindfolded child reach for an object, and describe it.

Uses Tactless Statements

To remediate the child's use of tactless statements, the child must be made aware of the effect these statements have on others. This is accomplished by having the child identify or express personal feelings as the recipient of statements.

The language practitioner and child may role play home, family, and school situations, where the language practitioner tests the child's reactions to tactless statements. The language practitioner should discuss with the child reactions to the following statements. For example "How did you feel when I said"

No, I don't want to.
You're silly.
I'm tired of this.
You're not my friend.

Remediating the child's use of tactless statements is accomplished by presenting the child with opportunities to use alternative ways of saying the same thing.

Tactless Statement	*Alternative*
I hate math.	I like reading better than math.
I won't do it.	I'd rather do something else.
I don't want to play ball.	I would rather ride my bike than play ball.
	Let's play checkers instead.

REMEDIATING PROBLEMS OF STYLE

Problems of language style involve characteristics of speech that prevent the smooth flow of ideas, detract from the content of what is said, or represent a disjointed combination of ideas that make it difficult to comprehend the meaning of the speaker. Included in the area of language style are

- false starts and mazes
- slurred speech and giant words
- incoherent sequence of details
- difficulty in word finding
- speech volume not adapted to the context
- speech rate not appropriate

False Starts and Mazes

False starts and mazes represent attempts by the child to revise or alter what has already been uttered. False starts occur at the beginning of sentences, whereas mazes are revisions in the middle of the child's utterance. To remediate this habit, the language practitioner must stress the benefits of taking time to organize thoughts before speaking. A timer may even be used so that the child is forced to take a minimum of 30 seconds to one minute to organize ideas before speaking. The tape recorder is another useful tool in helping children analyze their own speech patterns. Playback of a language sample can help point out false starts and mazes and set the stage for correction.

Slurred Speech and Giant Words

Slurred speech and use of giant words (several words indistinctly slurred as one) and rapid speech rate can be corrected by encouraging the child to slow the rate of speaking. Again, the tape recorder is valuable in self-analysis of speech rate. Playback of a language sample several days after it is obtained may be unintelligible to the child, making self-awareness the important first step in slowing down the child's rate of speech.

Incoherent Sequencing of Details

Incoherent sequencing of details can occur if the child has difficulty mentally organizing thoughts. Several activities should be provided for the child to visualize more concretely a sequence of events and to have time to reorganize and think before responding.

Picture sequence cards can help depict definite sequences of events and act as a visual cue in helping the child express the sequence. Use of familiar fairy tales, stories, and poems may also help the child increase ability to relate a sequence of events. After listening to a story the child may be asked to rearrange story cards depicting the correct sequence of activities in the story.

Difficulty in Word Finding

Word finding difficulty occurs when the child's vocabulary is limited and when the child has a lapse in recall of specific names for objects or events. To remediate this problem, oral practice and drill activities should be provided to increase immediate recall of vocabulary.

- Using picture cards to develop a repertoire of names of objects and events
- Using picture books and stories to increase vocabulary
- Labeling objects in the classroom, school, and home
- Discussing common activities with the child as they are occurring
- Introducing games that require the child to recall a name after being given a verbal description, e.g., "I'm thinking of something to eat. It's round, sweet, red, and crunchy." (apple)
- Developing concrete activities that stress vocabulary for: feelings, colors, nouns, actions, tastes, sounds, and smells.

Speech Volume Not Adapted to Context

When a child's volume of speech is not appropriate for the context of the situation, such as the use of a loud shouting voice inside the classroom, the language practitioner needs to discuss differences between times and places for use of a loud voice, and how the child may talk differently at home, in school, on the playground, at church, or at a sporting event. In addition, the language practitioner should provide opportunities to increase the child's awareness of intonation and stress in the voice.

One activity designed to do this is modeling a short sentence, placing stress on one word.

The girl *screamed*.	The dog ran *fast*.
The *boy* likes ice cream.	I ate it *all*.

The child must imitate the sentence, placing stress on the same word as the model sentence.

Another lesson may stress different connotations produced when sentences are intoned in different ways. For example, phrase cards may be made available for the child to choose and read. A second child may be selected to give a different intonation and, therefore, present a different meaning of the phrase.

Please don't do that.	Look at him go.
I'm tired.	Eat your dinner.
	That's just wonderful.

To help the child recognize differences in pitch and volume, the language practitioner should express phrases using different volumes and pitch and have the child imitate them.

She went home. (whispering)
I said no. (loud)
I can't do it. (low voice)
Oh boy! (high voice)

SUMMARY

The activities provided in this chapter are intended to extend language programming for the language delayed child by providing techniques for remediating problems of form, function, and style. Methods in refining and enriching the language process are expanded in Chapter 7.

REFERENCES

Mowery, C., & Replogle, A. (1977). *Developmental language lessons* (Cards 136–151). Boston, MA: Teaching Resources.

Why—Because Cards (1976). Wesbeck, Cambs, UK: Learning Development Aids.

Chapter 7

Language Activities for Enrichment

Extending beyond the scope of language intervention for the language delayed child is the language arts curriculum. The language arts curriculum is provided here as an addition to providing a remedial program for the language delayed child. Language practitioners must not only develop language in specifically deficient areas, but should also provide activities to enhance and enrich the process of learning language.

Though the language curriculum is more general in nature than the language intervention program and broader in the numbers of children it is intended to serve, it nevertheless has specific learning goals. These goals are to increase the child's ability to

- observe the immediate environment
- listen and comprehend
- attend and follow oral and written directions
- express thoughts in complete sentences and enhance the communication of thoughts

The activities found within this chapter have been designed to fulfill these program goals. They are intended to help the child achieve proficiency in the communication process. Although reading and writing are communication skills within the field of language arts, it is not the intent of this chapter to delve into these areas. Instead, this chapter will be devoted to the presentation of enrichment activities designed to enhance the receptive and expressive language processes. The language practitioner will be provided with various exercises to use with individuals or groups of children in increasing their ability to understand the spoken and written word and in increasing their verbal skills in self-expression.

To provide activities for the development of receptive language skills, several components must be considered. The child must learn how to attend to and follow

226

spoken directions. The child must learn the meaning of spatial, directional, and ordinal concepts as well as those of size and quantity. Experiences should be provided in classification and categorization, both important cognitive skills. Furthermore, comprehension skills must be developed, ranging from the simplest recollections of detail to more difficult interpretive skills. Instructional activities provided in the receptive language section will enhance the acquisition of these important skills.

To provide instruction in the area of expressive language, the language practitioner must consider many aspects. The language practitioner must develop activities designed to increase the child's vocabulary, keeping in mind that the acquisition of vocabulary consists not only of adding new words to the child's verbal repertoire, but also expanding the meanings of words already within the child's working lexicon. This process of vocabulary enrichment occurs as a direct result of activities designed to increase vocabulary acquisition.

Also to be considered are the skills enabling the child to recall and communicate details correctly. Consequently, many activities are designed to give children ample practice in expressing events and ideas and in sharing their perceptions with others.

Expressive language is also improved with activities enabling children to practice correct word order and transformations of sentences. Use of unique ways to express ideas using more compound and complex sentences is another step in helping children refine their expressive language.

Finally, the social function of expressive language is considered sufficiently important to warrant instructional activities. These activities are designed to enable children to speak in front of groups, to be aware of their own feelings, and to express themselves succinctly.

The activities for developing receptive and expressive language skills, coupled with supplemental techniques in programming for language enrichment, will enable the language practitioner to add new dimensions to the instructional program.

ACTIVITIES FOR ENHANCING RECEPTIVE LANGUAGE

The development of comprehension skills is vital to the process of understanding the spoken word and receiving verbal communication accurately. The language practitioner must work systematically to enable the child to master a hierarchy of comprehension skills. These skills range from comprehending oral language at a literal level to mastering the more complex evaluative level.

Figure 7-1 illustrates the comprehension hierarchy. These comprehension skills may be taught by the language practitioner in an effort to refine thought processes of the child.

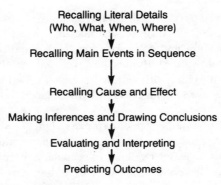

Figure 7-1 A Hierarchy of Comprehension Skills

A Hierarchy of Comprehension Skills

Recalling Literal Details

Developing the ability to understand and respond appropriately to lower level literal comprehension questions is an important prerequisite skill in the child's mastery of higher level comprehension skills.

Activity. One way of fostering the recall of detail at an initial stage is to simply make a single statement to the child such as ''The dog ran into the woods in the morning.'' The child is required to answer literal questions concerning the statement.

- Who ran into the woods?
- Where did he run?
- When did he run?
- What did the dog do?

This activity requires the child to attend to the question and listen to every element for details. Other suggested statements require the recall of details.

- When it was dark the boy ran home.
- When the girl got up, she rode her bike to town.
- In the afternoon the boy went swimming with his friend.
- The boy went to the candy store after school.
- In the summer the children like to sell lemonade at the street corner.

Activity. The difficulty of the previous activity may be increased by reading short passages or paragraphs to the children. They are required to listen to more details and recall specific information about what they heard.

Recalling Main Events in Sequence

Recalling and sequencing the main events of a story or descriptive passage is the second step in the comprehension hierarchy. Recalling main events is a logical outgrowth from recalling literal details. It does require some synthesis of detail, however, and requires the child to state details succinctly in one expressed thought.

Activity. The language practitioner may give the children practice in this skill by reading them short stories and asking the group to contribute by relating the events. The following set of questions is effective for eliciting the sequence of events.

- What or who was the story about?
- What did the subject of the story do?
- What did he do next?

Activity. Sequencing the events of a story may also be practiced by using story sequence cards. Several publishers of educational materials have marketed sets of picture cards that illustrate a story or event. These picture cards are divided into sets of four or six cards each. When arranged correctly they illustrate a logical order of events. The task of the child is to arrange these cards in the order in which they would naturally occur, or to create a sequence of events. The child must then describe the story.

Activity. Cartoons found in newspapers can also be used in this manner. The language practitioner may cut a cartoon story into segments and request a child to arrange them in order.

Activity. Another exercise for developing the ability to recognize sequential events is to have children describe a step-by-step procedure for making a familiar arts and crafts project, preparing an item to eat, or doing a familiar routine. The child must arrange or describe the events in order. The child may describe how to brush teeth, how to get ready for school in the morning, or how to play a favorite game. Emphasis should be placed on the logical order of events so that the child begins to think of events in proper succession.

Relating Cause and Effect

Understanding of cause and effect relationships, the third step in the comprehension hierarchy, can be developed initially by helping the child relate simple causal relationships in daily life.

Activity. Questions such as ''What happens when you turn on the water faucet?'' (water comes out) or ''What happens when you put water in the freezer?'' (ice is formed) serve to get the child thinking in terms of obvious causal relationships between events.

Activity. More complex relationships can be stressed in familiar stories, such as "Snow White and the Seven Dwarfs" and "The Little Red Hen." Questions such as "What Happened to Snow White when she ate the poison apple?" or "What happened when the Little Red Hen found out that no one would help her?" give the child practice in determining the effects of events in a story.

Activity. Commercially made materials designed to develop cause and effect skills are also available. One set of cards listed in Appendix B illustrates causal relationships in paired pictures. For example, one picture shows a boy in his living room lighting matches. The other picture shows the drapes in the living room on fire. The child, after matching the pictures, must describe the preceding event and what event followed as a result.

Activity. If no commercial materials are available, homemade materials such as pictures clipped from magazines can be just as effective. For example, the language practitioner may use a picture of a fire, one easily found in magazines. The language practitioner would ask "What do you think started this fire?" Utilizing the imagination, the child would think of a variety of causes contributing to the event.

Developing an understanding of cause and effect relationships aids the child in developing reasoning skills often used in the communication process.

Making Inferences and Drawing Conclusions

Making inferences and drawing conclusions, the fourth level of understanding depicted in the comprehension hierarchy, is a necessary step in the process of thinking critically and comprehending. It requires the child to filter the mass of detail found in a story or conversation and to make deductions based on the knowledge already formed by experience. To develop this skill, the language practitioner must develop a more open-ended line of questioning to allow children to draw their own conclusions and to generalize from the information.

Activity. To achieve this with young children, the language practitioner may read a simple story, purposely omitting the ending. The task of the child is to give an ending to the story by telling the final portion. In this exercise the child has to utilize all available facts and information in the story to draw a conclusion.

Activity. Another exercise designed to develop the child's ability to make inferences employs the use of single-illustration cartoons. The language practitioner clips a cartoon from a newspaper or magazine. After showing and reading the cartoon to the child, the language practitioner may ask the following questions.

- What message is the cartoon trying to tell us?
- Who are the characters in the cartoon supposed to be?
- Why is the cartoon funny?

The child must use visual imagery to summarize the illustrated detail and make an inference.

Activity. Mystery stories also lend themselves extremely well to developing this skill. Children enjoy a good "who-done-it" story and will be motivated to seek a conclusion regarding the character or the final outcome in an unknown or unexplained chain of events.

Activity. For younger children, riddles, puzzles, or open-ended stories provide the basis for developing the problem solving abilities necessary in drawing conclusions. Any puzzling or perplexing problem presented in riddle or story form serves as a springboard for discussion, allowing children to compare ideas and share conclusions with each other.

Activity. Unexplained pictures, scenes that seem to present discrepant or incongruous events, or pictures that the child finds fanciful or comical will also provide the language practitioner with activities designed to develop inferential skills. The language practitioner, by presenting such graphic enigmas, provides ground for inquiry. The language practitioner may lead the child through a process of asking questions, gathering information, and making decisions based on this investigation. More specifically, the child is requested to invent captions or to summarize events by synopsizing conclusions into one statement.

Evaluation and Interpretation

Evaluation and interpretation skills imply the synthesis of available information coupled with a subjective summary of the meaning this holds for the individual. The child must be provided with experiences in thinking critically to interpret the meaning of events.

In the process of evaluation the child learns how to form opinions on the moral or ethical nature of occurrences. The child learns to pass judgment on the truthfulness or reality of statements made. Furthermore, the child makes decisions on the purposes or biases revealed in different happenings.

Activity. To develop the skills of evaluation and interpretation, the language practitioner may give children the opportunity to appraise a review of a popular movie, television program, or play. After the language practitioner reads a review to the children, the following questions may act as a catalyst to promote critical thinking.

- Do you think you would like to see this movie? (read this book?)
- Why?
- Did the person reviewing the movie like it?
- What in the review let you know how the reviewer rated the movie?

These questions help the child understand individual choices in entertainment.

Activity. The child can also be requested to listen to and interpret a book review or to respond to the short description of a book found inside the book jacket.

- Would you like to read this book?
- Why?
- Would your friends like it? Why?
- Are the pictures attractive?
- Are the words hard to read?
- Is the book too long?

These questions may enhance the evaluative judgment of children and help them to understand the reasons for their personal choices in reading.

Activity. Children can be given practice in examining and expressing their own wishes and desires with advertisements from magazines as focal points for discussion. Pictured ads of food, toys, or clothing may be cut out and mounted on tagboard. Critical thinking skills can be developed by asking these questions.

- What is in this picture that makes you want to buy this product?
- What would you tell your mother about this if you wanted her to buy it?

Older children may be requested to think of answers to these questions.

- Which of your senses is the ad appealing to?
- What is the hidden assumption behind this product?

Activity. The common mail order catalog may be used to encourage children to pretend that they are going to buy a gift for each member of their family. The language practitioner centers the discussion on how the children perceive the wants and needs of their family members, their preferences for colors, their sizes, and their interests.

Activity. Children can also be asked to compare and contrast different accounts of the same event and to form opinions as to the credibility of each. The language practitioner can clip from two different magazines or newspapers stories recounting the same event and ask the children to listen to both accounts, determine how the two reports differ, and judge which of the two they believe to be the most accurate. Children can be asked to discriminate between statements of fact and statements of opinion. This exercise not only serves to develop the children's abilities to analyze and make judgments for themselves, but to reinforce the idea that articles are written with natural biases that the children should be aware of if they are to form their own opinions.

Predicting Outcomes

Predicting outcomes, the last step in the comprehension hierarchy, is the process of using all available information and evaluated opinion in anticipating future consequences. In addition, it encompasses the evaluation of human feeling in response to the events that have taken place.

Activity. Techniques for predicting outcomes can begin with very young children. They may be asked to respond to questions that require them to determine what will happen next or how a person will feel after an event has taken place. For example, the child is shown a picture of an emotionally charged event, such as two children fighting. The child is asked to observe the picture and then answer questions such as these.

- What is happening in the picture?
- What do you think will happen after the fight is over?
- How will the boys feel after the fight is over?

Activity. Similarly, the child may be asked to think of alternative endings to a story. Given a familiar children's story, such as Snow White, the child gives optional conclusions, varying the characters or the sequence of happenings or changing the events themselves.

Activity. Another means of helping children develop the ability to predict outcomes is by discussions utilizing fanciful topics.

- What would happen if we had no telephones?
- What will the world be like in the year 2050? What will people be like? What will the earth look like? What kind of food will we eat? What will schools be like?

Questions such as these function mainly as instigators of thought. Children should be given practice in using their creative thinking skills to predict and anticipate the future.

The hierarchy of comprehension skills serves as a multifaceted tool for instruction.

- It serves as a reminder that children should constantly be provided with experiences for developing a variety of levels of comprehension. The language arts program should provide more than just the lower level skills of literal comprehension. It should also provide exercises in the more complex levels of understanding, developing critical thinking, and the evaluative process.

- It emphasizes that the process of teaching evaluative skills can, and should, be initiated at a very early age. The language practitioner need not wait until children are reading to develop comprehension skills. Much can be accomplished with oral activities specifically designed to follow the sequential hierarchy of comprehension. The language practitioner must constantly read to the children, exposing them to problems and events of daily life, as well as to children's literature. Oral discussions serve as the mode of expression for comprehension in young children.
- It reinforces the idea that listening, comprehending, and speaking are interrelated components of the process of communication. The environment should provide for activities designed to enhance all three areas.

ADDITIONAL ACTIVITIES FOR ENHANCING RECEPTIVE LANGUAGE

Developing Classification Skills

To develop the child's ability to associate and differentiate patterns, the language practitioner should provide the child with opportunities to learn to classify objects.

Activity. The language practitioner shows the child three pictures, two of which represent the same class, such as foods. The third picture should represent another class, such as animals. The child is asked to select the ones that go together. Other categories may include vehicles, tools, musical instruments, household appliances, furniture, clothing, and others.

Activity. Another activity to enhance vocabulary in specific word classes is to make picture collages containing a variety of examples of a particular class. This can be accomplished by having the child examine magazines for particular items. For instance, if the language practitioner were helping the child develop labels for clothing, the child would be encouraged to find examples in magazines to cut out and paste together in a clothing collage.

Activity. To develop classification skills using descriptive words, children can hunt for pictures that illustrate those words. For example, the language practitioner might ask the child to look through magazines to find things that are "hot." Pictures of the sun, a cup of steaming soup, coffee, a stove, etc., can be easily found and judged by the child to be hot. Similarly, the child can find objects that represent cold, big, little, empty, full, or a variety of other descriptive attributes.

Activity. To develop classification of objects according to function, proceeding from specific to general, the language practitioner might show children a group of pictures such as an apple, a pear, a hamburger, a bike, an ice cream cone, a ball, a jump rope, and other pictures. After the language practitioner asks "Find the ones we can eat'' or ''Find the ones we can play with,'' the child's task is to sort the pictures accordingly.

Activity. A similar activity designed to teach children to categorize objects according to function requires them to go from the general class to specific examples within that class. Children are encouraged to find pictures in magazines in these classes: things we wear, things we eat, or things we play with.

Activity. Another categorization activity can be used to develop oral responses to word classes. The language practitioner gives the category, e.g., fruits or games. The task of the children is to name as many examples of that class as they can recall.

Activity. The child should be able to express a one-word answer when the language practitioner asks a simple word association question. For example, if the language practitioner asks ,''What do we eat?'' the child may answer ''food.'' Other categorizations might include these.

- What do we ride in?
- What do we wear?
- What do we drink?
- What can we plant?
- What do we live in?

Following Directions

Activity. To develop the ability to attend and follow directions, short games can be played with the child to enhance the receptive process. For a very young child, the goal may be the achievement of a short one-phase direction such as ''Touch the table'' or ''Drop the block.'' As the child succeeds at one-phase directions, another phase is added. ''Stand up and clap your hands'' or ''Close your eyes and touch your knee'' are examples of two-phase directions. Three- and four-phase directions may be attempted later.

Activity. This game can also be utilized to enhance the ability to follow directions. For this game the children will need crayons and paper. As the children listen the language practitioner orally states one phase of the directions at a time. The children's task is to draw what the language practitioner describes, step by step. As soon as the children complete the first phase, the language practitioner gives them the second phase.

- Draw a dog.
- Draw a bone for the dog.
- Give the dog a brown collar.
- Make the dog a doghouse.

Developing Analogies and Comparisons

Activity. To develop a sense of analogies, children should be encouraged to complete the following sentences. The language practitioner models the first part of the sentence, and the children are to supply the missing word.

- Grass is green. The sky is _____.
- Cats meow. Dogs _____.
- Birds sing. Cows _____.
- Bugs are little. Elephants are _____.
- Rabbits are fast. Turtles are _____.
- The sun is hot. Ice is _____.
- Horses run. Fish _____.
- Snakes crawl. Birds _____.

Activity. To develop skill in using analogies, the language practitioner can present situations that illustrate similes. For example, the language practitioner asks the group of children what some of the largest objects they can name are. They may respond with elephant, house, or similar objects. The children are then asked to make silly sentences out of that comparison. For example "I have a cat. It is as big as *an elephant*." The children respond, using the large objects they named.

If asked to name the reddest thing they can think of, the children might answer fire engine, apple, etc. The language practitioner then asks them to complete this sentence: "My nose is red. It is as red as _____."

Other analogies can be developed in the same manner.

- My sister is small. She is as small as _____.
- My dog is hungry. He is as hungry as _____.
- My mother is pretty. She is as pretty as _____.
- My friend was mad. He was as mad as _____.
- The boy is silly. He is as silly as _____.

Other similes to be developed include

- as strong as _____
- as smooth as _____
- as soft as _____
- as hard as _____

- as dark as _____
- as long as _____
- as short as _____

Developing an Understanding of Abstract Concepts

Activity. To develop a clearer concept of shapes, children are first asked to match shapes, then to name them. After they are able to identify the shape by naming it in isolation, they are taken on a walk to identify the shapes that are contained in objects found in the environment. For example, children may see that a clock face is round, like a circle, and that the wheels on a car are also circular. Or they may identify the rectangular or square shape of a cardboard box. Children can be encouraged to make a construction paper picture using only three cutout shapes—a square, a circle, and a triangle. The child could even be asked to make a picture using straight popsicle sticks to see how lengths can be combined to form a picture.

Activity. To learn the proper use of concepts involving comparative and superlative modifiers, especially in comparing sizes, the language practitioner can provide concrete experiences to point out the comparison between objects or persons. For example, in discussing taller and shorter, the language practitioner can measure the children and draw their figures on paper to express relative height. After the visual comparison is made, the pictures may be labeled. Sentences such as "Jim is taller than Sue. Bob is the tallest in the class. Ann is the shortest in the class" may be stressed both orally or in written form. A variation of this might include asking the children to draw two children, one taller than the other.

Activity. To teach the comparative adjectives longer and shorter, objects of varying lengths are introduced. The child is asked to point to the object that is longer. In a series of successive discrimination tasks, the child will generalize the concept of longer to objects that are closer and closer in length. Three or more objects are used to teach the superlative form of the adjectives longest and shortest. Similarly, the child can be trained through the use of proper reinforcement techniques to make finer and finer discriminations.

Other comparative and superlative adjectives can be taught in a similar manner, through successive discriminations. Examples of these adjectives include

- big-bigger-biggest
- small-smaller-smallest
- high-higher-highest
- wide-wider-widest
- low-lower-lowest
- fat-fatter-fattest

Activity. To enhance the child's ability to understand spatial concepts, the child should be given objects or pictures to manipulate. An empty box can be used to demonstrate relationships with other objects such as blocks, beads, toy animals, etc. The language practitioner gives the child opportunities to practice these directional concepts.

- Put the block in the box.
- Put the box under the chair.
- Put the toy on the table.
- Put the bead beside the box.

Activity. A variation on the previous activity would include asking children to position themselves relative to a chair, table, or other object in the room. For example, the language practitioner may request the following of children.

- Stand *on* the chair.
- Stand *beside* the chair.
- Get *under* the table.
- Sit *in* the chair.
- Stand *in front of* the desk.
- Stand *in back of* the chair.

Activity. The words top, middle, and bottom are directional concepts that are vital to the learning process. If the child has not mastered these concepts, pencil and paper tasks can present great difficulty. Likewise, instructions that require the child to start at a certain place on the page or to find specific items located on the page may be confusing. To teach the concept of top, the language practitioner may point to the top of a bookshelf or blackboard and request that the child name items positioned above. Similarly, the concepts of middle and bottom can be developed using

- a three-drawer filing cabinet
- desk drawers
- three stacked blocks
- a sandwich or hamburger
- children climbing a playground slide ladder
- a stack of books
- a column of numbers
- figures printed at the top, middle, and bottom of a sheet of paper

The child should be exposed to many examples of the three directional concepts. Asking the child to point to or name the objects in these three different positions, with proper reinforcement procedures, will greatly increase the likelihood of a correct response in other situations.

Activity. Teaching the ordinal concepts first, second, and third can be achieved using the children themselves as examples. Every time the group of children lines up for movement to other activities such as lunch, recess, or library, the occasion can be used to reinforce the ordinal concepts by naming who is first, second, or third in line. Frequently, discussing children's placement in line relative to others enables the child to generalize the ordinal concepts.

An additional activity might be a race between the children. Discussion of who came in first, second, or third will reinforce the ordinal concepts.

Activity. To introduce the concepts of up and down, the child is presented with two objects during each trial and asked to point to the object that is up or down. By having successive discriminations provided, the child will generalize the concepts. While the children are outside on a climbing apparatus the concepts of up and down can be illustrated again, this time by pointing out which child is up or down in relation to the others.

Activity. To develop directional concepts in the learning environment, the language practitioner can draw a map illustrating the placement of rooms in the school or clinical setting. The rooms represented should be those familiar and significant to the activities of the children, such as the office, the library, and the cafeteria. Photographs may also be taken of staff members such as the secretary, librarian, principal, custodian, and cooks, and they can be pasted in their respective rooms on the map. This provides children with a graphic idea of where different personnel are located in the building. Consequently, if they are requested to take messages or to find a particular staff member, they can easily consult the map to find the person and location.

Activity. To establish receptive understanding of the difference between the concepts of fact and fantasy, the language practitioner should introduce to the child a series of real and absurd sentences. The child's task is to determine whether the situation could happen in reality or if it is fantasy. These statements are examples of sentences that illustrate this activity.

- An elephant dances in the refrigerator.
- A man wears a hat.
- Monkeys can sing.
- Monkeys can swing by their tails.
- Zebras can roller skate.
- Birds can fly to the moon.

TEACHING ABSTRACT LANGUAGE CONCEPTS THROUGH CONCEPT ANALYSIS

Teaching abstract language concepts has always posed a great challenge to the language practitioner. This challenge is greatly increased if the child's language delay is associated with low mental functioning or learning disabilities. This chapter proposes a methodology for teaching abstract concepts.

A concept, as defined by Engelmann (1969), is a listing of characteristics shared by all those and only those instances in a particular set. Specifically applied to an instructional situation, Thiagarajan, Semmel, and Semmel (1974) defined a concept as a group of stimuli that evoke an identical learner response. Merrill and Boutwell (1972) stated that concepts must have certain features that are critical for defining or understanding an idea. They pointed out, for example, that the concept "ball" must include the critical attribute of roundness, whereas the finger holes in a bowling ball represent irrelevant or noncritical attributes.

A strategy that has great potential for use in teaching language concepts is generally known as "concept analysis." This teaching technique concerns itself with identifying the critical and noncritical attributes of the concept to be taught.

Becker, Engelmann, and Thomas (1975), Markle and Tieman (1970), and Thiagarajan et al. (1974) have developed models using concept analysis to enhance the processes of generalization and discrimination.

The differentiation theory of Gibson and Levin (1975) and the attention theory of Zeaman (1973) support the use of concept analysis principles. Both theories point to the importance of enhancing the relative stimulus attributes, a principle maximized by comparison of critical and noncritical features in concept analysis.

In teaching abstract concepts two further issues must be considered. In *The Conditions of Learning*, Gagne (1970) admonished that one must concentrate on helping the child generalize the concept to novel situations. Ausubel (1973) cautioned against rote memorization as a primary teaching vehicle. Ausubel pointed out that

> Teachers frequently forget that pupils become very adept at using abstract terms with apparent appropriateness—when they have to— even though their understanding of the underlying concepts is virtually nonexistent (p. 38).

Therefore, a concept analysis model must present an approach to language instruction that not only teaches the specific language concept, but also provides the child with the ability to identify and use the same concept in a variety of situations.

The authors advocate the following model of concept analysis for the teaching of abstract language concepts (Figure 7-2). To utilize this model, the language practitioner must develop an instructional plan based on five phases.

Identifying the Concept

In this first phase, the language practitioner simply identifies the concept(s) to be taught. For the purpose of illustration, we will suppose that the language practitioner wants to teach the concept "mammal."

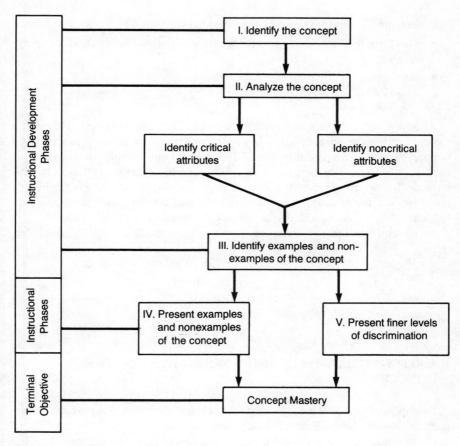

Figure 7-2 Concept Analysis Model

Analyzing the Concept

This phase actually consists of two steps: identification of critical attributes and identification of noncritical attributes. Critical attributes have characteristics that, taken together as a set, differentiate one concept from other concepts (Hertlein & Whitney, 1976).

The entire set of attributes must be present to define a particular concept. With a mammal as a concept example, the critical attributes might be

- body covered by hair (fur or wool)
- mammary glands
- lungs

- four limbs (arms and legs, flippers, paddles)
- gives birth to living young (except for the duckbilled platypus and the spiny anteater)
- two parents
- capable of movement

At first glance, many attributes appear to be critical to a concept. However, closer examination will reveal that they are common to more than one concept, are not part of the critical set defining the concept and, consequently, do not serve to accurately differentiate between concepts. Noncritical attributes have characteristics that do not differentiate one concept from others. Although the list of noncritical attributes could be infinite, it is essential for the language practitioner to identify those that would tend to confuse the learner.

Again with mammal as a concept example, some noncritical attributes might be

color	number of parents after birth
sex	dietary habits
size	life span
age	

IDENTIFYING EXAMPLES AND NONEXAMPLES OF THE CONCEPT

Examples of the concept contain the set of critical attributes, whereas nonexamples are those lacking the set of critical attributes.

For mammal, examples of the concept could include

• man	• cow
• cat	• horse
• dog	• mouse
• monkey	

For mammal, nonexamples of the concept could include

• snake	• lizard
• duck	• frog
• fish	• shellfish
• insects	

PRESENTING EXAMPLES AND NONEXAMPLES

The actual presentation of examples and nonexamples to the child should utilize a variety of media. For mammals, live examples and nonexamples could be used as well as movies, photographs, and drawings. If drawings are to be used, they should be as realistic as possible.

Concept examples teach the child to generalize to other cases within the same concept, whereas nonexamples teach discrimination between differing concepts. It is especially important with language delayed children to use a large number of examples presented in a variety of situations. These situations should also include noncritical concept attributes. Examples for the concept "mammal" might be the presentation of "man" and "boy," which would account for the noncritical attributes of size and age. Similarly, the presentation of several "men" and "women" would account for the noncritical attributes of sex and number. To avoid confusing the learner, it is recommended that mastery of the examples be established before introduction of nonexamples.

PRESENTING FINER LEVELS OF DISCRIMINATION

Examples and nonexamples should be presented in a manner that calls for increasingly finer levels of discrimination by the learner. Essentially, what might be termed a "funnel approach" is used. Initially the difference between the example and nonexample should be very clear. For instance, it would be a good idea to contrast "man" (example) with "rock" (nonexample). As the learner masters these clear contrasts, finer discrimination will be required. For instance, "anteater" (example) could be contrasted with "turtle" (nonexample).

The following examples of analyzed language concepts serve to further illustrate to the reader the process of concept analysis.

1. Identify the concept.
   The concept is "work."
2. Analyze the concept.
   The critical attributes are
   a. living
           human, or
           animal
   b. effort
           mental, or
           physical

The noncritical attributes might include
  a. occupation
  b. employment
       unemployed, or
       employed
  c. remuneration
       paid or
       not paid
  d. difficulty
       hard or
       easy
  e. sex
       male or
       female
  f. race or ethnicity
       black
       white
       yellow or
       brown
  g. age
3. Identify many examples and nonexamples of the concept.
   The concept of "work" may include
   a. adult females in work situations
   b. adult males in work situations
   c. female adolescents in work situations
   d. male adolescents in work situations
   e. female children in work situations
   f. male children in work situations
   g. persons of various racial or ethnic groups in work situations

   Nonexamples of the concept "work" could include
   a. adult females in nonwork situations
   b. adult males in nonwork situations
   c. female adolescents in nonwork situations
   d. male adolescents in nonwork situations
   e. female children in nonwork situations
   f. male children in nonwork situations
   g. persons of various racial and ethnic groups in nonwork situations
4. Present examples and nonexamples.
   When the language practitioner presents examples and nonexamples of the
   concept "work," it is important for him or her to depict individuals of
   differing race and ethnic backgrounds in both work and nonwork situations.

Similar treatment should be given to both sexes and to individuals representing different age groups. Pictures of individuals in work and nonwork situations are one of the easiest and most practical ways to present this concept.

5. Present finer levels of discrimination.

Initial examples should clearly differentiate between work and nonwork situations. For example, a construction worker clearly engaged in physical activity (work) could be contrasted with someone sleeping (nonwork). Finer examples requiring much greater concept mastery might include a student at a desk doing homework (work) and a student sitting in a chair resting (nonwork).

The following concept analysis is presented for the purpose of illustrating how the lower level concept of shape can be taught to a language delayed child.

1. Identify the concept.
   The concept is "round."
2. Analyze the concept.
   The critical attributes are
   a. circular
   b. spherical
   c. globular
   d. constant curve

   The noncritical attributes might include
   a. size
   b. color
   c. thickness
   d. weight
   e. position
   f. location
3. Identify many examples and nonexamples.
   For "round," examples of the concept could include
   a. baseball
   b. basketball
   c. golfball
   d. wheel
   e. globe
   f. marble
   g. pipe
   h. bowl
   i. phonograph record
   j. hoop

k. doughnut
l. drinking glass
m. crayon
n. ring

Nonexamples of the concept might include
a. square
b. any angle
c. corner
d. straight line
e. flat surface (desktop, tabletop, floor, or wall)
4. Present examples and nonexamples.
   It is relatively easy to present examples and nonexamples of the concept "round," because they are readily available in almost any teaching environment or clinical setting.
5. Present finer levels of discrimination.
   Initial examples might contrast a circle with a square or a ball with a flat surface, and progress to increasingly more subtle differences.

The concept analysis model provides a process by which the language practitioner can systematically develop and teach abstract language concepts to children. Concept analysis is easy to implement, economical in terms of time needed to prepare teaching units, and inexpensive. Thus it becomes a very effective method for teaching abstract concepts to language delayed children.

Recalling Visual and Auditory Detail

To foster recall of detail from verbal images and auditory descriptions, the language practitioner can provide simple riddles for the child to guess. In this process the child will have to listen to the verbal cues given by the language practitioner to determine the answer. The following are examples of simple riddles that encourage the child to attend to cues and respond appropriately.

- It can fly.
  It lives in a nest.
  It is a _____.
- It is a fruit.
  It is red.
  It is an _____.
- It lives in the ocean.
  It can swim.
  It is a _____.

- It is big and gray.
  It has a trunk.
  It is an _____.
- It is a tool.
  It can hit nails.
  It is a _____.
- It is red.
  It grows in the ground.
  It is a _____.

Activity. "I spy" is another game that encourages attention to details such as shape, color, and position. The language practitioner says "I spy something round and white. What is it?" The child scans the room to pinpoint the object in question. If the child responds correctly, then that child is given a turn to describe an object to be found by the others playing the game.

Activity. To develop the ability to describe events in a visual stimulus, the child is requested to dramatize a situation illustrated by a thought provoking picture. The child is then asked to give a factual account of the events illustrated in the picture. Other children in the class can be asked to describe the dramatization.

Activity. To increase ability to remember visual detail, there are two related activities that can be used. The first is a game in which the children watch as the language practitioner places several objects on the table. After they scan the objects for several seconds, the children are asked to close their eyes, during which time the language practitioner removes one object. When the children open their eyes, their task is to determine which object is missing. The difficulty of this task can be increased by placing more objects on the table and by removing more than one object from the table.

Activity. A related activity helps children become more aware of the visual detail of parts of the human body. Using a large paper or cardboard manikin or model of the body with removable parts, the language practitioner can provide experiences in recalling body parts. The language practitioner asks the children to close their eyes. During this time the language practitioner removes an ear, an eyebrow, an arm, or other body part. After the children open their eyes, they are asked to name the missing body part.

ACTIVITIES TO ENHANCE EXPRESSIVE LANGUAGE

Developing an Expressive Vocabulary

Activity. Children should be encouraged to learn and use a variety of descriptive words. Realistic experiences provide children with the base for language and increase the use of new words in different contexts. To develop sensory words, a tasting party encourages learning the meanings of the following words.

- salty
- sweet
- sour
- hot
- spicy
- cold

Activity. Hearing is a crucial sense, and children need to be able to use core words to communicate the information their sense of hearing conveys. Words such as soft, loud, high, low, and others can be developed by having children listen to variations in voice, music, and rhythms.

Activity. A variation of the previous activity could be presented to increase children's awareness of the senses they use to gain information about objects and events. For example, they could be encouraged to pick up a picture card from a deck of cards showing a variety of sensory objects. Foods, musical instruments, fragrant objects, and scenic pictures might be represented. After choosing a picture card, children must determine which sense is used to learn about it— hearing, smell, vision, taste, or touch. The children, in discussing these objects, may discover that some objects fit more than one category. For example, a hamburger belongs in the taste category, the smell category, and the vision category. In determining the class to which the object belongs, children will discuss likenesses and differences of these pictured objects. In this manner, sensory words are introduced and developed.

Activity. Another technique often used to develop vocabulary, especially in a specific case or category of words, is to provide an actual experience using real or simulated objects from that category. In the case of teaching food vocabulary, the language practitioner can set up a grocery store in the classroom, to which the children may contribute empty cartons, boxes, and cans that they collect at home. Open-ended discussion and specific activities will develop vocabulary in the foods class as children learn to label, point to, or identify specific items.

There are several variations to this activity. If the language practitioner plans to help children develop labels for toys, a miniature toy store is set up in the room. The children should be encouraged to bring in toys to be used temporarily in the toy store. To develop a vocabulary of farm animals, a farmyard may be set up, using building blocks, clay, construction paper, or similar materials. Plastic farm animals are added as the children learn to label and identify the animals.

Activity. To enable the children to develop descriptive words in their vocabulary, the language practitioner can conduct an oral discussion requiring them to make associations with a key word. For example, the language practitioner may give the key word "elephant" and ask the children to think of words that describe it. Words such as big, gray, and slow may come to mind as the children associate words characteristic of the key word elephant. This activity can be used with other key words such as flower, house, cat, and school.

Activity. Labeling objects in the room provides the child with names for familiar objects. Labeling can be done in oral exercises in which only five or ten items in the room are discussed during any one session. Children should be encouraged to identify the object by pointing, then to name the item, and at a more advanced level, describe its function.

As children mature and reading skills become more refined, these objects should be labeled in writing so that the children become familiar with the way object names are written. Labeling both verbally and in a written format can increase the children's vocabulary of common environmental objects.

Activity. To develop a receptive and expressive vocabulary of action verbs, the children may participate in this activity. The language practitioner selects one child to pantomime an action, such as sweeping the floor or washing the face. The other children are allowed to guess the action being depicted. After the action word is named correctly, the children state orally what the child was demonstrating. "Johnny was sweeping" or "Johnny was washing his face" exemplify the nature of the sentences to be elicited. Each child should be encouraged to describe the action using the proper verb. Other action verbs that can be pantomimed in this manner include

- dancing
- brushing teeth
- hopping
- clapping
- sleeping
- sewing

- batting a ball
- bouncing a ball
- rolling cookies
- tying shoes
- combing hair
- painting

- eating
- drinking
- playing an instrument
- kicking a ball
- swimming
- kneading bread

Description of Visual and Auditory Events

Activity. To enable the child to accurately describe events, the language practitioner shows a silent movie or a storybook with no written text and then asks the child to describe the details of the story. Different accounts of the movie or story can be recorded and compared for detail. In repeating this exercise, by showing the film or the book for a second time, the children can also check the accuracy of their own statements.

Activity. To encourage the accurate description of visual images, the following activity is suggested. The language practitioner prepares a set of small picture cards depicting animals, objects found around the house, toys, or other objects familiar to children. Each child takes a picture card. Then, without showing the card to the others, the child gives a one sentence clue about the picture. For example, if the child selected a picture of a bike, the clue "It has two wheels" may be given. If, after the children have had ample opportunity to guess the child's picture, no one identifies the object, the child gives an additional clue. "You can ride on it." The game continues until the children guess the object.

Developing Problem Solving

Activity. To develop the problem solving skills needed in communication, children should be encouraged to interact together and reach consensus as a common body. The language practitioner may present the class with a problem such as "What do you do when you're riding in the car and you run out of gas?" Other open-ended problems may be presented such as "What would you do if you saw a friend stealing a toy from another child?" The children are to be given five or ten minutes by themselves to work out a solution to the problem. Emphasis should be placed on giving each child the opportunity to present an idea to the group, yet the children should also be encouraged to think out and express a solution arrived at by consensus. This exercise makes children aware of the nature of compromise in the communication process.

Activity. Another oral exercise in problem solving involves asking the children "Imagine you are going to a very cold place far away. What clothes would you need to take along? How would you get there? What would you do when you got there? How would you live?" These questions require imagination, thought, and some awareness of the world. To develop a solution to these questions, the children must be able to listen to other ideas, share their own thoughts, and express answers satisfactory to all included in the discussion.

Activity. Children should also be encouraged to express or describe events and different life styles after looking at a visual stimulus. The language practitioner may choose a colorful picture from a popular geographical magazine and ask the children to determine who the people are, what the people are doing, where they are going, the time of the year, or other questions relating to distinguishing features.

Expressive Language for Social Communication

Activity. Many times the language disordered child feels self-conscious in speaking before others. The child is often misunderstood, which results in a reluctance to attempt further verbal communication. The language practitioner must find ways of dealing with this hesitancy to talk. One successful method of accomplishing this is to program into the group language session a time in which the children are responsible for expressing themselves to other children. This activity, not unlike the traditional "sharing time," serves as a means of helping children become more comfortable in speaking. The children should be encouraged to use their time to describe a game, a new toy, or a family activity. In approaching oral language on a one-to-many basis, the children gain experience in relating details, describing a sequence of events, or expressing daily occurrences. Exercises such as this increase children's ease and confidence in talking before a group.

Activity. Writing letters, greeting cards, or notes can be a means of getting the child to express an idea and fulfill a social function of language: communication with others. Dictation by the child serves as a means of eliciting the child's thoughts. If, for example, the child wishes to write a thank you letter to a resource person who conducted a field trip, but has no writing or spelling skills, the child may be successful in dictating what was liked about the experience. The language practitioner takes the child's dictated remarks and writes them down on paper, to be sent or given to the receiver. The following is an example of a child who dictated a letter that was sent to a policeman who took the class on a tour of the police station.

Dear Officer White:

I liked the police car. And I liked the way you put the handcuffs on Billy.

from

Marty

This actual letter was quite an accomplishment for a child exhibiting expressive language difficulties. It showed the organization of thought derived from a concrete experience.

Activity. Children need to commit to memory certain types of details or factual information such as birthdays, addresses, and phone numbers. Children can learn these common types of information by constructing a tagboard house similar to their own. On the door the address and phone number of the child is printed. Class games may be played to give children ample practice in orally stating their addresses and phone numbers.

Developing Syntax

Activity. Appropriate syntax, or word order, is stressed using the following activity. The language practitioner presents the children with sentences mixed up in sequence. Their task is to unscramble the sentences and say them in the correct order.

- Pie the boy ate. (The boy ate pie.)
- Like I ice cream. (I like ice cream.)
- Dog the see I. (I see the dog.)
- Is mad the boy. (The boy is mad.)

Activity. To develop the ability to recognize component parts of sentences, and to determine possible words that fulfill the function of these word classes, the children can be given practice in determining the missing elements of sentences. The language practitioner orally presents the child with a sentence, omitting a key word. The child must respond by supplying a word that would complete the sentence and still make sense. For example, the following incomplete sentences are offered for use.

- I see a _____.
- The bug _____ me.
- The boy _____.
- I saw the girl _____.
- You can play with _____.

Activity. The child can also be given practice in transforming simple declarative sentences into questions. The language practitioner presents a verbal stimulus—a short, declarative sentence. The child's task is to rearrange the same words to make a question.

> *Language Practitioner*: The dog is hungry.
> *Child*: Is the dog hungry?

Activity. Similarly, the child is given the opportunity to transform affirmative statements into statements using negatives. The language practitioner presents the child with a statement such as "The dog bit the boy." The child must use a negative in transforming the statement, e.g., "The dog did not bite the boy."

ENRICHING THE LEARNING ENVIRONMENT

The language practitioner should strive, at all times, to develop an atmosphere that encourages talking. Of necessity, there must be periods of quiet during the school day for individualized instruction and for developing independent working skills. However, in providing for enriching language activities, more use can be made of group instruction. One of the purposes of working with groups is social interchange. Therefore, certain periods of the day must be set aside for developing language skills important for interpersonal communication. The following techniques are suggested to broaden language experiences using activities that are quite divergent from traditional instructional processes. They bombard the children with experiences and specific use of language. Also, they expose the group of children to a variety of modes of expression, encouraging listening skills, thinking skills, and, more importantly, opportunities for talking.

Poetry

Poetry can enhance the phonological development of the child. By listening to and practicing rhymes, the child will hear and use patterns of intonation and stress and will be provided with practice in using rhythm in speaking, a very important voice quality.

The child who learns to repeat a number of poems will gain practice in memorization skills. By listening to and using poetry, the child gains a sense of rhyming words.

There is a multitude of poetry activities that may be used to enhance language. Several will be mentioned here.

Activity. One successful means of enhancing rhyming skills is to present the child with a two-line poem, leaving off the last rhyming word. The child is to supply the missing word that completes the rhyme. For example, the language practitioner may use these simple two-line poems.

- I see a cat.
  The cat has a _____. (hat, rat)
- Look at the dog.
  The dog is on a _____. (log)
- Look at me.
  I am in a _____. (tree)

These can be expanded to include four-line poems as well.

I like ice cream.
I like peas.
I like flowers
That make me _____. (sneeze)

Activity. Children also enjoy using their own names to create a rhyme.

- Bill, Bill.
  Took a _____. (pill)
- Andy, Andy.
  Got all _____. (sandy)
- Jack, Jack.
  Sat on a _____. (tack)
- Jean, Jean.
  Ate a _____. (bean)
- Jim, Jim.
  Went for a _____. (swim)
- Ted, Ted.
  Went to _____. (bed)

Activity. Favorite nursery rhymes can also be used to develop thinking skills. The language practitioner reads a nursery rhyme such as "Pussy Cat."

> Pussy Cat, Pussy Cat,
> Where have you been?
> I've been to London to visit the Queen.
> Pussy Cat, Pussy Cat, what did you there?
> I frightened a little mouse under the chair.

The language practitioner uses these questions to initiate the thinking process.

> Why was the cat going to see the Queen?
> What happened when he got to London?
> What do you think the Queen did after the cat chased the mouse?

Activity. To develop a sense of rhythm through poetry, rhythm sticks may be used. The poem "Hickory Dickory Dock" lends itself to this exercise. While the language practitioner establishes a beat with the rhythm sticks, simulating a ticking clock sound, the children recite the poem.

> Hickory Dickory Dock.
> The mouse ran up the clock.
> The clock struck one.
> The mouse ran down.
> Hickory Dickory Dock.

Variations in the tempo of the rhythm will cause the children to become aware of rhythmic beat, because they will have to vary their rate of recitation to match the beat of the rhythm sticks.

Dramatics

The area of dramatics includes several different components. They are

- dramatic play
- creative dramatics
- puppetry
- role playing
- mimetics
- story plays

In dramatic play, children are provided with time to act out familiar scenes of daily life in a "free play" situation. In creative dramatics, children dramatize stories, skits, or events. In puppetry, children use puppets as characters portraying a story. Role playing involves acting out events and situations as real characters. In mimetics the children learn to pantomime single actions using motor responses. A story play is a series of mimetics acted out by children while the story is narrated. Story plays are also effective and enjoyable activities that serve to get children responding to and interpreting language.

Dramatic Play

In dramatic play, children can be encouraged to act out scenes they experience in daily life. Although much of the content of dramatic play comes from children's spontaneous ideas, the language practitioner may also lend structure to the dramatic play activity by suggesting topics to be dramatized. These suggestions might include

- playing house
- a trip to the grocery store
- a visit to the doctor's office

- an airplane ride
- going on a picnic

Dramatic play gives children opportunities to use and demonstrate the sequencing of events in order of their occurrence; it provides empathetic understanding of the role of family members and people in the community and practice in the process of communicating with others.

Creative Dramatics

Creative dramatics can include the application of novel solutions in creating or performing familiar or unfamiliar stories. Children may be given the opportunity to act out familiar stories in children's literature such as

- ''Rumpelstiltskin''
- ''Rapunzel''
- ''The Little Red Hen''
- ''The Three Billy Goats Gruff''

Children should be encouraged to act out a story as it is normally told, using their own words and actions. Or they may vary the events of the story, adding new ones or changing the traditional endings.

Children may also be provided with the opportunity for creating their own fairy tales, fables, or stories. Creative dramatics gives children the opportunity to use language and provides the language practitioner with activities to use in emphasizing speaking in complete sentences and clear enunciation of speech sounds.

Puppetry

Puppetry is a variation of creative dramatics, with one significant difference. With the use of puppets, a substitute character is created, one that transfers the identity of the character from the child to a puppet. Because of this, many children who were previously too self-conscious to portray a human or story character will often readily assume a role if a puppet is used.

Children enjoy both finger puppets and hand puppets. Puppets come in assorted sizes, colors, and characters. If the language practitioner were to purchase or make puppets for the children, the most versatile would be those that could assume a variety of roles. Characters such as the Muppets illustrate nonspecific roles and can be used to create a variety of situations.

A puppet theater can be easily created by cutting a child-high window and a back door out of a cardboard refrigerator carton. A simple curtain may be sewn from scrap material and attached by gathering on a string of elastic tacked at both ends.

Children should be given several opportunities to create stories with the use of puppets. Puppetry serves to increase children's comfort in speaking before others, enhancing their overall ability to communicate more easily.

Role Playing

Role playing is a more structured form of dramatics. In role playing, the involved adult may structure the situation by suggesting topics or events to be acted out. Usually these events are of a problem solving nature. By also suggesting an event and identifying the characters to be portrayed, the child is given the experience of acting out a solution with another person. Many situations lend themselves to role playing.

- Pretend you are a salesman selling a car.
- Pretend you are a policeman giving a ticket.
- Act out a parent and child having a talk.

Mimetics

Mimetics, the act of imitating or pantomiming single events, is an activity designed to help children interpret and characterize language. The language practitioner presents an action to be portrayed, and the children perform the event through pantomime. Some concepts for mimetics include

- a snake slithering through the grass
- an elephant walking
- a monkey in a tree
- a person swimming
- a person sweeping the sidewalk

Story Plays

Story plays are a series of mimetic activities performed in a story sequence. The language practitioner may narrate the story while the children perform the actions. Examples of possible story plays that could be simulated might include

- a trip to the barber shop
- a visit to the county fair
- going on a walk through the jungle
- going on a picnic

The following story play is provided as an example of how the language practitioner might present a story while the children perform the events as it is being told.

A Trip to the Jungle

Language Practitioner:	"A family went to Africa on a trip to the jungle. When they got off the plane, they rode in an old jeep on a bumpy road."
Children's Action:	Children pantomime riding in a jeep, being jostled from side to side.
Language Practitioner:	"When they came to a clearing, they set up camp. Father set up the tent."
Children's Action:	Pounding in tent stakes.
Language Practitioner:	"Mother unpacked the suitcases."
Children's Action:	Opening suitcases and shaking out clothing.
Language Practitioner:	"And the children went for a walk. Because the jungle was so quiet, the children tiptoed as they went."
Children's Action:	Tiptoeing.
Language Practitioner:	"Soon the children were frightened by a noise overhead."
Children's Action:	Looking upward with frightened faces.
Language Practitioner:	"Oh, it was only a silly monkey jumping from limb to limb in a tree."
Children's Action:	Pretending to jump here and there.
Language Practitioner:	"Then they heard a rustling in the grass. It was a snake slithering away."
Children's Action:	Crawling like a snake.

Language Practitioner:	"Then they heard an elephant slowly walking through the brush. The elephant stopped to scratch his back on a tree. He swayed as he walked deeper into the jungle."
Children's Action:	They walk like elephants with arms for trunks, gently swaying from side to side. They pretend to scratch their backs by rubbing against a tree.
Language Practitioner:	"Then they heard a loud, scary CRACK! Oh, it was thunder! It started to rain hard, so the children ran as fast as they could back to the shelter of the tent."
Children's Action:	Running back to camp.
Language Practitioner:	"And the children told their parents all about the animals they saw in the jungle."

This type of story play can be used to help children develop interpretive skills and increase their ability to listen to stories and dramatize the actions through body movement.

Music

Music provides another means of oral expression for children. If music is an integral part of the curriculum, its benefits will be realized. It can provide another means of building vocabulary, establishing a sense of internal rhythm, developing an awareness of pitch and intonation in voice, and creating an understanding of language concepts such as loud, soft, fast, and slow. Providing practice in singing promotes the development of syntax and memorization skills. The musical activities provided here, however, are offered in addition to exercises stressing only singing activities, thereby giving another dimension to language learning.

Activity. To develop an awareness of rhythmic patterns, the language practitioner can clap out a pattern, then ask the group of children or an individual child to repeat the pattern by clapping it back. This develops a rhythmical response, much like rhythmical qualities used in speaking and singing.

Activity. Another activity designed to develop this internal sense of rhythm is having the children perform actions to a musical beat, rhythm, or song. Bouncing a ball to music, walking or hopping to a beat, and dancing or pantomiming with the rhythm are all exercises designed to encourage the children to interpret and to respond motorically to musical stimuli.

Activity. Singing games and chants help develop synchronization and choral responses, and they provide uses of language through motor responses. Games such as London Bridge, The Farmer in the Dell, and various jump rope chants provide the children with opportunities to memorize and use language verses in an entertaining way.

Activity. Music and rhythms can also be used to develop concepts. To develop the concepts of loud and soft, the language practitioner uses the volume control on a record player, a musical instrument such as a drum, or other rhythm instruments to illustrate loudness and softness. The children are requested to make successive discriminations in distinguishing between loud and soft. Similarly, successive discriminations illustrating the concepts of fast and slow can be used in helping children gain an understanding of tempo in music.

Field Experiences

Field trips, or field experiences as the authors prefer to call them, provide the child with concrete opportunities to observe and investigate the community. They offer the language practitioner a chance to develop new vocabulary and to help the child utilize language in a social activity. Some of the more important outcomes in utilizing field experiences as an instructional activity include

- developing new vocabulary
- teaching children how to ask relevant and pertinent questions
- establishing appropriate social behaviors while out in the community
- building a base of information
- learning concepts

Field trips should not be taken without advance preparation. Careful planning and organization will maximize the benefits these experiences will have in the development of language. If careful attention is taken in planning the new vocabulary to be learned, in preparing children to ask relevant questions, and in stressing the application of concepts, the children will undoubtedly gain much more in the learning process.

There is a multitude of sites for field trips. Table 7-1 lists several, along with the anticipated learning outcomes to be expected from a field trip to that site. The language practitioner may investigate places in the surrounding community for additional possibilities unique to the area.

An aid in the effective use of field trips is the instant developing camera. Photographing events and persons met on a field experience and bringing the

Table 7-1 Planning Field Experiences for Specific Language Outcomes

Field Experience	Anticipated Learning Outcome
A restaurant	Information on food preparation Experience ordering a meal from the menu
Fire station	Concepts of protection of people and property Information on how firemen fight fires Specific vocabulary
The city library	Information on library services offered Knowledge of how to use the library facilities
A nursery or greenhouse	Information on how plants are grown on a large scale in business Concepts of plants and life cycle of growth Specific vocabulary
The police station	Concepts of towns and cities and their protection Concepts of law and justice Specific vocabulary Experiences observing fingerprinting, the police car, and handcuffing
The hospital	Concept of health care for humans Specific vocabulary Information about medication Knowledge of surgical procedures
The veterinarian	Concept of health care for animals Concept of prevention of diseases common to animals (rabies, distemper, etc.) Concept of animal control Specific vocabulary
The home	Specific household vocabulary (labels for furniture, appliances, rooms) Concept of maintenance and care of a home
The post office	Concept of communication Concept of transportation of mail Information on how mail is processed

photographs back to class is very useful and motivating for continuing discussion. Children can be encouraged to verify experiences and share perceptions of the trip if they have photographs to help them remember.

Audiovisual Aids in Developing Language

Films, filmstrips, tapes, charts, study prints, and books can be used as supplemental materials to reinforce language concepts and vocabulary taught in the classroom. If carefully planned and utilized, audiovisual materials can serve as valuable tools for helping the child gain information through the sensory processes of vision and hearing.

To make the best use of materials available, careful planning is again advised. The indiscriminate use of films and other materials can render media ineffective in the learning process. The language practitioner should plan specific learning outcomes resulting from the use of media if maximum results are to be achieved.

Unit planning may follow a monthly schedule so that new concepts are developed each month. Or other convenient intervals may be selected, depending on the group of children and their interest in the topic. The language practitioner should preplan in advance of the school year, scheduling the topics and concepts to be covered in the course of the year's study and ordering audiovisual materials directly related to these topic areas.

Manipulative Play

Manipulative play, or engaging in games designed to use manual dexterity, can provide children with opportunities to initiate social interactive language with their peers. Giving children time to engage in activities requiring the sharing of table games and similar activities helps them develop communication with others in an informal play atmosphere. Several types of classroom materials lend themselves to eliciting this type of language. They include

- beads
- clay
- legos
- building blocks

- puzzles
- toy animals
- dolls
- toy cars and trucks

One needs only to watch children in their creative use of such manipulatives to realize the stimulus these toys provide in getting children to communicate with each other.

Displays and Exhibits

Finally, the language practitioner can make use of interesting exhibits or displays to provoke curiosity, encourage the learning of new vocabulary and concepts, and increase expression and use of oral language.

The language practitioner may display an item such as a bird's nest on a table in the room. This single item will initiate discussion and cause the children to find out more about the construction of nests by seeking information from books, pictures, or resource persons.

Other interesting items accomplishing the same purpose include

- magnets and iron objects
- a spider in a jar spinning a web
- a water table filled with different density objects
- an ant farm
- unique insects
- scales for weighing and balancing objects
- small animals such as hamsters or guinea pigs
- a coin or stamp collection
- photographs from a vacation

Placing these exhibits in the room will lead to much discussion. The language practitioner can then guide and channel the discussion to accomplish the purposes set out for language instruction.

SUMMARY

The activities provided in this chapter can serve as catalysts for the creation and use of other exercises designed to enhance and increase language production. The activities designed to enrich receptive and expressive language, as well as other exercises designed to enrich the learning environment, should provide the language practitioner with ideas for planning and implementing the language curriculum.

REFERENCES

Ausubel, D. (1973). *Educational psychology: A cognitive view* (p. 38). New York: Holt, Rinehart, & Winston.

Becker, W.C., Engelmann, S., & Thomas, D.R. (1975). *Teaching 2: Cognitive learning and instruction* (p. 75). Chicago, IL: Science Research Associates.

Engelmann, S. (1969). *Conceptual learning* (p. 9). Sioux City, SD: Adapt Press.

Gagne, R. (1970). *The conditions of learning* (p. 183). New York: Holt, Rinehart, & Winston.

Gibson, E., & Levin, H. (1975). *The psychology of reading* (p. 82). Cambridge, MA: MIT Press.

Hertlein, F., & Whitney, R. (1976). Concept analysis: An approach to instructional programming. *Breakthrough, 2*, 5–7.

Markle, S.M., & Tieman, P.W. (1970). *Really understanding concepts: Or in Frumious pursuit of the jabberwock* (p. 20). Champaign, IL: Stipes Publishing.

Merrill, D., & Boutwell, R. (1972). *Instructional development: Methodology and research* (Working Paper No. 33, May). Provo, UT: Brigham Young University, Department of Instructional Research and Development. (ERIC Document Reproduction Service No. ED 082 455).

Thiagarajan, S., Semmel, D., & Semmel, M. (1974). *Instructional development for training teachers of exceptional children: A sourcebook* (p. 195). Bloomington, IN: Council for Exceptional Children.

Zeaman, D. (1973). One programmatic approach to retardation. In D. Routh (Ed.), *The experimental psychology of mental retardation* (p. 78). Chicago, IL: Aldine Publishing.

Chapter 8

Evaluating Language Programs

The wise selection and use of commercially published language materials are vital to the success and effectiveness of the language intervention program. The language practitioner, usually on a restricted budget, must make the most of the resources available. Therefore, decisions about the choice of materials must be based on all possible information available on specific programs. The language practitioner must examine programs to compare and contrast them to determine which best suit the needs of the children to be taught. Decisions affecting a choice of language program should be based on rigorous criteria for evaluating programs and for differentiating one program from another.

The authors have included in this chapter criteria for evaluating language programs as well as guidelines for evaluating computer software language programs.

CRITERIA FOR EVALUATING LANGUAGE PROGRAMS

The authors offer here a set of questions or criteria to be applied in evaluating commercially prepared intervention programs. Evaluating programs using a standard measure of comparison results in an objective appraisal on which a decision can be based.

Exhibit 8-1, "Criteria for Evaluating Language Programs," provides the language practitioner with a structure for comparing language intervention programs. It is intended to provide a graphic method of identifying the characteristics of language programs for the purpose of comparison and selection. It will aid the language practitioner in clarifying the features of each program and determining whether the program meets the needs of the children to be served.

Major considerations in evaluating a language program include

- content of the language program
- measures contained in the program for evaluating the child's progress

264

- training required of the language practitioner to implement the program
- characteristics of administration or implementation
- cost

The language practitioner should consider these general areas along with the specific questions presented in Exhibit 8-1. This will provide the language practitioner with a structure for the selection and adoption of language intervention programs.

Content

The first consideration in evaluating a language program is content. The language practitioner must look carefully at the intent of the program to determine whether its components address a broad range of language problems. First, the language practitioner must determine the focus of the program. Does it concentrate on receptive or on expressive language? Is it a developmental approach for nonverbal children or does it teach functional language skills? Is it for children just beginning to develop one-, two-, and three-word responses, or is it for children already using kernel sentences? Does it concentrate on specific morphological or syntactical problems? Examining the content of the program and answering these questions should provide the language practitioner with information on the breadth of the language hierarchy included. If the language practitioner is working with a limited budget, it is preferable to select a program that develops a wide range of language skills, from the least complex to the more complex. In this manner the greatest number of children will benefit from the program.

In addition to determining the focus of the language program, the language practitioner must examine the program to discern whether it contains concise instructional objectives. The inclusion of clear-cut objectives for language instruction will aid in determining the primary emphasis of the instruction. Furthermore, instructional objectives become a guide for language programming. They greatly enhance the development of an intervention plan for teaching children language and enable the language practitioner to monitor language development in a child's individualized language plan by providing explicit performance standards.

Another consideration in evaluating language programs is sequence. Are the objectives, units, or phases of the program sequenced appropriately? Is the sequence of instruction consistent with what is known about the normal acquisition of language? Are earlier, less complex constructions taught before those that are usually acquired later? Is the program task analyzed, breaking the language tasks down into units that can be mastered more readily? Are branching steps provided for occasions when modification of the sequence is necessary?

Exhibit 8-1 Criteria for Evaluating Language Programs

Considerations	Program 1 (Name)	Program 2 (Name)	Program 3 (Name)
Content What is the focus of the program? Does it contain objectives? Is it sequenced appropriately? Does it provide for generalization to spontaneous language? Are materials attractively designed to motivate and interest children?			
Evaluation of Progress Are pre- and postassessment measures included? Does it contain a continuous monitoring system or method of collecting data in charts/graphs.			
Training Is special training required? Can parents or paraprofessionals also use it? Are consultants provided?			
Implementation What is the administration time required per day? How much time per week is required for recording? Can it be used with groups or is it to be used with individual children?			
Cost What is the initial cost? What is the cost to maintain the program?			
Comments			

In language training, the practitioner may observe that the child learns the specified construction in the instructional setting, but that it is not used appropriately in other environments. With that in mind, the question must be asked "Does the program contain techniques or methods that provide for the transfer of the language skill to spontaneous language?" If so, does it also offer a means of probing for maintenance of the skill at a later time? Programs that address these issues of generalization facilitate the mastery of language at a much higher and more practical level.

If a program can maintain the child's interest by providing for colorful stimulating activities, there is a higher probability that the child will attend to a task and perform the desired behaviors. In appraising language programs, therefore, the language practitioner must see to it that the materials are attractively designed so that children's motivation and interest are sustained.

Content provides perhaps the most important consideration when examining and evaluating language programs. The degree to which content corresponds with the needs of children and with the instructional philosophy of the language practitioner will determine whether the program is to be considered for adoption.

Evaluation of Progress

The proper placement of the child within the program and subsequent determination of target behaviors are extremely important in the process of language intervention. If a program contains pre- and posttest assessment measures, or procedures for placing the child within the program, the process of evaluation is greatly facilitated. In addition, the language practitioner must maintain a system of data collection so that modification or subsequent instruction is based on objective information directly related to the child's daily progress. For these reasons the language practitioner must ascertain whether the language program being considered for purchase contains adequate assessment measures, as well as a continuous monitoring system for evaluating progress.

Training

Frequently, language programs are not sold without mandatory training to ensure that the program is used correctly. The language practitioner must determine whether special training is required as a prerequisite to purchase. Similarly, it must be determined who can use the program. Can parents and paraprofessionals be trained to use it? Are resource personnel provided for periodic consultation when questions arise? Proper training in the use of a program provides for the appropriate use of all the materials and components contained.

Implementation

The practicalities of implementation, such as administration time and group versus individual training, are important factors to be examined when selecting a language intervention program. The language practitioner must look at the complexity of the program to determine how much time selected procedures will take, not only in the instructional phase of the program, but also in data collection. The language practitioner must consider how much instruction time per day is suggested for each child, or how many minutes a typical lesson takes. In addition, how much time per week is needed for charting data or maintaining the recordkeeping system? Can the program only be used for individuals, or is grouping possible in language training? Consideration of the pragmatic aspects of administration and implementation will help differentiate one program from another. Answering questions concerning daily instruction will assist the language practitioner in determining whether the program is suited for the children to be served.

Cost

In comparing the costs of language intervention programs, the language practitioner must determine not only the initial cost of the program, but also the subsequent costs in maintaining the program. Are the program components copyrighted, making it illegal to duplicate materials? In addition, does the program require yearly replacement of expendable materials such as data sheets, placement tests, or other component parts? Knowing the initial and subsequent costs of the language programs considered for purchase is often the decisive factor in the selection of a language intervention program.

Use of Program Evaluation Form

Keeping these considerations in mind, the language practitioner may compare and contrast programs using Exhibit 8-1 in the following manner. The name of the first program to be examined is entered in the column labeled ''Program 1.'' After scanning the program to ascertain the general scope of the program, the materials it contains, and the lessons it includes, the language practitioner may begin to look for answers to the specific questions relating to the program. The chart is designed so that the examiner's responses to the questions can be jotted down in the space provided, or the question can be answered with a simple ''yes'' or ''no.'' Once the examination of one program is completed and all questions are answered, a similar procedure may be followed with other programs being evaluated.

By using the criteria provided in the chart, the language practitioner will be able to examine the relative components of each program to decide which one has the most positive features for the children being served. This comparative information will provide objective data on which to base a decision and will ensure that the right program and materials are selected for purchase. Selecting the most appropriate language training program will increase the overall effectiveness of the language intervention process.

COMMON CAUSES OF PROGRAM FAILURE DUE TO INSTRUCTIONAL ERROR

Despite hard work, extensive planning, and good intentions, language training programs sometimes fail or have limited effectiveness. In many cases, this results from ineffective instructional (teaching) strategies. When this occurs, the instructional process should be carefully examined for the following common causes of language program failure.

Inappropriate Instruction

Many language practitioners discover that programs are not teaching what they were intended to teach. This instructional error is more common than one would imagine. For example, it is not uncommon to find programs for oral language practice without specific objectives established for each child. This is a problem often found in programs stressing group instruction, where some children receive instruction they do not need, whereas others do not receive the specific training suited to their language problems. The language practitioner must be constantly alert to the specific deficits of individual children and must provide program lessons suited to each one's needs.

Inappropriate Student Response Required

In this type of instructional error the language practitioner has not required the child to exhibit the response that is actually desired. For example, the language practitioner may require the child to respond in complete sentences when the child is only capable of two-word phrases. Conversely, a child who is capable of responding in complex sentences may be required to use the minimum response, thereby preventing the child from practicing more refined forms of language.

Another common error of this type involves requiring a great deal of expressive language in an instructional program that is intended to teach receptive language. More specifically, the child is incorrectly required to make oral or verbal responses to tasks typically requiring only motor responses. The language practitioner must be aware of target behaviors to be mastered and make sure that the learner responds in the appropriate mode.

Inadequate Reinforcement

In this instructional error the language training is not reinforcing enough to sustain the child's interest. Typical characteristics pointing to ineffective reinforcement can be seen in a child who does not attend to lessons, who exhibits a high degree of error, or who appears to be disinterested in the stimuli presented. To remediate this problem, every effort should be made to make the language activities as enjoyable as possible. This is known as "embedding the reinforcer," where the training sessions and the very act of learning are stimulating to the child. Sometimes external reinforcers may be needed to sustain interest in the learning task at hand. One of the most common and effective external reinforcers is adult attention in the form of praise and approval.

Reinforcement should be specific to the desired behavior rather than general. Children need to know exactly what behavior is being reinforced or what behavior is required of them. The language practitioner should never take positive behavior for granted. The practitioner must constantly seek ways of stimulating the child, making language training an enjoyable reinforcing experience.

Inappropriate and/or Insufficient Practice

Often, too much of the instructional period is taken up with direction giving and what is known as "teacher talk," leaving the child with too little time to practice the desired language skill. The training sessions must be organized and devoted to obtaining the maximum amount of language practice possible. Children must be given several opportunities to express themselves, interact with the language practitioner and others, and use new language. This process may be enhanced by allowing for patterned practice of constructions previously learned. In addition, the child must be provided with environmental experiences that encourage the generalized use of language. Furthermore, parents can be encouraged to follow up the instruction by providing extended practice in the home environment.

To develop language competence, children must use language. They must be able to practice what they have learned as a basis for modifying and refining their language performance.

Failure To Specify and To Require Mastery from the Student

The final instructional error centers around language skill mastery. Too often the language practitioner leaves a skill before the child has truly mastered it, later to be disappointed and confused when the child can no longer exhibit the skill. This is known as the "I thought I taught that" syndrome. The best way to ensure mastery is to have the child exhibit the particular language skill repeatedly in a variety of situations. Only if the practitioner plans for generalization will the language program guarantee mastery of skills. The language program and the language practitioner must provide frequent review to ensure maintenance of language skills.

These five areas represent potential sources of failure for the language intervention program. The language practitioner is capable of correcting many instructional errors by frequently evaluating and monitoring the instructional process and by making modifications in the training program when necessary.

CRITERIA FOR EVALUATING COMPUTER SOFTWARE LANGUAGE PROGRAMS

The explosion in the development of computer software has extended into the field of communication disorders. Software available at this point in time includes, but is not limited to, the following categories.

- drill and practice of a variety of language constructions
- augmentive communication programs
- computer speech synthesizers
- computerized analysis of language samples
- programs to facilitate the writing of Individual Education Programs (IEPs)
- word processing programs for report writing
- computer assessment of articulation
- computer tests of pragmatic language skills

The language practitioner faced with such a variety of programs should be aware of considerations for the evaluation of software. Informed evaluation of language programs software will prevent costly mistakes in purchasing. Using the same framework used to evaluate commercial language programs, the authors have provided a set of questions and issues to be considered when selecting software to meet the needs of the language intervention program planned by the language practitioner.

Content

The first consideration in selecting language software is whether the program really accomplishes what it purports to do. Furthermore, will it accomplish what the language practitioner has set as instructional goals for a particular child or group of children? Is the program designed as a tutorial for learning a new skill, for drill and practice of previously learned constructions, for simulation of a set of skills applied to a real life event, or for problem solving?

In terms of the features the program contains, the language practitioner should consider the following. Does the program have the capability to correct errors? Does it have the capability of saving data? When new improvements in the program have been made, is there an opportunity for the user to send in the program for upgrading? Is a backup disk provided? Does it provide branching steps? Is the program copy protected? Does the program have a warranty?

In the area of learner use, how fast is the stimulus presented, and does the program provide feedback to the learner? Are the quality of the graphics and presentation good? Is the stimulus interesting enough to capture and maintain the learner's interest?

Evaluation of Progress

Proper documentation of data and analysis is important for the language practitioner to determine whether the child is mastering the identified skills. The program should contain some method of saving data and/or data management over several sessions. Does the program contain a means of retrieving diagnostic and progress reports? Can graphs, charts, and other statistical analyses be made?

Training

Busy professionals need computer software that is easy to learn and use. The language practitioner should examine the following features to determine whether the program is "user friendly." Is a preview trial period provided so that the user may determine whether the program is suitable to the needs of the child and the language intervention process? Is a representative available for technical assistance if a problem occurs? What is the length of the manual? Are instructions for use clear and concise?

Implementation

Ease of use is perhaps the prime consideration when selecting language software. Often, only by trying the program will the language practitioner determine whether it is easy to use. Other considerations of implementation include the amount of time required for entering data, as well as the amount of time the computer takes to analyze data. Is the program menu driven, making selection of functions more clear? And, finally, are special complicated entry codes required for entering data?

Cost

With the price of computer software ranging from approximately $30 to $700, cost becomes an important consideration. In addition, the language practitioner must weigh the alternatives of leasing versus purchasing of a language program. Another question to be posed is whether the software publisher offers a free upgrade or trade-in of the program when improvements are made. Can the language practitioner receive money back or a replacement if the software is proven defective? And, finally, what is the cost of peripherals to the computer needed to run the program? Does it require two disk drives? Is a printer needed? Are a joystick or other peripherals needed?

SUMMARY

Providing criteria for evaluating commercially published language programs and computer software facilitates the objective selection of materials for the language intervention process. Knowing program and software characteristics and being aware of common sources of failure in the language intervention process should enhance the effectiveness of language practitioners in their efforts to provide quality programming and training for language delayed children. Appendix A and Appendix B provide the reader with descriptions of a number of language programs, software, and related instructional language resources that may be considered for inclusion in a language intervention program.

Appendix A

Bibliography of Language Intervention Programs and Software

Keeping in mind the considerations for evaluating language programs cited in Chapter 8, the authors present here brief descriptions of a number of commercial language programs. These descriptions contain the name and copyright date of the program, the authors, the publisher, and the target population of children to be instructed. In addition, an attempt has been made to specify what, if any, techniques of evaluating pupil progress are included in the program. The specific language focus of the program has been determined, as well as a description of the program components and materials included. The programs are arranged in alphabetical order.

Name: **Concept Formation**, c. 1978

Author: Elizabeth A. Tabaka-Jeudes

Publisher: Communication Skill Builders, Inc., 3130 N. Dodge Blvd., P.O. Box 42050-J, Tucson, Arizona 85733

Target Population: For the young elementary child who exhibits a delay in the acquisition or development of concepts.

Focus: Receptive language

Evaluation of Pupil Progress: No daily recording forms or system of monitoring are included. However, a pre/post test is included for assessment of acquisition of concepts.

Content/Description: This program consists of a series of activities to teach basic concepts such as in, on, over, corner, between, right-left, first, second, third, alike, and others. The author suggests that the language practitioner follow a four-step sequence in teaching the concepts.

That sequence includes

1. Introducing the concept
2. Following directions and making identity statements
3. Responding to yes/no questions
4. Responding to "wh" questions

Name: **Communicative Competence: A Functional-Pragmatic Language Program**, c. 1980

Author: Charlann S. Simon

Publisher: Communication Skill Builders, P.O. Box 42050-X, Tucson, Arizona 85733

Target Population: Students with pragmatic language problems, age 6 years to adult.

Focus: Pragmatic language

Evaluation of Pupil Progress: Pre/post test is included. Recordkeeping forms, objectives, and carry-over activities are included.

Content/Description: This program comes complete with filmstrips for discussion, a photo diagram book of sequences, 644 stimulus cards, spinner boards for use of pragmatic principles, and a manual.

This program concentrates on giving students opportunity to improve form, function, and style in communication.

Name: **Curriculum and Monitoring System Expressive Language Program (CAMS)**, c. 1977

Authors: Vonda Douglass and Richard Baer

Publisher: Walker Educational Book Company, 720 Fifth Avenue, New York, New York 10019

Target Population: All ages of developmentally delayed children with severe to moderate expressive language problems. This program teaches expressive language skills normally acquired between birth and five years of age.

Focus: The focus of the program is to teach expressive language skills, beginning with sound formation and proceeding through simple kernel sentences.

Evaluation of Pupil Progress: The CAMS Expressive Language Program contains a placement test, consisting primarily of phrase and sentence imitation tasks, daily data sheets for monitoring progress, and a summary sheet for synopsizing data.

Content/Description: This program consists of 41 objectives, each containing several sequenced and highly structured steps. The child must meet criterion on each step before proceeding to the next one. The hierarchy of expressive utterances is sequenced developmentally and increases in level of complexity as the student progresses through the program. The authors recommend the use of pictures cut from magazines and glued to heavy paper.

The program, packaged in a spiral binder, contains 41 objectives, a placement test, data sheets, and a summary sheet. The CAMS Expressive Language Program is intended for use with individuals. A slide-tape presentation is available for training users in the total curriculum, use of the programs, and scoring procedures.

Name: **Curriculum and Monitoring System (CAMS) Receptive Language Program**, c. 1977

Author: Jana Jones

Publisher: Walker Educational Book Company, 720 Fifth Avenue, New York, New York 10019

Target Population: Children of varying chronological ages who do not understand oral directions, commands, or concepts.

Focus: Receptive language

Evaluation of Pupil Progress: Placement tests are included with the CAMS Receptive Language Program, as well as daily monitoring sheets and a summary sheet for synopsizing progress.

Content/Description: The CAMS Receptive Language Program consists of 15 objectives such as attending to sound, responding to name, locating body parts, following commands in phases, demonstrating the use of objects, and understanding prepositions through the placement of objects. Each objective consists of from three to nine carefully sequenced and task analyzed steps. The child must meet criterion on each of these steps before proceeding to the next objective. Several concrete objects, e.g., a table, chair, ball, blocks, and other objects are needed to teach these objectives. This program is intended for use with individuals. A slide-tape presentation can be purchased for training in the purposes and uses of the CAMS materials and on the scoring system.

Name: **Developmental Language Lessons**, c. 1977

Authors: Charlane W. Mowery and Anne Replogle

Publisher: Teaching Resources Corporation, 50 Pond Park Road, Hingham, Massachusetts 02043

Target Population: Varying ages of language delayed children.

Focus: Expressive language

Evaluation of Pupil Progress: The authors suggest assessment of language deficits through the use of Developmental Sentence Scoring (DSS) by Laura Lee, 1974. Included in the program is the Profile of Syntactic Needs, which is to be used to prescribe the individual's language program, and the Criterion Test form, for testing the structures at different environmental levels.

Content/Description: The Developmental Language Lessons (DLL) program was designed to teach syntactical structures in the eight categories provided in Laura Lee's DSS. After obtaining a tape-recorded sample of the child's language and analyzing it with the DSS, the language practitioner determines at what level in each category the child is performing. The language practitioner then uses the Profile of Syntactic Needs to establish language goals for the child, which can be taught with the use of activity cards included in the program. The DLL card file contains 413 cards and corresponding activities to be used to teach responses within the eight categories. Within these categories, the following constructions are sequenced according to developmental norms.

- Indefinite pronouns
- Personal pronouns
- Primary (main) verbs
- Secondary verbs
- Negatives
- Conjunctions
- Interrogative reversals
- "Wh" questions

The DLL may be used with groups of children who have homogeneous language needs.

Name: **Developmental Syntax**, c. 1976

Authors: Lila Coughran and Betty Z. Liles

Publisher: Learning Concepts, 2501 North Lamar, Austin, Texas 78705

Target Population: For children of varying ages who exhibit specific errors in syntax and morphology.

Focus: Expressive language. For remediating specific deficits in the usage of

- Articles
- Personal pronouns
- Possessive pronouns
- The verbs "is" and "are"
- The verbs "has" and "have"
- Past tense of regular and irregular verbs
- Plurals

Evaluation of Pupil Progress: The authors suggest the use of commercial assessment measures for placement purposes. For monitoring daily progress, the program includes a therapy record for use by the language practitioner.

Content/Description: The program contains eight components, corresponding to the most common syntactical errors of children. Each program includes techniques that have been used in traditional articulation therapy.

- Ear training
- Production and carry-over
- Generalization in a different context

The Developmental Syntax Program offers suggestions for reinforcement and includes a criterion for mastery. The program is to be used with individuals, in training sessions not lasting over seven and one-half minutes each. Other materials included are a set of black and white cards illustrating relationships of the eight programs and a set of black and white posters for carry-over activities.

Name: **Ecological Communication System (ECO)**, c. 1986

Author: James D. MacDonald and Yvonne Gillette

Publisher: The Psychological Corporation, Harcourt Brace Jovanovich, Inc., P.O. Box 9954, San Antonio, Texas 78204-0954

Target Population: All ages of children who need early intervention in language. High risk infants, parent education programs, and learning disabled children.

Focus: Early language intervention. The program is for beginning stages of interaction and communication.

Evaluation of Pupil Progress: Assessment of early language skills is included. Also included are observation scales, interview schedules, and program planning strategies.

Content/Description: Four areas of interaction are stressed.

1. Social play
2. Communication
3. Language
4. Conversation

Adult-child interactions are developed to build pragmatic skills in the child.

Name: **Emerging Language 2**, c. 1976

Authors: John Hatten, Tracy Goman, and Carole Lent

Publisher: Communication Skill Builders, Inc., 3130 North Dodge Blvd., P.O. Box 42050-J, Tucson, Arizona 85733

Target Population: Children 2 to 10 years old who have not yet acquired language.

Focus: Expressive language

Evaluation of Pupil Progress: Reference is made to the measurement of goals. However, data sheets and evaluation measures are not included as components of this program.

Content/Description: The Emerging Language 2 consists of 136 objectives for language instruction, each with a suggested sample activity. The objectives are sequenced according to normal language acquisition. The program begins with teaching one-word responses and progresses to two- and three-word phrases, kernel sentences, and transformations. Also included is an appendix that deals with negation in sentences.

Name: **Fokes Sentence Builder Program**, c. 1976

Author: Joann Fokes

Publisher: Teaching Resources Corporation, 50 Pond Park Road, Hingham, Massachusetts 02043

Target Population: For language delayed and normal children of varying ages.

Focus: Expressive language

Evaluation of Pupil Progress: A response form is included for daily charting of correct/incorrect responses and the nature of the errors made by the child. A response chart is included for graphing percentage of errors.

Content/Description: Essentially a slot filler program (see Chapter 6), the Fokes Sentence Builder Program strives to help the student internalize the rules of sentence structure by providing a visual representation of each grammatical class within a sentence. In a typical lesson the language practitioner determines the sentence pattern to be developed. The child is encouraged to manipulate the filler cards, creating novel sentences of the same pattern. The lessons are developmentally sequenced. The program contains a sentence line, a vinyl mat divided into slots, and five sets of 200 cards representing

- Who (subjects)
- What (objects)
- Is doing (verbs)
- Which (adjectives)
- Where (prepositional phrases)

These categories can be manipulated to create varying sentence patterns for practice. Also included are sentence markers, to identify the type of sentence used, and sentence inserts, to hold the place of grammatical elements of the sentences.

Name: **Fokes Sentence Builder, Expansion**, c. 1977

Author: Joann Fokes

Publisher: Teaching Resources Corporation, 50 Pond Park Road, Hingham, Massachusetts 02043

Target Population: Normal and language disordered children of varying ages.

Focus: Expressive language

Evaluation of Pupil Progress: Response forms are provided to include new categories beyond the original program. Response forms can help the language practitioner analyze errors. Response charts for graphing percentage of error are to be used from the original program.

Content/Description: The expansion of the Fokes Sentence Builder provides additional categories to develop more complex sentences. These categories include "whose" (possessives), "how" (adverb phrases), and "when" (adverb phrases). These categories are represented by 77 cards packaged in three boxes. Also included is a small plastic clock for developing time concepts, a sentence line, a sentence insert, and a teacher's guide. The materials must be used in conjunction with the categories and other materials provided in the original Fokes Sentence Builder Program.

Name: **Functional Speech and Language Training for the Severely Handicapped**, c. 1978

Authors: Doug Guess, Wayne Sailor, and Donald Baer

Publisher: H&H Enterprises, Inc., Box 1070, Lawrence, Kansas

Target Population: Persons of all ages who lack language, both receptive and expressive.

Focus: Functional expressive language

Evaluation of Pupil Progress: This program contains scoring forms for each step of the program, summary forms for capsulizing data, skill tests to check mastery in most steps, and a sample graph for charting percentage correct over training sessions.

Content/Description: The Functional Speech and Language Training for the Severely Handicapped consists of 60 steps in four parts.
   Part I—Persons and Things. This involves identifying and labeling.
   Part II—Actions with Persons and Things. This consists of obtaining three- and four-word responses to sentence patterns such as "What do you want?" and "What am I doing?"
   Part III—Possession and Color. This develops phrases with the possessive-noun pattern and the adjective (color)-noun pattern.
   Part IV—Size, Relation, and Location. This part stresses phrases using prepositional placement and adjective-noun patterns.

Each of the four parts consists of several training steps in which the student must attain a set criterion for mastery. Further training is offered in "Programming for Generalization" suggestions that reinforce skills learned at each step.

Name: **Language Acquisition Program for the Retarded or Multiply Impaired (LAP)**, c. 1974

Author: Louise R. Kent

Publisher: Research Press, 2612 North Mattis Avenue, Champaign, Illinois 61820

Target Population: Severely retarded children of varying ages.

Focus: Receptive and expressive language

Evaluation of Pupil Progress: The LAP contains an inventory for placement, a performance graph for displaying results of the inventory, data sheets for recording correct and incorrect responses, and program sheets for monitoring mastery of program steps.

Content/Description: The LAP is designed for use with individuals. However, with some structure, the language practitioner may be able to work effectively with two children. The program consists of three components. The preverbal component emphasizes attending skills. The verbal-receptive component teaches a limited receptive vocabulary such as object names, room parts, and body parts. The verbal-expressive component teaches the child to imitate single words and two-word combinations. The author suggests objects to be used in teaching the constructions. Also included in the LAP are basic procedures for using reinforcement in training and a section on manual communication.

Name: **Let's Talk for Children**, c. 1983

Authors: Elizabeth H. Wiig and Candice M. Bray

Publisher: The Psychological Corporation, Harcourt Brace Jovanovich, Inc., P.O. Box 9954, San Antonio, Texas 78204-0954

Target Population: Language delayed children, ages 4 to 9 years.

Focus: Pragmatic language

Evaluation of Pupil Progress: Skills targeted for training may be monitored with a progress checklist.

Content/Description: Forty-one skills in four categories are included.

1. Ritualizing
2. Informing
3. Controlling
4. Feeling

Materials include a professional guide, a manual for activities to be used in the home, 50 color picture cards, 50 communication activity cards, progress checklists, reinforcement stickers, and puppets.

Name: **A Sourcebook of Pragmatic Activities**, c. 1984

Authors: Elizabeth Booth Johnston, Barbara Derickson Weinrich, and Ann Randolph Johnson

Publisher: Communication Skill Builders, P.O. Box 42050-X, Tucson, Arizona 85733

Target Population: Communication disordered students, ages 4 to 12 years.

Evaluation of Pupil Progress: Unknown

Content/Description: This book consists of 90 lessons in six areas of pragmatic problems.

1. Topicalization
2. Conversation
3. Register
4. Syntactic forms

5. Effective language use
6. Nonverbal communication

Name: **Syntax One**, c. 1976

Author: Carolyn Ausberger

Publisher: Communication Skill Builders, Inc., 3130 North Dodge Blvd., P.O. Box 42050-J, Tucson, Arizona 85733

Target Population: Children 5 years old and above, who exhibit a lag of at least 1 year in syntactic skills.

Focus: Expressive language

Evaluation of Pupil Progress: There are no placement tests available, but two types of data sheets are included in the kit for monitoring progress. Daily data sheets help the language practitioner monitor correct/incorrect responses. Monthly conversation evaluation sheets assist the language practitioner in conducting periodic checks of the child's spontaneous language from tape-recorded samples.

Content/Description: Syntax One, a slot filler program (see Chapter 7), is intended for use with individuals or in groups. It is suggested that if children are taught in groups, it is necessary that they each have a set of the materials. The materials include syntax wheels, which enable the child to manipulate the fillers to be used in each grammatical slot. Chart pictures are included for carry-over. The program also contains a student booklet, which consists of lessons to be used by parents at home. These lessons reinforce syntactical forms learned in the clinical setting. With each take-home lesson is a perforated form, which the parent may tear off and return to the language practitioner, indicating when the carry-over activity was completed.

The lessons are arranged following 12 goals, each of which contains four sequenced steps. These goals begin teaching one-word responses and progress through five-word sentences. Branching steps are provided within each step should the child have difficulty meeting criterion on any given step.

Name: **The Teaching Research Initial Expressive Language Program**, c. 1975

Authors: John J. McDonnell, H.D. Bud Fredericks, and David N. Grove

Publisher: Teaching Research Publications, Monmouth, Oregon 97361

Target Population: Children of any chronological age whose expressive language does not exceed five- to six-word phrases.

Focus: An expressive language program for severe language delayed children. The terminal behavior of the program is the expression of five or more word kernel sentences.

Evaluation of Pupil Progress: An initial placement test is included in the program for determining the phase for initial instruction. For daily monitoring of progress, data sheets are included.

Content/Description: This program consists of eight sequenced phases and corresponding instructional objectives, ranging from establishing eye contact through imitating three-, four-, and five-word sentences. Included in the materials are an instructor's manual, data sheets, placement tests, and a set of 342 black and white picture cards depicting a variety of nouns and verbs. The instructor's manual includes an extensive description of behavioral techniques to be used in the language training process. The program is to be used with individuals.

LANGUAGE SOFTWARE

Name: **First Words**, c. 1982
      First Words II, c. 1985

Authors: Mary Sweig Wilson and Bernard J. Fox

Publisher: Laureate Learning Systems, Inc., 110 East Spring Street, Winooski, Vermont 05404

Target Population: First Words is intended for students with a language age of 18 months to 2 years. First Words II is for students with a language age of 1 to 4 years.

Focus: Vocabulary development

Evaluation of Pupil Progress: Lesson summary monitors the student's correct responses

Content/Description: Two visual choices are presented to the child. The child is then given an auditory stimulus, such as "Find the _____." The child must move the cursor to select one of the named pictures. First Words teaches 50 high frequency nouns. First Words II teaches 50 more high frequency nouns.

Name: **Following Directions: One- and Two-Level Commands**

Author: Eleanor Semel

Publisher: Laureate Learning Systems, Inc., 110 East Spring Street, Winooski, Vermont 05404

Target Population: Elementary students who exhibit a delay in the development of concepts.

Focus: Language concepts

Evaluation of Pupil Progress: Unknown

Content/Description: Two diskettes contain eight lessons. The student is asked auditorially to position objects in the following positions.

- Above-below
- In front of-in back of-next to
- In front of-behind-beside

- In front of-behind-between
- Upper-lower-left-right
- Through-under
- Ordinal 1st, 2nd, 3rd
- Ordinal behind-beside-in front of

Name: **Language Stimulation Software**, c. 1986

Authors: Robert Volin and Michael Groher

Publisher: Aspen Systems Corporation, 1600 Research Boulevard, Rockville, Maryland 20850

Target Population: This program is intended for students needing practice in using language constructions. Some reading ability is needed.

Focus: Expressive language

Evaluation of Pupil Progress: Data from 11 student users of each program may be stored. The percentage of accuracy and response time are analyzed.

Content/Description: Eight software programs offer practice in the use of the following eight constructions.

1. *Sentence completion: semantics.* This program asks the student to use semantic cues to choose nouns and verbs to complete sentences.
2. *Rebuilding sentences.* The student unscrambles sentences to form grammatically correct sentences.
3. *Grammatical judgments.* The student uses grammatical understanding to correct faulty sentences.
4. *Associative naming: mixed cues.* The student selects correct vocabulary nouns and verbs based on functional or definitional stimuli.
5. *Sentence completion: syntax.* The student must complete sentences using correct morphemes.
6. *Selecting modifiers.* The student completes sentences using modifiers.
7. *Reading comprehension: Inference.* The student reads short paragraphs and makes inferences.
8. *Reading comprehension: Reference.* The student reads short paragraphs for specific information.

Name: **Microcomputer Language Assessment and Development System (Micro-LADS)**, c. 1984

Authors: Mary Sweig Wilson and Bernard J. Fox

Publisher: Laureate Learning Systems, Inc., 110 East Spring Street, Winooski, Vermont 05404

Target Population: Preschool and elementary students who need practice in acquisition of language constructions.

Focus: Expressive language

Evaluation of Pupil Progress: This program can provide a lesson summary of student performance.

Content/Description: This program consists of seven training diskettes, emphasizing the following language constructions.

1. Noun plurals/noun-verb agreement
2. Verb forms
3. Prepositions
4. Pronouns
5. Negatives
6. "Wh" questions, passive and deictic expressions
7. Prepositions II

Name: **SHANE Augmentive Communication Series**, c. 1987

Author: Howard Shane

Publisher: The Psychological Corporation, Harcourt Brace Jovanovich, Inc., P.O. Box 9954, San Antonio, Texas 78204-0954

Target Population: Severely physically handicapped children, adolescents, and adults.

Focus: Synthesized speech communication program for functional interaction.

Evaluation of Pupil Progress: Functional use of software by student determines effectiveness of synthesized communication. This program is not intended for collection or analysis of student data.

Content/Description: Seven programs are offered in this series.

1. *Message Maker*: the student can produce synthesized speech and key phrases.
2. *Message Maker Scan*: using a single keystroke, the student can produce synthesized speech.
3. *Touch and Speak*: the student can select from up to 615 preprogrammed messages, using a keystroke, power pad, or switch. The student may also combine available characters to develop customized phrases.
4. *Scan and Speak*: using a cursor, the student may select from a scanned group of messages to produce synthesized speech.
5. *Environmental Control*: For students with severe motor handicaps. This program enables the user to control other devices in the environment, e.g., the t.v., radio, and other appliances.
6. *Desk Top*. This program enables the user to integrate electronic communication, word processing, and a math scratch pad for calculations.
7. *Communication Board Construction*: This program is for the language practitioner who plans to individualize a communication board for specific users and purposes.

Appendix B

Related Language Resources

A necessary addition to a language intervention program is the supplementary material that provides visual stimuli for eliciting verbal responses from children. These resources may include picture cards, games, activities, and audiovisual instruments to be utilized in the language training process. Several of these resources have been included as suggested materials to be used in language instruction. They have been arranged in alphabetical order.

Name: **Alike, Because, Level I,** c. 1974, 1978

Publisher: Teaching Resources Corporation, 50 Pond Park Road, Hingham, Massachusetts 02043

Description: This resource consists of a binder containing full color flip pictures. The pictures may be manipulated to form associations based on similarities among objects.

Name: **Color, Object, Number Grouping Cards**

Publisher: Developmental Learning Materials, 7440 Natchez Avenue, Niles, Illinois 60648

Description: A set of cards depicting objects of differing number, object, and color to be used in classification activities.

Name: **Functions**

Publisher: Teaching Resources Corporation, 50 Pond Park Road, Hingham, Massachusetts 02043

Description: A set of 70 picture cards designed to depict associations based on function of objects. For example, a set of five cards may illustrate rags, paint, a ladder, a pail, and a brush, which can be classified according to their common functions.

Name: **Games Kids Like,** c. 1975

Author: Dianne Davis Schoenfeld; Harry J. Murphy, Consulting Editor

Publisher: Communication Skill Builders, Inc., 3130 North Dodge Blvd., P.O. Box 42050-J, Tucson, Arizona 85733

Description: A three-ring binder containing 40 games and activities designed to reinforce speech and language skills. The games may be reproduced for use by the language practitioner.

Name: **The Language Master,** c. 1965

Publisher: Bell & Howell Company, 7100 McCormick Road, Chicago, Illinois 60645

Description: The Language Master and accompanying card program are audiovisual instructional devices for providing language practice. The double sound track cards permit both an auditory model and a track for recording the student. The student may first listen to the auditory model, then respond and record on another track to practice patterns in oral language.

Name: **Language Skills: Categories—Clothing and Household Items,** c. 1973

Publisher: Teaching Resources Corporation, 50 Pond Park Road, Hingham, Massachusetts 02043

Description: A set of full color cards illustrating two categories—clothing and common household items. These cards may be used to help develop vocabulary or to develop classification skills.

Name: **Language Skills: Categories—Foods and Animals,** c. 1973

Publisher: Teaching Resources Corporation, 50 Pond Park Road, Hingham, Massachusetts 02043

Description: A set of full color cards illustrating the classes of animals and foods. They may be used to develop classification skills and vocabulary.

Name: **Language Skills: Categories—Varied,** c. 1976

Publisher: Teaching Resources Corporation, 50 Pond Park Road, Hingham, Massachusetts 02043

Description: A set of cards depicting tools, musical instruments, sports equipment, reading materials, buildings, measurement devices, vehicles, and common household items. These cards may be used in classification and categorization activities.

Name: **Language Structure Simplified, Kits 1 and 2,** c. 1975

Author: Bethanie Millstein

Publisher: Educational Activities, Inc., Freeport, New York 11520

Description: These two kits provide visual stimuli (picture cards and sentence patterns) for teaching basic sentence types and syntax. Kit 1 contains pictures and sentence strips covering plurals, comparative adjectives, pronouns, prepositions, and future, past, and present tense verbs. Kit 2 contains pictures and sentence strips on negatives, subject-verb-object sentence patterns, progressive pronouns, "wh" questions, descriptive adjectives, and verb tenses.

Name: **Living Parts and Wholes**

Publisher: Teaching Resources Corporation, 50 Pond Park Road, Hingham, Massachusetts 02043

Description: Children can be encouraged to match parts to the whole of familiar animals and people with this set of 36 photo cards. It develops attention to visual detail and the part/whole relationship.

Name: **Match Me—Opposites,** c. 1975

Publisher: Trend Enterprises, Inc.

Description: A set of full color activity cards designed to illustrate opposite or polar relationships. Some of the opposite pairs include go-stop, left-right, up-down, night-day, etc.

Name: **Match Me—Singular and Plural Activity Cards,** c. 1975

Publisher: Trend Enterprises, Inc.

Description: A set of 32 full color cards representing plurals, both regular and irregular. Some of the plurals depicted include snail(s), shoe(s), kite(s), leaf(ves), etc.

Name: **Motor Expressive Cards I**

Publisher: Developmental Learning Materials, 7440 Natchez Avenue, Niles, Illinois 60648

Description: A set of small full color picture cards designed to show associations. The cards may be matched in pairs, stressing the identification of objects that go together. Examples of associated pairs include a milk carton and an empty glass, a coat and a hanger, a hammer and a nail, a key and a lock.

Name: **Motor Expressive Cards II**

Publisher: Developmental Learning Materials, 7440 Natchez Avenue, Niles, Illinois 60648

Description: A set of small full color cards designed to show associations. The child matches objects that go together. For example, a boy and a bike, a saddle and a horse, a thread and a needle, a stamp and a letter depict common associations.

Name: **Parts and Wholes**

Publisher: Teaching Resources Corporation, 50 Pond Park Road, Hingham, Massachusetts 02043

Description: A set of pictures grouped in 23 sets of three, each containing a whole and two-component parts. The child is to match the cards depicting the whole and part relationships.

Name: **Opposites**

Publisher: Teaching Resources Corporation, 50 Pond Park Road, Hingham, Massachusetts 02043

Description: A set of 40 cards designed to illustrate opposite relationships. Pairs such as hot-cold and big-little are depicted.

Name: **Parts of Speech Complete**

Publisher: Teaching Resources Corporation, 50 Pond Park Road, Hingham, Massachusetts 02043

Description: Five decks of cards to be used in syntactic development of particular word classes and increasing vocabulary. The five classes represented include nouns, verbs, adverbs, adjectives, and prepositions.

Name: **People, Places and Things**

Publisher: Teaching Resources Corporation, 50 Pond Park Road, Hingham, Massachusetts 02043

Description: The cards develop associations between people, objects, and locations. The cards come in four major categories: occupations, stores, recreation, and sports. The child takes a large card and matches smaller cards that are associated with the major category.

Name: **Pictures Please,** c. 1978

Authors: Marcia Stevenson Abbate and Nancy Bartell LaChappelle

Publisher: Communication Skill Builders, Inc., 3130 North Dodge Blvd., P.O. Box 42050-J, Tucson, Arizona 85733

Description: A notebook of 1,232 illustrations grouped according to nouns, prepositions, verbs, pronouns, and modifiers. It is designed to be used in teaching vocabulary and increasing syntactic development. It also contains activity sheets, a cross-referenced index, recording sheets, and instructions.

Name: **Positions**

Publisher: Teaching Resources Corporation, 50 Pond Park Road, Hingham, Massachusetts 02043

Description: A deck of 50 full color cards designed to depict objects and persons in prepositional placement. Sample relationships depicted include a boy jumping on a bed, a girl sitting on the floor, and a man climbing up a ladder.

Name: **Sentence Building Sequential Cards**

Publisher: Developmental Learning Materials, 7440 Natchez Avenue, Niles, Illinois 60648

Description: A set of ten sequences consisting of three cards each. The purpose of the cards is to give the child practice in relating sequential events, not only through a motor response, but in expressing the sequence orally. On the first card of the sequence an object or agent is represented, on the second card an action is illustrated, and on the third card another object is depicted. The task of the child is to arrange the pictures in sequence; then the child should be encouraged to express a complete sentence about the sequence.

Name: **Sequence Picture Cards**

Publisher: Teaching Resources Corporation, 50 Pond Park Road, Hingham, Massachusetts 02043

Description: A set of picture cards depicting several sequenced stories. For example, a flower is seen growing in three phases. The task of the child is to arrange them in sequence.

Name: **Sequential Picture Cards IV**

Publisher: Developmental Learning Materials, 7440 Natchez Avenue, Niles, Illinois 60648

Description: A set of six sequences of four cards each designed to be arranged in logical order of occurrence. The story themes include making cookies, visiting a haunted house, the construction of a building, a storm, buying a record, and a flight to the moon.

Name: **Singulars and Plurals 1 and 2**

Publisher: Teaching Resources Corporation, 50 Pond Park Road, Hingham, Massachusetts 02043

Description: These sets of picture cards contain pairs of picture cards depicting singular nouns and their plural forms. Regular and irregular plurals are represented.

Name: **Why-Because Cards,** c. 1976

Publisher: Learning Development Aids, Park Works, Norwich Road, Wisbech, Cambs, England

Description: A set of cards consisting of matched pairs. One part represents a cause. The other represents the event resulting from the cause. The task of the child is to view both cards and determine the cause and effect relationship.

Name: **Wipe Off Cards: Associations,** c. 1972

Publisher: Trend Enterprises, Inc.

Description: A set of 12 cards, designed to illustrate associations. Each card is laminated so the child can mark the answers in crayon and wipe them off for reuse. Each card consists of four horizontal rows of pictures with a sample picture. The task of the child is to find the one that goes with the sample picture.

Name: **Wipe Off Cards: Categorizing,** c. 1974

Publisher: Trend Enterprises, Inc.

Description: A set of 12 laminated cards that can be marked in crayon and wiped off. A general category such as clothing is stated at the top of each card. The child is to find all the objects that belong in the category and mark the responses. Other categories include kitchen things, furniture, fruits, forest animals, transportation, sports equipment, vegetables, farm animals, tools, things to eat, and places people live.

Index

About the Authors

Martha L. Cole, M.Ed., is an elementary school principal. Prior to that she was a teacher of children with communication disorders in Las Cruces, New Mexico. She has served as the president of the New Mexico Federation of the Council for Exceptional Children and has been a practitioner in the field of early childhood education and special education for over 20 years. She has served as a clinical/ demonstration teacher at the Exceptional Child Center, Utah State University, and has taught university-level courses in the areas of special education and early childhood education. She has given numerous presentations and workshops on the language development of language delayed and nonlanguage children.

Jack T. Cole, Ph.D., has been an elementary teacher, counselor, school psychologist, and special educator. He is currently an associate dean and director of the Educational Research Center at New Mexico State University. He holds the rank of professor in the Department of Special Education and Communication Disorders. Dr. Cole has published, taught, consulted, and directed grants in the field of special education. He has been actively involved in regular and special education for over 20 years.